GRANTA

IN TROUBLE AGAIN
A Special Issue of Travel Writing

20

Editor: Bill Buford
Assistant Editor: Graham Coster
Associate Editor: Piers Spence
Advertising and Promotion: Monica McStay
Subscriptions: Claire Craig
Assistant to the Editor: Anya Schiffrin
Design: Chris Hyde
Research: Margaret Costa
Editorial Assistants: Vicky Ross, Alicja Kobiernicka
Contributing Editor: Todd McEwen
Executive Editor: Pete de Bolla
Photo Editor: Harry Mattison
US Editor: Jonathan Levi, Granta, 250 West 57th Street, Suite 1203, New York, NY 10107, USA.

Editorial and Subscription Correspondence: Granta, 44a Hobson Street, Cambridge CB1 1NL. (0223) 315290.
All manuscripts are welcome but must be accompanied by a stamped, self-addressed envelope or they cannot be returned.

Subscriptions: £15.00 for four issues. Overseas add £2 postage.

Granta is photoset by Hobson Street Studio Ltd, Lindonprint Typesetters and Goodfellow and Egan, Cambridge, and is printed by Hazell Watson and Viney Ltd, Aylesbury, Bucks.

Granta is published by Granta Publications Ltd and distributed by Penguin Books Ltd, Harmondsworth, Middlesex, England; Viking Penguin Inc., 40 West 23rd St, New York, New York, USA; Penguin Books Australia Ltd, Ringwood, Victoria, Australia; Penguin Books Canada Ltd, 2801 John Street, Markham, Ontario, Canada L3R 1B4; Penguin Books (NZ) Ltd, 182–90 Wairau Road, Auckland 10, New Zealand. This selection copyright © 1986 by Granta Publications Ltd.

Cover photograph by Don McCullin

SUPPORTED BY THE
E A S T E R N
Arts
ASSOCIATION

Granta 20, Winter 1986

ISBN 014-00-8597.1

CONTENTS

Marguerite Yourcenar

Mishima
£9.50   85628 145 X   PUBLISHED
Yourcenar's brilliant study of the famous Japanese writer. Includes   ·
analysis of the *Sea of Fertility* and *The Sailor Who Fell From Grace With The Sea*.

The Bodleian Library and its Treasures

£29   85628 128 X   148 col/60 b/w   192 pages   MARCH, '87
The Bodleian Library of the University of Oxford was the first great public library in England and is one of the largest libraries in the world, holding about four and a half million volumes.

For the first time in its four hundred year history this famous Oxford library, one of the oldest in Europe, opens its doors and shows off all its magnificent treasures in one volume.

The essays are magnificently illustrated in colour and black and white pictures from the Bodleian collections. Each chapter is written by the relevant Keeper.

John Murray

Kin
£9.95   85628 161 1   PUBLISHED
"The ground is so well-trodden . . . but John Murray's gifts as a writer nevertheless brings a freshness to the subject . . . He is a fine writer."
Daily Telegraph

"Mr. Murray is an eccentric stylist but his book maintains an intelligent gusto and a pulse of emotional reality." *The Guardian*

For a complete list please write for our catalogue.

Editorial and Publishing:
Cobb House, Nuffield, Henley-on-Thames, Oxon RG9 5RU.
Telephone (0491) 641496. Telex 825751 J M Dent G.

AIDAN ELLIS

A Letter to our Subscribers

Dear Subscriber

Over the past year the size of <u>Granta</u>'s readership has grown at a phenomenal rate, and our subscriptions are now maintained on a computer. To ensure a fast, efficient service, there are a number of things to bear in mind:

■ If you have problems with your subscription please let us know as soon as possible.

■ We can deal with your queries much more quickly if you quote your subscriber number when writing. You will find this on the top line of your mailing label.

■ Should you change your address, please inform us in good time. Hundreds of copies of the magazine are returned after each dispatch because subscribers have moved without telling us.

■ Please use your postcode in all communications with us. This will ensure that your copy of <u>Granta</u> reaches you without unnecessary delays.

■ We occasionally exchange our mailing list with other publications whose aims are broadly similar to our own. If you would rather not receive mailings from these publications, simply write and tell us, and your name will not be included.

■ One final thing. In the next issue of <u>Granta</u> we will enclose a readers' questionnaire, in which you will have the chance to let us know some of your thoughts about the magazine: what you like about it, what you don't like. A questionnaire of this sort is the best opportunity for us to discover how we can improve <u>Granta</u>, and we look forward to your reply.

Yours sincerely,

Claire Craig

Claire Craig
Subscriptions Manager

P.S. *If you're not already a subscriber, isn't it about time you became one? See details on page 244.*

PICADOR
OUTSTANDING INTERNATIONAL WRITING

HOUSE
Tracy Kidder, author of the Pulitzer Prize-Winning *The Soul of a New Machine*

In this luminous book, Tracy Kidder watches the construction of a new house from conception to reality. In intimate detail we see the ambitious owners, the architect who gave form to their dreams, and the carpenters who pounds the nails. Kidder delves deep into the lives of them all, artfully weaving their stories into his portrait of the project that brings them all together.
'The stuff of real drama' *New York Times Book Review*
£3.95   Published **5 September**

A BOOK OF TRAVELLER'S TALES
Eric Newby

A great traveller pays tribute to his illustrious predecessors and contemporaries with this marvellously entertaining anthology of the very best travel writing from all ages and places. With more than 300 writers represented, this is a veritable Who's Who of travellers from 430 B.C. to the present day. From Alexander the Great to Queen Victoria, from Ibn Battuta to Paul Theroux, from Evelyn Waugh to Cecil Beaton, this is an anthology that will provide hours of entertainment and enlightenment.
£4.95   Published **10 October**

THE MAN WHO MISTOOK HIS WIFE FOR A HAT
Oliver Sacks

An enthralling collection of clinical tales which border the thin divide between fact and fiction, and show us all the poignancy of losing faculties which most of us don't even know exist. As Professor of Clinical Neurology at the Albert Einstein College of Medicine, New York, Oliver Sacks sees a remarkable cross-section of some of life's more unusual problems, such as the distinguished musician of the title, who couldn't distinguish between the shape of a hat and his wife's head.
'It is a wonderful book, by which I mean not only that it is excellent (which it is) but also that it is full of wonder, wonders and wondering' *Punch*.
£3.50   Published **7 November 1986**

THE MADWOMAN'S UNDERCLOTHES
Essays & Occasional Writings 1968-85
Germaine Greer

Strong, fearless and often controversial, Germaine Greer has never shied from putting her opinions into writing. This feast of views, taken from sources as diverse as *Oz* and the *Sunday Times*, is both a reflection of an era and the changing ideas and styles of Germaine Greer. Whether the topic is John F. Kennedy, vaginal deodorants or the aftermath of Bangladesh, the essays are always stimulating, often explosive, sometimes angry and sometimes funny.
Hardback **£9.95**   Published **10 October**

BREAKFAST IN HELL
A Doctor's Experiences of the Ethiopian Famine
Myles Harris

Before the full extent of the catastrophe was known in the West, Dr Myles Harris spent four months in Ethiopia on attachment to the Red Cross. With ruthless honesty and acute intelligence, he examines every factor that contributed to the Ethiopian tragedy, from the naivete of the relief organisations to the Kafkaesque bureaucracy of Mengistu's communist regime. This is a real-life journey into the 'Heart of Darkness', an angry, impassioned and vitally important book about unremitting villainy.
£3.50   Published **7 November 1986**

THE WORLD OF THE SHORT STORY:
A Twentieth Century Collection
Edited by Clifton Fadiman

This collection of stories by some of the finest writers of our time has a special appeal: they are not the ones which usually appear in anthologies. Readers will meet some famous and familiar talents in fresh and unexpected masterpieces of the form. Sixty-two stories from sixteen countries range from the 'moderns' of the century's dawning – Maugham, Colette, Lawrence – to current practitioners such as Updike, Carver and Joyce Carol Oates.
Hardback **£14.95**
Published
7 November 1986

CENTURY HUTCHINSON
Brookmount House, 62-65 Chandos Place, London WC2

FIDEL: A CRITICAL PORTRAIT
Tad Szulc

After more than twenty-five years in power, Fidel Castro has allowed a biographer to look at his extraordinary life through personal conversations and full access to his closest associates and companions in arms.

For the first time, in exclusive detail, Tad Szulc reveals the dramatic inside stories behind the revolution that toppled Batista, the Bay of Pigs and Cuban missile crisis, Fidel's volatile relationship with Nikita Kruschev, his real feelings about John F. Kennedy, as well as his present political aspirations.

With fascinating insights too into Castro's personal life, Tad Szulc creates the definitive portrait of one of the twentieth century's most complex and controversial characters.

June 1987   £14.95

IN SOUTHERN LIGHT
Alex Shoumatoff

'Travelling to Zaire and up the Amazon with anyone is an adventure; with Shoumatoff it's grand adventure.' Russell Banks

February 1987   £12.95

WORLDS APART: Travels in War and Peace
Gavin Young

A memorable collection of pieces summoning up more than twenty years of travel and adventure in some of the world's most exciting and remote places, from unknown wars in remote Indian hill towns to battles in the Walled City of Kowloon.

March 1987   £14.95

JERUSALEM
Colin Thubron

'This is a rare book, and one to read and reread.' Observer

'Mr Thubron obviously knows and loves every stone of the city.' Guardian

'Of all the books I have read on this dustily irresistible city, Colin Thubron's most vividly conveys its atmosphere.' Gerald Kaufmàn, Listener

February 1987   £5.95

METHUEN
■ MODERN FICTION ■

JOE ORTON
Head to Toe
Out of print from 1971 until now, Orton's fantastic, erotic and satirical fable follows the fortunes of Gombold on his peregrinations from the head of a creature some hundred miles high through the giant's nether regions and on towards his toes...

'Worthy of Swift' Auberon Waugh
£3.95

MAEVE KELLY
Necessary Treasons
An exciting, insistent and highly original narrative of the lives of women in contemporary Ireland — and the 'necessary treasons' that they are all forced to commit.

'A landmark in Irish feminist writing' FORTNIGHT
£3.50

PETER HANDKE
The Left-Handed Woman
'The writing is all exact observation of dangling nerve-ends...A clever, claustrophobic text. You can smell the airlessness behind the double-glazed windows on the German housing estate...' GUARDIAN

'Dazzling lucidity' Ian McEwan
£2.95

RONALD BLYTHE
The Stories of Ronald Blythe
'Blythe transmits dreams of the past and fantasies of the present with a creamy, conscious grace. His stories are compelling, atmospheric, as rich in detail as the dark cluttered parlours of aunts. This is a seductive writing...' SUNDAY TIMES
£3.95

PETER HANDKE
Slow Homecoming
'Pained, chapped, gritty trilogy... extraordinary odyssey' OBSERVER

'German literature's last surviving romantic, a modern day solitary-cum-nature poet' SUNDAY TIMES
£3.95

BENEDICT KIELY
Nothing Happens in Carmincross
'Written with zest and grace, humour and irony in a style that is totally individual...It must be read by everyone interested in Irish writing and the peculiar tragedy of the Irish situation.' IRISH TIMES

'Richly, grimly funny' OBSERVER
£3.50

methuen

GRANTA

BACK ISSUES

Thursdays are unthinkable without it

From your newsagent. 80p

REDMOND O'HANLON

AMAZON ADVENTURE

Having spent two months travelling in the primary rain forests of Borneo, I thought that a four-month journey in the country between the Orinoco River in Venezuela and the Amazon in Brazil would pose no particular problem.

I re-read my nineteenth-century heroes: the seven volumes of Alexander von Humboldt's *Personal narrative of travels to the equinoctial regions of the New Continent during the years 1799–1804* (1814–29); William H. Edwards's *A Voyage up the River Amazon* (1847); Alfred Russel Wallace's *A Narrative of Travels on the Amazon and Rio Negro* (1853); Henry Walter Bates's *The Naturalist on the River Amazons* (1863) and Richard Spruce's *Notes of a Botanist on the Amazon and Andes* (1908).

There are no leeches that go for you in the Amazon jungles, an absence which would represent, I felt, a great improvement on life in Borneo. But then there *are* many of the same amoebic and bacillary dysenteries, yellow and blackwater and dengue fevers, malaria, cholera, typhoid, rabies, hepatitis and tuberculosis—plus one or two very special extras.

There is Chagas' disease, for instance, carried by various species of assassin bugs that bite you on the face or neck and then, gorged, defecate next to the puncture: when you scratch the itch that results, you rub the droppings and their cargo of protozoa into your bloodstream; between one and twenty years later you begin to die from an illness whose symptoms are at first like malaria and later like AIDS. Then there is *onchocerciasis*, river-blindness, transmitted by blackfly and caused by worms which migrate to the eyeball; *leishmaniasis*, which is a bit like leprosy and is produced by a parasite carried by sandflies (it infects eighty percent of the Brazilian troops on exercise in the jungle in the rainy season): unless treated quickly, it eats away the warm extremities. And then there is the odd exotic, like the fever which erupted in the state of Pava in the 1960s killing seventy-one people, including the research unit sent in to identify it.

The big animals are supposed to be much friendlier than you might imagine. The jaguar kills you with a bite to the head, but only in exceptional circumstances. Two vipers, the fer de lance (up to seven-and-a-half feet long) and the bushmaster (up to twelve feet, the largest in the world) kill you only if you step on them. The anaconda is known to tighten its grip only when you breathe out; the electric eel can only deliver its 640 volts before its breakfast; the piranha only rips you to bits if you are already bleeding and the giant catfish, which merely has a penchant for taking off your feet at the ankle as you do the crawl.

The smaller animals are, on the whole, much more annoying: mosquitoes, blackfly, tapir-fly, chigger, ticks, scabies-producing *Tunga pentrans* and *Dermatobia hominis*, and the human botfly, whose larvae bore into the skin, eat modest amounts of you for forty days and emerge as inch-long maggots.

But it was the candiru, the toothpick-fish—a tiny catfish adapted for a parasitic life in the gills and cloaca of bigger fish—which swam most persistently into my dreams on troubled nights.

In Borneo, when staying in the longhouses, I learned that going down to the river in the early morning is the polite thing to do—you know you are swimming in the socially correct patch of muddy river when fish nuzzle your pants, wanting you to take them down and produce their breakfast. In the Amazons, on the other hand, should you have had too much to drink, say, and inadvertently urinate as you swim, any homeless candiru, attracted by the smell, will take you for a big fish and swim excitedly up your stream of uric acid, enter your urethra like a worm into its burrow and, raising its gill-cover, stick out a set of retrorse spines. Nothing can be done. The pain, apparently, is spectacular. You must get to a hospital before your bladder bursts; you must ask a surgeon to cut off your penis.

Then, in consultation with my friend at the Radcliffe Infirmary in Oxford, Donald Hopkins, the inventor of the haemorrhoid gun, I designed an anti-candiru device: we took a cricket-box, cut out the front panel and replaced it with a tea-strainer.

Released so brilliantly from this particular fear, I began, in earnest, to panic. Alfred Russel Wallace's resolution seemed the only one possible. Attacked by fever in his dugout on the Rio Negro in 1851, Wallace collapsed, was delirious for two days, and, recovering, vowed 'never to travel again in such wild, unpeopled districts without some civilized companion or attendant.' That was the answer: I would persuade the civilized companion of my Borneo journey, the poet James Fenton, to visit the Venezuelan Amazons with me. He would be flattered to be asked. He would be delighted to come.

After supper at the long table in James's kitchen (a map of Borneo still hung on the wall), half-way through a bottle of Glenmorangie, I judged the time was ripe.

'James,' I said, 'you are looking ill. You are working far too hard writing all these reviews. You need a break. Why don't you come to the Amazon with me?'

'Are you listening seriously?'

'Yes.'

'Are you sitting comfortably?'

'Yes.'

'Then I want you to know,' said James, shutting his eyes and pressing his palms up over his face and the top of his bald head, *'that I would not come with you to High Wycombe.'*

I asked everyone I knew. I went to see the poet Craig Raine. 'It will increase your stock of metaphors,' I said.

'It will increase my stock of parasites,' said Craig.

I rang the photographer Don McCullin.

'To be frank with you,' said Don, 'I thought you might get round to me sooner or later. You've come to the right man. It makes sense. Look, I don't want to be rude or anything, Redmond, but I've looked at a lot of pictures in my time, and, well, frankly, *yours are the worst I've ever seen.* But I'm not interested. I've done it all. I cleaned up on the Xinqu for Norman Lewis, and that was enough for me. Just at the moment, just for now, I want to get drunk a lot. And I also want to make love to Laraine a lot—and where you're going you can't do either.'

And then I thought of Simon Stockton. I met Simon years ago, before he left England for Germany to run his own discotheques. He ran a nightclub in Hamburg until the police found his partner lying on a park bench with a bullet through his head. Simon had had his passport stamped UNDESIRABLE ALIEN and been deported.

He started again as a croupier, worked his way up from club to club and now helped to run the Kensington Sovereign. He would be a push-over. His secret ambition, I knew, was to abandon his wild, professional night-life and become something really peaceful, like a war photographer. I gave him a ring. It would be my first visit to a casino.

S imon, in his mid-thirties, suave in a dark suit, met me by the guard at the reception desk.

'Come on through and try to keep calm,' he said. 'We've got big punters tonight. Everyone's tense.'

We sat at the bar. Simon clicked his fingers and a Malay brought a bottle of claret. Through a glass partition we watched the players hunched round the roulette and blackjack tables. Wives and mistresses sat on stools behind their husbands or lovers, anxious, chain-smoking. I still could not believe that Simon really wanted to come with me.

'Of course I'm coming. It's the biggest opportunity of my life. I've bought a 500 millimetre mirror lens for the birds. I wouldn't miss it for the world. And besides, after fifteen years in this joint, I need a break: it's the Amazon or the bin for me.'

'And there again,' Simon added à propos of nothing in particular, 'I'm good on the violence. See that?' He lifted the hair off his forehead to reveal a long, recently healed scar. 'Eight stitches. Some maniac lost all he'd got and thought I'd put the hex on him. Smashed me over the head with an ashtray. The doorman butted him in the stomach and we did him for assault.' Simon nodded at a waiter and a tray of oriental dishes arrived.

'What do they generally do,' I asked, 'when they lose everything?'

'They go home and top themselves,' said Simon, his mouth full of monkfish. 'We get a lot of that, but it's not our fault—just that we happen to be at the end of the line.'

'You'll be bored in the jungle.'

'I can handle it,' said Simon, turning round briefly to scan the tables. 'There's nothing I can't handle. Why, we had three Iraqi's in here only last week. Some Arab gangster thought we were cheating and these boys were his minders. So I promised them everything— my Aunt Sally, the cat, the piggy-bank, *everything*—while the car-jockey called the police. When the Old Bill rolled them we found their pockets were just wide slits: they'd got the hardware strapped down their thighs, eighteen inches long and curved at the ends. *It was the dimensions.* Right out of order, in my opinion.'

I was staring through the glass partition, admiring the half-naked girl croupiers standing by the dull lights above the green baize when an elderly Japanese scowled, beckoned a flunkey, muttered something and despatched him to Simon.

'Fatso,' said Simon, 'you just got yourself thrown out.'

'Thrown out?'

'For smiling.'

'Smiling?'

'Yeah. You were smiling at the girls. You upset Mr Yamamoto there. He thinks you put the jinx on him. You are interfering with his astral powers. You'll have to go. They're *gamblers*, you see. They come here to *gamble*. It's called a *casino*. If you want girls you go to something called a *brothel*.'

Outside on the pavement, we stood in the drizzle and looked at Waterhouse's masterpiece, the great Victorian romanesque façade of the Natural History Museum, sheltering the very collections which Bates and Wallace and Spruce had visited before setting out for the Amazons.

'Isn't it beautiful?' I said. 'Do you often slip over there when you're on a day shift?'

'Frankly, Redmond,' said Simon, turning to go back down the steps past the uniformed doorman, 'I've never set foot in the place.'

I stood in the rain, unable to move, and continued staring at the building across the road.

When I was about four-and-three-quarter years old, a mistle-thrush dropped half an empty egg-shell in front of me. Being unaware at the time of the empty cosmos, of the unfeelingness of causal connections, I concluded that this message of brown and purple blotches on a background of browny-white had been intended just for me.

I began an egg collection and kept it in a box on top of the chest of drawers by the window which looked out over the kitchen-garden and across the small fields, thick hedges and woods of the cheese country to the distant scarp of the Wiltshire downs. I took one blackbird's egg from a clutch of five in their rough cup lined with dried grass hidden in a thicket by the laburnum tree. I found a thrush's egg in its mud-rounded nest in a bush by the pond. I raided the nest of a flycatcher that returned each year to rear its young on a ledge against the Bathstone front of the house. With a teaspoon I scooped out the white, brown-speckled egg of a wren from its dome of dead leaves built into the leaf-litter behind an old wall-pinioned greengage tree. And, one day, sitting in the front of my father's two-seater canvas canoe on Bowood lake (which was part of his parish), I lifted the covering from a floating mound of weed moored in a lily-bed and removed the chalky egg of a great crested grebe. It was the pride of my collection.

When I was seven, my father gave me the two volumes of T.A. Coward's *The Birds of the British Isles and their Eggs,* my first proper books, which he had been given by *his* father, who used to watch birds and geologize with Coward all over Cheshire in the early 1900s. And he also gave me T.A. Coward's own custom-built binoculars which Coward had left to my grandfather: in fact a pair of matching telescopes, slim, black, brass tubes through which, one day, I hoped to see all the birds that Coward had seen, as mysterious in their marsh and coastland, on their moors and mountains and forests, as Thorburn had depicted them in his tempera plates.

On the first week of the school holiday I persuaded my father to take me to the Natural History Museum. It was all different then: you could actually go to the mahogany egg cabinets and pull out the drawers. And there were all the eggs of all the birds in the British Isles, thousands of them, lying in whole clutches, on their beds of cotton wool in the wood partitions under the glass. It was the guillemots' eggs that really astonished me—they had a whole cabinet to themselves: they were white, yellow, blue, green, purple, red or brown; and they were smeared or lined or blotched or spotted with all kinds of different colours. If these were the eggs of just one species, how could you ever hope to know enough? It was all variety and surprise and difference. Perhaps it was *that* feeling, I now thought, standing in the rain on the Cromwell Road, which I had really been searching for—and had found—in the primary rain forest in the heart of Borneo, that sudden moment when you were not even sure if the something that was flying across the river in front of you was a bat or a bird or a butterfly. And it was that feeling which I vowed to experience again, if I could, in the vaster forests of the northern Amazons.

There was a hand on my shoulder.

'Are you all right, sir?' It was the doorman. He had a

compassionate look on his craggy face. He had seen it all before.

'Not want to go home? Is that it? Listen, sir. It's always best to go straight home when you've had a spot of bad luck. You'll feel better in the morning. If you haven't the money for a cab, sir—if you don't mind my saying—the Kensington Sovereign will lend it to you. It's the policy.'

Over the next two months I made an unerring selection from different camping shops of seriously defective equipment. Exasperated, I once again invoked the talismanic name of my uncle, Colonel Egerton-Mott, who had run Special Operations Executive in Borneo against the Japanese during the war, and went to see the sponsors of our Borneo journey, 22 SAS.

At their headquarters near Hereford I was absurdly pleased to see that I had been promoted, from Training Wing to Regular Stores.

'Well done, lad,' said the quartermaster as we walked from his office to the equipment shed. 'I liked your book on Borneo. You made us sound almost human.'

Then I got that wrong, too, I thought, as we passed a platoon of young soldiers on the apron making a last check on their Bergens before jumping into two parked lorries. They were fit and lean and possessed with a ferocious energy. They didn't even *look* human.

In the stores I had a reunion with Ernie and Eddie and signed for two complete sets of the jungle equipment I had taken to Borneo, plus an outfit of special lightweight jungle fatigues (large) and a floppy camouflage hat. Over-excited, I put on the clothes. I felt tough at once. I was ready for anything.

'We can't let him go like that,' said Ernie, sounding genuinely distressed.

'Why not?' I said. 'Am I missing something?'

'No,' said Ernie, 'it's just that you're a disgrace to the Regiment. You look like Benny Hill.'

A week later, I took Simon's share of the equipment down to his house in a suburb of West Drayton. It was easy enough to find: the villa was distinguished from the row of look-alikes because Simon had painted it purple all over, and an enormous blown-up photograph of his head entirely blocked off the left upstairs window.

It was three in the afternoon and Simon came to the door in his flannel dressing-gown.

'Hi, Fatso. Brought the kit? Lob it in here,' he said, helping me carry the Bergen into the room on the right. Against one wall, there was a stack of tuners, amplifiers, record and tape decks topped with shelves of records. An enormous television and several video machines stood by the window. In the corner a wooden girl with big wooden breasts held out an ashtray. We spread the olive-drab basha-top, the canvas hammock, the mosquito net and the pole-bed across the carpet on top of one pair of small, red dancing shoes, one pair of black fish-net stockings, one black suspender belt, and one black G-string with a tiny, scarlet, silk heart sewn on to the front.

'It's okay,' said Simon, 'she's asleep upstairs. She wears anything I ask her to, comes on a Thursday night, and goes away again on Friday. She *never* gives me any aggravation.' Simon asked if I wanted a tour of the house—his 'maximum-pleasure dream-machine'—and we walked across the corridor.

'This is the front room. We take tea in here when very special guests, like Mother, come to pay their respects. We eat little cakes.'

On our way upstairs, we passed a large inscription, REMEMBER REMEMBER THE FIFTH OF NOVEMBER. 'It's the day my wife left me,' Simon said, without looking round. 'I'll never forgive her.'

Out of the landing window, I saw an old plum tree, and from its lowest branch there hung a bedraggled Snoopy doll, a riding-hat on its head and a shredded target pinned to its chest. It swayed, slightly, in the breeze.

'That,' said Simon, 'is actually my ex-wife. That's her crash-helmet. Whenever I get depressed I take my cross-bow, lean out and bolt her one.'

'And this,' he said, flinging open a door marked DANGER HIGH VOLTAGE OVERHEAD CABLES, 'is the master bedroom.'

He switched on a red light. It was a darkroom, the window obscured by black shutters and a light-proof ventilator. Tables ran round the edge of the room, with filing cabinets beneath them. There were two big Durst enlargers, a set of developing and fixing trays and three plumbed-in washing sinks. The cameras and lenses were neatly arranged on a shelf. There were Bowens flashlights, tripods, folded umbrellas and a pile of cones and bowl reflectors. But the chief glory of the room was the girls. They pouted from Simon's sofa in soft-focus black-and-white. They sat naked in full Cibachrome in Simon's flower-bed. They perched in sepia on the knob of his banisters and giggled. They sprawled long and languorous on his carpet. They were caught by remote-control on the bed, with the master himself undressing them.

I was getting a sense of what our conversations in the jungle might be about. 'Simon,' I said, 'they must actually like you.'

'Of course they do,' said Simon, 'it's only natural. They love me to death. But it's wham, bam and thank you mam with me, I'm afraid. Not like you. How long you been married? Fifty years?'

Simon led me across the passage and opened another door. We peered inside.

'This is the romper-room.'

A very young girl lay asleep on the double bed. She was half-covered by a duvet, curled in the foetal position. Three Siamese cats snuggled together, pressed into the hollow between her buttocks and the back of her thighs. Her yellow hair fell forward across the pillow.

'She works in the casino,' Simon whispered. 'I'm in charge of personnel. I'm not kidding, Redmond, I'm *exhausted* with pretty girls. I'm *man-handled* by them. There are days when I can hardly call my dick my own.'

We sat down at the table in the room Simon called the kitchen. It looked more like a spaceship.

'You're a busy man, Simon.'

'True, but it's just a problem I have,' he said, reaching over to a wine-rack and pulling out a bottle of Châteauneuf-du-Pape. 'You see, Redmond, I want to change my life. I really do. On this trip, I want you to educate me. You tell me what books to read. Come to that, why are we going on this trip, anyway? Why aren't you still teaching in Oxford, you fat berk? *That's* the life. Free port, as much as you want, laid down *hundreds* of years ago. Young students all over you.'

Ten years ago, I taught English literature at Oxford, but I was only on trial. 'I taught my undergraduates the wrong century, just before their exams.'

'Shit a brick. I thought you were safe to go with. I thought I could trust you.'

'They made the same mistake.'

'Jesus.'

'It's all right,' I said, 'We're going to take a nineteenth-century route. And that *is* my period.' I explained that we would follow Humboldt up the Orinoco river and through the Casiquiare region. Then we would pick up Spruce and Wallace on the Rio Negro, go down to Manaus and join Bates, and then maybe go up the Purus. But Simon was clearly panicking; for that matter, so was I. 'I've been wobbling round our local wood every morning,' I said to reassure him, 'I'm fitter than I used to be.'

'Are you, hell,' said Simon, pouring himself another glass.

It dawned on me later, as I was driving back to Oxford that evening, that it was too late to change anything. I was not just going to the jungle. I was going to the jungle with Simon.

Caracas, Venezuela

I left Simon reading *Pride and Prejudice* in the flat I had rented in the centre of Caracas and took a taxi to the Country Club to meet Charlie Brewer. Charlie Brewer is the great explorer and photographer of Venezuela. His hobby is dropping by helicopter on to jungle mountains and then abseiling into their caves and sink-holes. He has led so many scientific expeditions into the interior that thirteen plant species, one plant genus, one bird species and one acquatic insect (*Tepuidessus breweri*) now bear his name. Every taxi driver in Caracas knows Charlie Brewer and will tell you about his term of office as Minister of Youth. To publicize Venezuela's claim to land that now belongs to Guyana, Charlie gathered a band of young admirers and invaded the territory. Guyana mobilized its army and air force. Charlie unscrewed an old brass name-plate proclaiming 'British Guiana' on a frontier post, and withdrew. The communist government of Guyana was not amused. The capitalist government of Venezuela was not amused. Charlie lost his job.

I found him sitting at a table in the cloister of the central quadrangle, surrounded by flowers and sipping a glass of water. Charlie, it seemed, believed that the best introductions are accomplished in an hour-long session of weight-lifting; I had been hoping for an hour-long session with a couple of bottles of wine.

We exchanged greetings, and he picked up an athlete's bag from the paving stones, swung it on to his shoulders, and pointed to a leather pouch on the table. 'Bring that,' he said while leading me to my first visit to a gym since I was sixteen. 'And give it to me if there's trouble.'

The pouch was heavy, and I looked inside. It was a large, black Browning automatic.

'Everyone out there,' Charlie explained, 'wants to kill me.'

Later, sitting in a dry-heat room, surrounded by men sweating and joking in front of directional heaters, I asked Charlie about our proposed route, following Humboldt.

'It's ridiculous,' he said. 'Those rivers are as big as the sea. You won't find your birds and animals. But there's a little stream, the Maturaca, that also connects the Orinoco and the Rio Negro. It's marked on the maps and we know it was used to smuggle *salsaparilla*—a plant that helps you to piss in the final stages of syphilis—from the Spanish to the Portuguese possessions in the seventeenth century. But it's not been travelled since. Go find the way into it from the north. It's wild country. The trees meet overhead all the way and the streams are criss-crossed with fallen trunks. You just have to cut your own way through. The last people to try, the Border Commission officers, were lost in there for two months in 1972 and gave up. The country is so remote that Neblina itself, the highest mountain in South America outside the Andes, was not discovered until 1953.'

We took a cold shower.

'You will come to my apartment,' shouted Charlie from his stall. 'I have low-level radar and high-level NASA infra-red satellite maps of the area. It is a small obsession of mine.'

One wall was hung with assorted blow-pipes. Books and papers lay everywhere. An adjoining room contained a Sten gun, a Hasselblad, a combined .22 rifle and .410

shotgun, a 7 x 8 Pentax with a wooden carrying handle, a 12-bore shotgun, a Linhof panoramic, a 16-bore shotgun, a pair of Olympuses and a case of lenses. On the floor stood a large radio transmitter. On a spare piece of table were a plan and various bits of a knife.

'This,' Charlie explained, taking a complete knife out of a drawer, 'is the Charlie Brewer Explorer Survival Knife. It has a six-and-a-quarter inch stainless steel blade, with a Rockwell Hardness of fifty-six to fifty-eight, and a two-and-three-quarter inch saw extending from the handle to the point. On the left here is a 180-degree clinometer for calculating the height of mountains; on the right instructions for five ground-to-air signals and a six-centimetre ruler. This small hole in the blade is for sighting when used as a signalling reflector; this hole converts into wire cutters. It can also be made into a harpoon with another special device of mine. This end-cap screws off, and inside the hollow handle there's a compass and a waterproof container with the Morse code printed on its sides in which you'll find six fish hooks, a monofilament nylon fishing line, two lead sinkers, one float, an exacto blade, two sewing needles, three matches, a flint stick and a suture needle with suture material attached. It's made by Marto of Toledo and imported into the US by Gutman at $150. But you and Simon can have one. It's good for skinning alligators. And when the Yanomami have had a go at you you can sew each other up round the arrow holes.'

'The Yanomami?'

'The most violent people on earth. Some anthropologists think they were the first peoples to reach South America from the North. They have very fair skins, occasionally green eyes. They are the largest untouched group of Indians left in the rain forest. The other Indians are terrified of them. My friend Napoleon Chagnon called his book about them *The Fierce People*. I'll give you a copy. It's all perfectly understandable—they grow a few plantains, but basically they're hunter-gatherers and there's not much food in those forests. So when times are hard they kill the new-born girls. Then there are never enough women to go round, so they fight over them. They have formalized duels, and hit each other over the head with ten-foot-long clubs. They also raid other tribes for women and kill the men with six-foot-long arrows tipped with curare. And on top of all that they've no concept of natural death, so if anyone dies from a fever it's meant to be the result of malign magic worked by an enemy shaman, and the death must be avenged.'

I stood there stupidly, holding the enormous Brewer Explorer Knife. 'And this still goes on?' I asked.

'They are killing each other,' said Charlie, '*right now*.'

The route Charlie planned for us meant chartering a small plane in Puerto Ayacucho on the Orinoco River and flying south to San Carlos on the Rio Negro. On Charlie's infra-red satellite map, San Carlos was the only squiggle in the whole area, and after San Carlos there was nothing.

In San Carlos we were to hire Charlie's men, their first job this year and their last, at eight dollars a day: Chimo, an old motor man; Valentine, an old prow man; Galvis, a radio man; and Pablo, who was good with an axe. Charlie had it all worked out: I'd pay half their wages at the beginning, and then one week later—once the money had been spent and they had sobered up—we would start.

We were to travel north up the Rio Negro in two dugouts, turn east into the Casiquiare River, swing south down the Pasimoni, which narrows into the Baria, just after the Yatua. And this was the easy part. 'Almost at once,' Charlie said, 'you'll begin to see all kinds of monkeys, two species of otter, sloth, anacondas, tapir, peccaries, jaguar, deer, ocelot, everything.

'And here,' Charlie said, spreading out his fingers, 'the Baria divides into a thousand tributaries, and disappears entirely beneath the forest. You can say goodbye to sunlight. Believe me. I've flown over bits of it in a helicopter and you can't see the streams from the air.

'But you should keep going. You should try to reach Neblina by the Baria. Follow the strongest current and you'll get there. You'd be the first people to reach it by the Baria route. In 1953, Bassett Maguire and William and Kathy Phelps went by the Siapa River.'

'And at some point,' Charlie added, 'you might even come across some yoppo.' Yoppo, it seemed, was a drug that the Yanomami blast into each other's nose through a metre-long tube. It is meant to produce 'peripheral-vision colour-disturbances' and enables the shamans to summon their *hekura*, their tutelary spirits.

'It also produces severe shock in the ear, nose and throat system and the pain blows your head off. I've never tried it, and other Indians swear it causes brain damage. But you, Redmond, you'd probably like it.'

Back in the flat, Simon was curled up on the sofa, watching a football match on the television, *Men Only* spread open on his knees, a half-empty bottle of Chilean wine on the table beside him and another empty bottle discarded on the floor, together with three empty packets of Marlboro cigarettes, *Playboy, Penthouse, Fiesta* and *Pride and Prejudice*.

I took one of Charlie's knives out of its black metal sheath and laid it on the sofa. Its thick, highly polished blade with the jagged saw-top and engraved reminders for helicopter signals (V ASSISTANCE + MEDICAL) glinted in the table-light.

'Oh, God,' said Simon, looking down, 'that's *horrible*. That would give *Hitler* the screaming ab-dabs.'

'It's a present from Charlie,' I said, taking a seat. 'There's been a change of plan. We're going to try to be the first people to reach Neblina, the highest mountain in South America outside the Andes, via the vast Baria swamp. Then we'll be going down a river that nobody's been down since the seventeenth century, to try and find a fierce people called the Yanomami. Apparently they hit each other over the head in duels with ten-foot-long clubs and hunt each other with six-foot-long arrows.'

'Oh, thanks,' said Simon, concentrating at last. 'Out of sight. Thanks a bundle for telling me in London. I've *always* wanted to be slammed up the arse with an arrow and then whacked on the nut with a pole.'

A Day in San Carlos

On the first morning in the little frontier town of San Carlos, I woke up early, disturbed by a high-pitched, metallic chattering that came from the corner of the roof directly above my head. I switched on my small torch, and mesmerized three very black, very glossy, very furry bats a quarter of the way down the wall. They stopped talking, recovered their composure, moved crab-wise up to the runnels beneath the corrugated iron ceiling and disappeared. I lifted the mosquito net, swung out of bed and stepped on one of a pair of neatly formed, dryish and surprisingly large Cane toad turds. The trip had begun.

We were staying at a research station of the Venezuelan Institute of Ecology, courtesy of Juan Saldarriaga. Juan is a Colombian ecologist. He is dark, small, bearded, wiry and worried. He also loves to lecture his companions—about anything. I had met him on the airstrip of the capital of Amazonas, Puerto Ayacucho, and immediately liked him. After five minutes, I'd asked him to come with us.

Juan was perhaps the only man in South America with a real reason for joining us. He was obsessed with his theory that the rain forest was not the stable environment it was generally imagined to be, and he wanted to prove that at one time or another during the irregular dry periods almost all of it had burned down in patches, believing that such repeated small-scale devastations might account for the extraordinary diversity of species. To do that he needed to journey to the remotest possible areas and dig for carbon samples in soil that had not been disturbed by the shifting agriculture of the Indians, the burning and clearing of small pieces of jungle to grow plantains or manioc. And to do that he needed me. In return he would make available to me, at all times, the entire contents of his skull.

Simon emerged from his room, looking a little strained.

'Those friends of yours in the SAS,' he said, 'are they pygmies? It's their hammocks. You can only sleep in one if you're four feet long.' Simon banged his toothbrush on his head. Juan looked at him with curiosity. 'I can't say I go around slinging hammocks in the normal course of things,' Simon continued, 'but it can't be right. You *can't* be meant to sleep with your legs in the air and your knees locked and your hooter practically stuffed down your strides. It's the pits. It really is.'

'You're meant to sleep across it,' Juan pointed out.

'I've tried *that*. You wind up with your head on the floor and your nuts in the air. You might as well bung up a meat hook and string yourself to that.'

'We'll find you a proper hammock. The best ones come from Colombia. Do not fret.'

'I am *not* fretting. In England only girls fret. I am throwing a wobbly. In English it's called *throwing a wobbly*. And another thing. You can't breathe in that mosquito net. And then there's lizards throwing bricks about on the roof all night.'

'It's not lizards,' Juan said, 'it's rats.'

'Rats!'

Juan was trying to be helpful. 'I had a cat, but one day he made a shit in my dried soil samples. So I threw him out into the street. I threw him by the tail. Since a year already we have had no cat.'

'Charming.' Simon and Juan were already beginning their special relationship.

Galvis walked in, a tall man with a small moustache and a squeaky voice. He was one of the men Charlie had arranged for me to hire, and he had gathered the others—Chimo, the motor man; Valentine, the prow man; and Pablo, the one who was good with an axe. Chimo, it seemed, had also brought his nephew from Solano. The nephew was called Culimacaré because that was the name of his village. Chimo, Galvis explained, said we would need an extra man, that the journey to the Maturaca, the unknown river, would be very difficult. No one had been there before, and we would have to cut a way through with axes.

The door slammed right back against the wall. The man who entered the room had skin as thick and leathery as Professor Glob's dug-up bog people, tanned by several hundred years under the peat. The furrows, where his face met his neck, were folded like the sides of a bull's dewlap. He wore gum boots and had bulging thighs. His stomach was tremendous. He held a pipe in his gums, and wore a heavy-duty construction-worker's helmet. He stopped close in front of me. He smelled of shag, rank male sweat and beer. He looked me up and down. He was not reassured.

'Chimo,' he said.

I smiled and presented him with a machete out of the bundle I had ready under the table.

Chimo took it in one hand, looked at it carefully, drew his pipe out of his mouth and spat a small pond of gunge some six feet away to the right.

'Thank you, Chief,' said Chimo in Spanish, 'this is Brazilian. This is the worst machete you can buy.'

Simon, uncharacteristically, whispered in my ear. 'This is the real McCoy. *This is one big heavy.*'

'I want my wages in advance,' Chimo added. 'I need beer.'

I pulled out half his pay, 300 dollars worth of small Bolivar notes which I had prepared the night before.

Chimo took the notes and grunted. 'Culimacaré,' he said, and nodded towards his nephew who, I only then realized, was standing by the doorway. 'We need an extra man.'

Simon was behind me, clutching my sleeve. 'He's just trying it on. He probably wants you to hire his whole family.'

Culimacaré was small and manifestly strong. I tried to shake his hand, but he snatched it away. An extra thumb stuck up, I noticed, inactive and hooked over at the top.

'Welcome,' I said grandly, 'to the *Expedición Maturaca.*'

Chimo grunted again and walked over to Culimacaré: 'Now you can buy a gun.'

An old pock-marked man, wearing a helmet like Chimo's, and a well-built, very dark Indian of about forty entered the room.

'Valentine and Pablo,' said Chimo, 'now we're all here. Now you must pay up.'

I handed out the money, and we agreed to meet again in the morning. I had met the crew.

L ater that evening there was a knock on the door and Juan drew back the bolt. A distraught old man in shorts and T-shirt muttered something. Juan disappeared into his drying room and came out again carrying a jar and a big syringe. The visitor took them and left.

'*That's* a needle and a half,' said Simon, 'what's *he* shooting up?'

'It's not for him. It's formalin. His aunt died yesterday. He wants to preserve the body for the party tonight and the funeral tomorrow. You rot fast here.'

'Oh, God,' said Simon.

'Perhaps,' Juan continued, 'you would like to join them at their fiesta.'

Outside the family's hut, under a group of lemon trees, tables and benches had been arranged. Groups of men were drinking *aguardiente* and playing dominoes. Friends and relatives arrived bearing presents, a tin of coffee, a basket of manioc. A few girls were sitting in a circle playing pass-the-ring. Kids were dribbling a ball about at knee level, a little over-awed by the cadaver spread out on a table just inside the door. Candles stood at the four corners, and a water-filled bowl of herbs and cut lemons had been placed on the floor beneath the body to hide its smell.

'She was an old lady of seventy-five,' Juan said. 'She fell over and fractured her skull. But it is not just an ordinary death. She was the last speaker in San Carlos of the Baré language. There is a professor who can speak a little Baré, but that is not the same thing. The language is now dead.'

We walked back in the dark by a different route. Half-way home we came across a body lying on the path. It was Pablo, our axe-man, sleeping soundly, his legs splayed out, one arm over his head and the other straight out along the ground with a wad of notes in his clenched fist. They had been torn off where they stuck out between his thumb and forefinger. Juan felt in his pockets. Nothing.

'His friends wait until he is drunk,' Juan said, 'and then take all the wages you gave him. It is better to leave him here. It will not rain tonight. He will wake up before the morning.'

In the research station we were all preparing to go to our hammocks when the outside door swung violently open. Chimo stood on the path. He swayed from side to side and then lurched backwards against the fence.

'I just came to tell you,' he said, 'that I will be a responsible man in the morning.'

It was going to be a long trip.

The Baria

'Dateline: 27 May. Place: Baria River. Significant event: rain.
'Dateline: 28 May. Place: Baria River. Significant event: rain.
'Dateline: 29 May. Place: Baria River. Significant event: rain.
'Dateline: 30 May. Place: Baria River. Significant event: rain.

In all honesty, angel, Redmond is a selfish bastard. He pretends he likes it here. The Indians, of course, poor geezers, don't know any better. And that Juan is just a nasty little Dago who treats me like a moron. Good night. I kiss your tits. I miss you. Simon.

'Dateline: 31 May. Place: Baria River. What's new? I ask myself. No rain today, *that*'s what's new I tell myself. Hear that? . . . Right? No endless thundering buckets of piss crashing down on my head all day. Well, you can take it from me, angel-drawers, the whole ghastly business will start again tomorrow. Up-to-the-minute report: only three wasp stings this morning. No more than 10,000 ants. No hornets. Blissikins, you might say. Oh, yes, one more thing before I mosey on out to favourite pub: Fatso has got the right needle with me just because I wouldn't take a picture of some frigging horrible snake. And how do I know Fatso's got the right needle with me? I know Fatso's got the right needle with me 'cause he hasn't spoken to me for *two whole days*.'

Our first long trip turned out to be quite a short one, and there were, I can see, various reasons why Simon cracked and was eventually flown out of the jungle. For although we reached Neblina, becoming the first to do so via the Pasimoni-Baria route, and witnessed its nine-thousand-foot cliffs rising sheer out of the jungle, we didn't see much else. The Baria turned out to be a difficult waterway. All the birds of the open river had long since disappeared. The yelping toucans, the big Amazon parrots, the paired flights of macaws, the rattling cry of the ringed kingfisher, the giant herons, the anhingas, the swallow-tailed kites hawking termite swarms—they just weren't around. Even the big blue Morpho butterflies and the bats, the tiny bats that cluster unseen on dead branches in half-overgrown rivers and burst away like pieces of a kicked puff-ball as you approach—even they had gone. Instead we had two things: gloom and rain.

The gloom was cast by the great trees that met overhead, knotted together with lianas, thickened by epiphytic orchids and the umbrella-leaved bromeliads. The sun reached the black water channels of the Baria only when, because of a storm or a collapsing bank or old age, a tree fell, leaving a small gap in the canopy. And the rain blasted down through the trees like pig-shot, hour after

35

hour, falling straight and heavy, shutting you into your own small world. The noise was relentless, and we moved in a trance of washed-out emptiness.

On the day when we expected to find the Maturaca, I woke at four-thirty, and lay still for a moment. The rain had stopped. It was almost clear. Today we were to find our way out.

I unwrapped myself from my SAS groundsheet and sat up. I was covered with algae and fungus; I smelled of rotten butter. A nocturnal curassow was still booming above our heads. *Hum hum hum hum de hum hum*, its call is a set of simple, unvaried notes repeated every few seconds.

'That bird again,' Simon said, already looking a little disturbed. 'I can't bear it.'

'It's all right,' I said. 'Today we will find the Maturaca. We're nearly there.'

We had been in the jungle for thirty days, and, although I intended to look for the Yanomami after discovering the Maturaca, Simon, it appeared, had other plans. 'If it's five days down the Maturaca,' he calculated, 'followed by three days in a big boat down the Rio Negro, another five days to Manaus, then it's straight to the airport. I could be in London with Liz in two weeks. *In two weeks*, I'll eat beef and Yorkshire and peach melba and drink claret and roger her stupid, all ways.'

Simon and I were having our difficulties. It was possible that some of them stemmed from his reluctance to eat anything that we caught and cooked—piranha soup, say, or the occasional guan, a chicken-like bird, that Culimacaré had been lucky enough to shoot. Simon hated it whenever we gutted an animal, and had taken to eating only the spam and rice that we had brought along as reserve stores and now nearly exhausted. But most of our difficulties probably resulted from having to be together—always. That morning, listening to Simon's projected itinerary, I had one thought: homicide. But first we had to find the Maturaca.

I shone my torch across our tarpaulin and carefully noted the positions of two scorpions. There would be a scorpion, I calculated, under every eleventh leaf. They had been caught by the rising water, and, like all the other refugees of the jungle floor, had to camp with us on islands that were never more than ten yards by

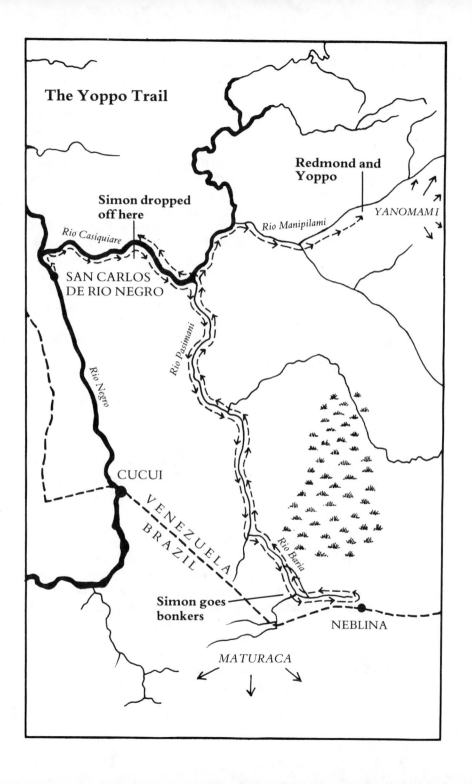

The Yoppo Trail

Redmond and
Yoppo

Rio Manipilami

YANOMAMI

Simon dropped
off here

Rio Casiquiare

SAN CARLOS
DE RIO NEGRO

Rio Pasimani

Rio Negro

CUCUI

V E N E Z U E L A

B R A Z I L

Rio Baria

Simon goes
bonkers

NEBLINA

MATURACA

twenty. I collected my wet clothes from the parachute-cord line strung up over our heads and shook them free of the insects crawling all over them. There was nothing particularly alarming in this morning's collection: no huge *veintecuatros*, so called because their bite hurts for twenty-four hours; no *catanare*, tiny ants that sting like wasps. I changed quickly out of my dry clothes, and made a brief tick check by torch-light.

Dawn filtered down. Frogs and cicadas began to call. The mosquitoes scrambled. Chimo, Culimacaré and Pablo cut fresh poles and we set off, punting our heavy canoes with difficulty. The channels were never very wide—fifteen feet at the most—but our ten-foot poles rarely touched bottom, and we had to push against the soft bank. Most of the time we couldn't punt at all, and had to pull the boats forward, standing on submerged branches up to our waists or necks, easing the hull over fallen trees, hacking a way through the branches. That morning, in two hours, we travelled two hundred yards.

Once in the water, pushing the boats along, we were never very comfortable. First, there were the ants, not the dangerous ones, but thousands and thousands of your ordinary, everyday biting ant, which went for your head and neck and had a knack for fastening on, just beyond reach, to the centre of your back.

Then there was the wasp and the hornet, which hung their nests from a twig or fixed them to the back of a leaf suspended over the water. As we cleared a passage with our machetes it was impossible to spot their yellow-brown cones. The cry '*Avispa!*' galvanized our limbs in the most extraordinary way: wherever you were, you dived for the water and, once there, you held your hat tight over your face to protect your eyes. On the back, a wasp-sting was tolerable; on the neck, very painful; and a hornet sting, anywhere, was very, very painful. By now Simon had developed, on principle, a dislike of water of any kind. With the cry '*Avispa!*', he was always the last to relinquish the boat, and always an easy target: Simon got stung on the *head* by everything.

By mid-afternoon we had turned into a channel some four feet wider than the lattice-work of waterways we had travelled that week.

'Maturaca!' Chimo announced. We had arrived.

Chimo celebrated our discovery in his characteristic fashion: facing forward and holding the punt pole out behind him like a rudder, he put his right leg up on the gunwhale, hooked his penis out of his trousers with his left hand, and, directing the jet under the raised leg, pissed with impressive volume and velocity to starboard.

'I am honoured to have such an uncle,' Culimacaré said in ritualistic response from the bow, 'because his pinga is so big.'

'That's because it's done so much work,' Chimo said, still hosing the river with undiminished velocity.

'Magic,' Simon said, 'magic, old mate. We're on the way.'

The normal dank, rotting smell of the river bank was displaced by the powerful, musky odour of otter droppings and urine; we passed a muddy patch of firm ground, big enough to camp on, which had been entirely cleared of its undergrowth.

We rounded a bend and came to a small pool where four little streams met, and there, barring our way, were the otters themselves. Five furry heads, flattened on top, stuck out of the water in a line.

Chimo imitated their chatter and they grew agitated. They looked at each other and then at the boats, before diving and surfacing right beside us.

'Jesus,' Simon said, 'knock it off will you, Chimo? They're huge. There's no room in here. I don't want my nuts nicked off.'

They had small, laid-back ears, large brown eyes, blotches of white on their big chests and efficient-looking teeth. Drops of water slid off their long side-whiskers.

'Go on, boys,' Simon said, waving his arms at them, 'piss off and scrag a fish.'

'They're just curious,' said Juan, laughing, 'they've never seen people.'

'That's why they thought we were fish,' said Simon.

We axed a way through two more trees and came out into a winding stretch. Poling round one of the bends I found myself staring into two enormous yellow eyes. A buzzard-sized owl sat on a low branch fifteen feet away, self-contained, pure white against the dull green of the glaucous leaves, a black mask of feathers round his eyes and beak. He looked at us for a moment, then stood up on his feathery legs, turned round as if every movement was an effort, and slipped easily away through the undergrowth on his brown, rounded wings.

'*Lechuza de anteojos*,' said Chimo, pointing at his own eyes with his forefinger and nodding his head.

I took Schauensee and Phelps's *Birds of Venezuela* out of my Bergen: there he was, a mere schematic representation of the real thing, outlined on Plate IX, a juvenile spectacled owl, not yet equipped with its 'chocolate-brown upperparts and broad breast band.'

Then something happened.

The dug-out had come to a standstill. I looked up. We had entered a new channel, but Culimacaré had run the bow into the bank. Chimo was resting on his punt pole, staring ahead. Nobody spoke, until Simon clasped his arms to his head and bent over.

'Oh God, oh God.' He rocked himself back and forth. 'Dear God.'

There were axe-marks everywhere. The channel had been cleared. The vegetation had been chopped down for the full length of the stream. Somone had come here before us. We were not going to be the first to re-discover the Maturaca. We had been forestalled, and it was all too late. I felt cold down my back, dull and blank in the head, wary, old.

'Who is it?' I asked.

Simon looked at me with incredulity. 'Who is it? *Who* is it?' He made a sound mid-way between a chuckle and being strangled. 'You idiot, it's us. *We did it.*'

A little way down to the left I recognized the bole of a big hardwood tree from several days ago. We had not discovered the Maturaca. We had not found the way out. We had gone in one big circle.

I suddenly felt very ill. 'It's all right,' I said. 'We've just come in a circle. We'll just have to go back and start again.'

Simon began to gag. 'It's all right?' he said. 'We've just come in a circle? We'll just have to go back and start over?' He was pounding his knee with his fist. Then he began pounding it with both fists. 'We're lost. It will take months.' He banged his forehead on the side of his pack. '*We're lost!*'

On our way back down our old track, poling quickly and silently, no one spoke, except Simon, who muttered over and over again: 'You've got to let me go, Redmond. I don't trust myself. I shall do something terrible. You've got to let me go, Redmond. I don't trust myself. I shall do something terrible.'

We drew level with one of the young otters we had seen before, who was eating something on the bank of the river. He looked round, considered us and then disappeared into the trees. Culimacaré punted up to the bank and picked up a dead paca, a large fruit-eating rodent with a furry coat like a baby fallow deer. Its broad nose and mouth were covered in foam. The paca had obviously died by drowning, the otter catching it from the river and holding it underwater. The otter had begun to eat at the back of the neck.

Chimo observed it. 'It's a gift from God.'

We stopped at one of our own old camp sites. We started a fire, placed water on to boil for scalding the paca skin, and put up our shelters and hammocks from the posts and cross-pieces we had made before. Pablo took Chimo's old, single-barrel shotgun, held together by a piece of wire, and paddled off on a hunt in the curiara.

I went for a swim fully dressed, washing myself and my clothes at the same time. I dried myself under my mosquito net, dusting my crutch in zinc-talc anti-fungus powder, put Anthisan on the bites of the day, Savlon on the cuts, Canesten cream on my feet which had begun to rot. I covered my entire body with sticky Jungle Formula, the everything repellent, and wondered how Humboldt and Wallace and Spruce had ever managed to survive.

There was a shot some way off, although it was difficult to judge the distance of noise where everything, even the sound of an explosion, was immediately broken up, stilled and smothered. Valentine and Chino laid the paca on a bed of palm leaves, pouring boiling water over it, and began scraping off the fur. They slit open the stomach, threw the guts in the water. The bladder driffed slowly away, and was finally pulled down from below by piranhas.

I took out my maps. One map indicated that the entrance to the Maturaca was to the north-west. Charlie's diagram showed that we were in the right place. The Operational Navigational Chart I had bought in London made a wild guess in heavy blue, put a large swamp to the north that I knew did not exist, and offered sound advice for pilots flying in an area that was vaguely—but only vaguely—to the east of Neblina: ABRUPT CLIFFS REPORTED IN THIS AREA. HAZARDOUS FLYING UNDER 13,000 FEET. On a fourth map the Maturaca did not even appear. I looked up and saw Pablo's canoe: it was almost sinking with the weight of a huge cayman. We hauled it out and measured it: six feet long. Its back was knobbed and ridged, and was the exact colour of the brown-black water; its tail was mottled with light patches like dim spots of filtered sunlight. We laid it down on its back on the muddy ground.

Chimo began to build a platform for smoking the meat; Galvis had almost finished preparing the paca soup. Pablo and the otter had temporarily dispelled the perpetual anxiety about finding food: maybe, despite everything, we could still find the Maturaca. Perhaps Simon would recover in a week or two. We turned the cayman over and Pablo opened it up with axe blows along its backbone. We cut out the dense flesh in sections and laid it on Valentine's platform. I slit open the distended stomach and released an appalling stench.

'Jesus,' said Simon, who, unnoticed, had come to watch.

I pulled out something that was covered in fur and slime. It was a small monkey with big circular eyes; it was intact apart from its tail, its little hands and feet still in place.

'No, no,' said Simon, stepping against a tree, holding the back of his hand to his nose, 'Just promise me, Redmond. Just promise me *you're not going to eat that as well.*'

It was a Nocturnal or Owl monkey—the only truly night-living monkey in the world, which comes out fifteen minutes after sunset, safe from every predator except the great horned owl and, it seemed, the cayman. I threw the tightly furred little body into the water.

Galvis announced that paca soup was ready. For Simon, Galvis had also cooked some rice and put out a tin of spam.

We sat down round the fire, but Simon remained standing. He was banging his mess tin with his spoon.

'Galvis,' he said, 'haven't you forgotten something?'

Juan translated, and Galvis looked confused.

'Galvis,' Simon continued, 'it is the eighth day.'

Juan translated.

'Galvis,' Simon said, 'where is my tomato ketchup?'

Juan translated, staring at Simon. 'Galvis says,' Juan answered, 'that your tomato ketchup is in the boat. But it is only the seventh and not the eighth day. You divided the stores and it is your rule. You are not allowed any more tomato ketchup until tomorrow. You must stick to that.'

'It *is* the eighth day. And I want Galvis to go to the boat and get my tomato ketchup.' Simon was still banging his tin. I suggested that it wouldn't be all that much trouble for Simon to go to the boat himself and get his own tomato ketchup.

'Just keep out of this. You don't know how to handle these people.'

'Simon, it is only a bottle of tomato ketchup.'

'*Precisely*. It is a bottle of tomato ketchup.'

Juan stood up and walked over to Simon. 'Here we are,' he said in a whisper, 'lost in this swamp. Everyone is trying to be cheerful, but everyone is very afraid. We do not know where we are. We do not know if we will ever return home. We have no food. We have only a half-eaten paca and a cayman. The rice and tins of meat that were meant for us to keep us from starvation are now almost gone. You have eaten them. And now you complain about a bottle of tomato ketchup.'

Simon turned on me. 'I'm going to kill this little shit. I warn you. I'm not going to butt his teeth in. I'm going to kill him.' Simon was breathing hard. He looked at Juan, then at me, and then at Juan. Then he threw his mess tin and spoon to the ground and walked to the bank by the black water, which had been steadily rising higher and higher, inching its way up the island. He looked up into the dark trees, and into six million square kilometres of jungle he screamed : 'WHERE IS MY T-O-M-A-T-O-K-E-T-C-H-U-P? WHERE IS MY T-O-M-A-T-O-K-E-T-C-H-U-P? WHERE IS MY T-O-M-A-T-O-K-E-T-C-H-U-P?' There was no echo from the soft leaves.

The Yanomami

It took us two weeks to return to civilization. Chimo and Pablo took Simon down river to the nearby army post, and the resident marines gave him a lift to San Carlos.

'Do not worry,' Juan reassured me. 'Perhaps it was only the

sudden withdrawal from drugs and alcohol. And then again, why *should* he like it here? But now we will find the Yanomami. Chimo knows one of the chiefs, Jarivanau. He once quarrelled with the big tribe, the Emoniteri, and there was a great fight over women and many men were killed. And so Jarivanau and his relations moved down to the Siapa.' And after five days travelling up the Siapa River, we found them.

We rounded a slow bend into a straight stretch and Culimacaré immediately pointed ahead and to the right.

'Mother of God,' said Chimo, 'there they are.'

Through the binoculars I could make out a large bongo with a cargo of naked people; two men paddled at the stern and two at the bow. As we gradually closed with them, the men stood up.

'Whoooo!' they yelled, a high-pitched shout of tremendous force.

When we were twenty yards away, Chimo asked: 'Jarivanau?'

'Jarivanau!' shouted a thickset man in the stern, pointing at his chest with a jabbing finger and waving us alongside. His head was close-shaved, and, as he bent forward to hold our gunwhale, I saw that the top of his skull was ridged and indented with four or five enormous scars.

In their boat, there were nine men, eleven women, ten children, eight dogs, one cat, one parrot and the right rear leg of an armadillo. Two old women sat in the middle of the dugout weaving baskets; in our honour, they each put on a khaki-coloured man's shirt leaving it open down the front. Almost everyone had a wadge of tobacco stuffed in the space between the lower gums and lip, distending their mouths, giving them a misleadingly Neanderthal-like profile. They were much lighter-skinned than Pablo or Culimacaré or Valentine or Chimo, much fairer, indeed, than I at first thought. Looking closely, I saw that they were covered in tiny blood-spots: they had suffered so badly from the blackfly that there was not a space left anywhere on their bodies for a fresh bite.

Several of the men had drawn black lines and circles on their forehead and cheeks, and one wore four-inch wooden plugs in his ears. The old women had smeared themselves with red onoto seed dye. Jarivanau, I noticed with a start of excitement, was clutching a narrow reed-cane pipe which was about two-and-a-half feet long and had a small black nozzle at one end. I recognized it from the description in Chagnon's *The Fierce People*. It was a yoppo pipe, the device for blasting a fearsome dose of hallucinogenic snuff up one's nostril.

I pointed at it and mimed holding the nozzle to my nose. Jarivanau grinned and nodded.

'You take that,' said Chimo, as we lashed our dugouts alongside theirs, 'and you'll be one mad Englishman.'

'It damages the brain,' Pablo said.

'It is very, very bad,' Juan said. 'It is addictive.'

Jarivanau flashed me an enormous smile and smacked his forehead with his free hand.

'I'll just try it the once,' I said, 'if it's OK with them.'

Pablo and Chimo started the two engines and the new convoy, three abreast, moved slowly up-river. The young women near the prow passed Galvis a large cooking pot, and he filled it with manioc and river water. All the Yanomami drank and then offered the remains to me. It was impossible to refuse such a draught of sawdust and friendship. I wondered, irrationally (we were far from any settlement), just how many parasite eggs I was inviting to hatch in my gut.

'Jarivanau,' said Chimo, pointing at a woman suckling her child in the stern and miming love-making by moving his pelvis forward and back, 'is she your wife?'

Jarivanau shook his head and put his arms round a young woman and a girl, who could not have been more than ten years old, sitting in front of him. He then stood up and pointed into the middle of the boat. A woman we had not noticed lay there, propped up against a carrying basket, emaciated, listless, her brown eyes huge in her sunken face. She tried to smile at us, but coughed instead. She turned her face away. Juan said that she had malaria and probably TB as well; we would take her with us on our return.

Chimo muttered: 'We'll take them a good long way, and then double back. There are too many people. If we camp together we'll lose everything. They'll have your trousers off you as you sleep, Reymono. We can visit them tomorrow evening.'

I nodded at the two old women next to me. They nodded back. They were on balance, I decided, a great deal cleaner than I was.

We slung our hammocks and then chopped up enough rotten logs to keep the fire burning all night, waiting until darkness fell and the blackfly disappeared before ladling out our piranha soup and manioc and standing round the cooking pot. Then it was definitely time to go to bed.

I hobbled under the mosquito net and rolled backwards into the hammock. Bending forward gingerly, I took out Chagnon and the torch. Once I had tucked the SAS mosquito net into the sides of the hammock and made a routine check for resident insects, I began the most delicious part of the day—a quarter-of-an-hour read in the knowledge that one was unlikely to be bitten by anything short of a jaguar.

I turned quickly to Chagnon's *Yanomamö, The Fierce People*. Having at last actually seen some Yanomamo head scars, I wanted to re-read Chagnon's description of how they were acquired, a description which, in Caracas, had once seemed impossibly exotic and remote and only half-believable.

In a graduated scale of violence, chest pounding duels are the friendliest formal exchange. Chagnon witnessed one such contest between two rival Yanomami groups:

> Two men, one from each side, would step into the centre of the milling, belligerent crowd of weapon-wielding partisans, urged on by their comrades. One would step up, spread his legs apart, bare his chest, and hold his arms behind his back, daring the other to hit him. The opponent would size him up, adjust the man's chest or arms so as to give himself the greatest advantage when he struck, and then step back to deliver his close-fisted blow. The striker would painstakingly adjust his own distance from his victim by measuring his arm length to the man's chest, taking several dry runs before delivering his blow. He would then wind up like a baseball pitcher, but keeping both feet on the ground, and deliver a tremendous wallop with his fist to the man's left pectoral muscle, putting all of his weight into the blow. The victim's knees would often buckle and he would stagger around a few moments, shaking his head to clear the stars, but remain silent . . . He then would

stand poised and take as many as four blows before demanding to hit his adversary. He would be permitted to strike his opponent as many times as the latter struck him, provided that the opponent could take it.

Club fights represent the next level of violence. These can take place both within and between villages . . . The clubs used in these fights are, ideally, 8 to 10 feet long. They are very wiry, quite heavy, and deliver a tremendous wallop. In general shape and dimensions, they resemble pool cues, but are nearly twice as long. The club is held at the thin end, which is frequently sharpened to a long point in case the fighting escalates to spear thrusting, in which case the club is inverted and used as a pike.

Most duels start between two men, usually after one of them has been caught *in flagrante* trysting with the other's wife. The enraged husband challenges his opponent to strike him on the head with a club. He holds his own club vertically, leans against it and exposes his head for his opponent to strike. After he has sustained a blow on the head, he can then deliver one on the culprit's skull. But as soon as blood starts to flow, almost everybody rips a pole out of the house frame and joins in the fighting, supporting one or the other of the contestants.

Needless to say, the tops of most men's heads are covered with long, ugly scars of which their bearers are immensely proud. Some of them, in fact, keep their head cleanly shaved on top to display these scars, rubbing red pigment on their bare scalps to define them more precisely.

Jarivanau, it seemed, had everything except the red pigment.

Yoppo

Late in the afternoon the next day, as we rounded a bend into a straight stretch, we came to a large plantation on the right bank.

Two rectangular huts were set close by the shore, their thickly-thatched roofs sloping right down to the ground on all sides. A haze of smoke diffused from them into the sky.

A few large palms were still standing, but all the trees had been axed and burned. We tied the boats up by the Yanomami bongo and went ashore through clouds of blackfly. There was a rustling noise low down at the end of the hut nearest us, and two of the young women who had been in the bongo the day before emerged, blinking in the sunlight and putting on their shirts. They stood looking at us, slapping themselves as the blackfly bit their arms and legs. Their glossy black hair was cropped short at the back of the neck and hung in a fringe across their foreheads. They were thick set and square-shouldered but no more than four-and-a-half-feet tall. The younger, Jarivanau's new adult wife, had a match-stick poked into a hole just below the centre of her lower lip, the ignitable end towards us. It wiggled up and down as she talked, ceaselessly, her own emphatic language. She had also, I noticed, deep round holes at the corners of her mouth. We stood there, talking together, enclosed in our different languages and enclosed, too, in our very own columns of furiously swirling blackfly.

Chimo, perhaps tiring of being bitten, mimed that we would return with food when it was dark and have a fiesta. And '*tengamos la fiesta en paz*,' he added to himself, 'let us have no trouble.'

As night fell we unloaded our ordinary stores from Chimo's dugout, and set off downstream with the presents; with bowls of manioc; with ready-cooked spaghetti; and, the centre-piece, our giant pot full to the brim with agouti and armadillo risotto.

Jarivanau came out to greet us and helped carry our cargo as we crouched low through the tiny door into the hut. Several small fires were burning on the mud floor to either side of the tall building, and Chimo hung up our two kerosene lanterns, but it still took time for our eyes to adjust to the thick murk. Each family had a part of the hut to itself, where short and narrow split-vine hammocks were hanging.

Feeling big and awkward I sat down, undid my canvas bag, took out my Polaroid and a manual camera and flashgun, and fearing that it might constitute a nineteenth-century imperial insult, I shared out my handfuls of precious beads. The women took them eagerly, turning to each other and talking very fast. Trading had begun at once: the large, cheap, plain red ones, it seemed, were worth about eight of the small, multi-coloured, expensive, hand-painted variety.

Galvis, coming into his own and telling the Yanomami loudly in Spanish that he was a cook to be reckoned with, built up one of the fires from a pile of split logs and wedged the pot of risotto on top with an arrangement of short poles.

Jarivanau squatted down and beckoned Chimo to sit beside him. He patted the top of his own shaved, smashed skull and then ran his fingers through Chimo's wiry frizzle. He punched his own muscled stomach and then felt, with obvious amazement, the massy curve of Chimo's rounded paunch. Chimo took his pipe out of his mouth and, to order, with scarcely a pause, produced one of his gigantic, Le Pêtomane-like farts. Everyone laughed. The tension eased. The rest of the men sat down.

Juan and Culimacaré produced fish hooks and shared them out, fifty to each man. Pablo measured out ten-metre lengths from our spools of fishing line. Jarivanau and a small, wiry man tried to re-measure their gifts, by stretching the fishing line diagonally from the big toe of the left leg to the forefinger of the right arm. The calculations, however, soon conjured up that look of blank pain and unfocused anger that only mathematics can produce, and, with a sudden grin and a shrug, they gave up.

Galvis announced the start of his banquet by banging the side of the cauldron with his ladle.

'Kings, Chiefs, Ministers and all you young ladies with beautiful breasts,' he sang in Spanish, 'dinner is served.'

'We thank God and the Virgin for this food,' said Chimo, crossing himself. He took me by the elbow: 'From now on, we must not annoy the Mother of God. Reymono, she must help us to stay alive.'

Galvis piled up one of our mess tins with hot risotto and cold spaghetti, added a fistful of dry manioc, and handed it to the nearest Yanomami woman. Jarivanau stopped Galvis, snatched the tin away and took it instead to his favourite wife, the healthy-looking girl with the matchstick in her lip. She in turn fed her son, who was perhaps five years old and wore two small rods in his little ears. Jarivanau then gathered up each family's wooden bowls and supervised their filling and distribution, disappearing, lastly, into the darkest corner of the hut and forcing the emaciated girl with malaria, and her equally frail child, out of their hammock and on to the mud floor, where he fed them. The Yanomami licked their bowls clean and came back for more. It was easy to forget how desperate a business finding enough food can be.

When they had finished, I picked up the Polaroid, fitted a bar of flash bulbs and, in the ensuing silence, took Jarivanau's portrait. The dogs yelped at the burst of light and crept behind the pile of yucca. Everyone tensed. The men stood up.

I gave the still-wet print to Jarivanau; gradually, the image appeared. The Yanomami jostled round warily and then, as his face became unmistakable, they grinned with delight. I took everybody's picture, handing them out, and slipped in shots with the Minolta in between takes.

Galvis, perhaps realizing that he was temporarily free of mosquitoes, dry, and surrounded by half-naked girls, burst into song. In his high tenor he sang the sad songs of the llanos, the latest Venezuelan pop songs, and then, exhausted, he turned to his audience and indicated that now they should sing their songs to us.

The girl with the matchstick marshalled all the young women into a line and began a high-pitched, nasal, dissonant chant to which the others provided a chorus. They stood quite still as they sang their eerie song, impassive, unsmiling, without moving their hands and feet, and after about five minutes they all sat down. We clapped and shouted for more, but Jarivanau, shaking his head, got up, went to his hammock and came back bearing his yoppo pipe and a small glass phial of brown powder.

He squatted in the middle of the mud floor and two other young men joined him. Neither of them had shaved their heads, but one was disfigured by a deep, badly-healed scar which ran from his right shoulder down his right arm to his elbow. Jarivanau beckoned to me and I went and squatted in line.

'Reymono,' Chimo said, 'don't be a fool. You don't know what you're doing.'

'Don't do any more stupid things,' Juan said. 'It damage the brain. It hurt the head.'

'It's all right,' I said, grinning, feeling extremely nervous.

'How the hell do you know?' Juan asked.

'I've read about it,' I said.

Juan was disgusted: 'Read about it! Read about it!'

'You take the camera,' I said.

'I'll take you being sick,' said Juan, 'like the dogs.'

Jarivanau and the two men smiled at me.

'Kadure!' said the one with the scar, thumping his chest, introducing himself.

'Wakamane!' said the other.

I shook hands.

'Reymono!' I said, completing things.

Jarivanau tipped a handful of powder into his thick palm. He cupped it into the open end of the yoppo pipe and flicked the barrel to distribute it evenly. Kadure took the nozzle, inserted it in his left nostril and shut his eyes. Jarivanau drew in an enormous draught of air, expanding his high chest, and blew long and card down the tube. Brown dust hissed out of the nozzle, up Kadure's nose, but also, such was the force of the blast, mushroomed out at the edges and clouded his face. He dropped the tube, put both hands to the back of his head and sat, staring at the floor, gasping. Brown slime trickled out of his nostril, down his lip and into his mouth. Jarivanau re-loaded the pipe and waited. Kadure dribbled a long stream of saliva down his chest. He bent forward, pummelled the ground with his fists and inserted the nozzle in his other nostril. Jarivanau blew. Kadure put his hands to the back of his neck, his face contorted. 'Whooooaaa!' he said. He started to his feet, grabbed a support post and was horribly sick.

Jarivanau, ignoring his distress, ministered to Wakamane. At the second blast, Wakamane sat, shaking, coughing and spitting for some moments, his hands clasped as the back of his head, brown gunge glistening down his lip and chin and throat. 'Whooooaaa!' he said, collecting himself and struggling, very slowly, to his feet. He began a powerful stamping to and fro, his arms bent above his head as if carrying a small planet which, but for his support, would crash to earth. His eyes unfocused, his lungs tugging for breath in

51

desperate spasms, he called to his *hekura*, his spirits, in a deep, monosyllabic chant, pausing only to spit. After ten minutes, drained and faltering, he sat down, withdrew into himself and became quiet.

It was, I realized with panic, my turn.

Jarivanau blew the dust into my left nostril. At once someone seemed to hit me just above the bridge of the nose with a small log. I put my hands to the back of my head to stop it detaching itself. Someone else eased a burning stick down my throat. My lungs filled with hot ash. There was no water, anywhere. Jarivanau offered me his re-loaded tube. Bang. My ear, nose and throat system went into shock. I sat unable, it seemed, to breathe, my hands pressed to the back of my head, my head between my knees. And then suddenly I was gulping oxygen through a clogging goo of ejaculating sinuses. I mouthed for air as yoppo-stained snot and mucous from nasal recesses whose existence I had never suspected poured out of my nostrils and down my chin and chest.

The pain went. I realized that I was still alive, that it was all over and that I was taking the best breaths I could remember (well, you would, after such a clear-out). I looked up. To my surprise, Kadure and Wakamane were squatting on either side of me and put their arms briefly across my shoulders. The Yanomami seemed the most welcoming, the most peaceful people on earth. I felt physically invulnerable: a mere bash on the head from a club, I thought, could not possibly do me any damage. The hut had grown larger. There was more than enough room for us all. I could sit on the mud floor happily for ever. Given the opportunity, I could have seen across vast distances; as it was, every detail in front of me was extraordinarily clear. It all seemed so safe and familiar: the frayed, red-dyed, split-vine hammock; the worn rim of a wooden bowl; the hand-smoothed bands a third of the way up the central support posts. Indeed, given enough yoppo, it occurred to me, becoming a Yanomami would be a desirable and simple matter. I recalled that *hekura*, the tutelary gods who lived in the rocks and in the mountains until summoned to live in our chests, were meant to appear as small shards of light, a migraine of spirits. I searched the periphery of my field of vision. Nothing. But in it, instead, very obviously, sat the matchstick girl.

She sat, cross-legged, no more than ten feet away. She gave me a smile of the most enormous, encouraging kind; it was not simultaneous, this smile, in its spread to the left and the right across her cheeks: the matchstick tilted first one way and then the other. I smiled back, giddy, overcome with slow tenderness and deep desire. We had, after all, more time than any man and woman could possibly need: it stretched away in all directions across six million square kilometres of jungle. She appeared to be perfect in every way. I admired her, slowly. I stroked, in imagination, her cropped neck. I ran my hand through the round tuft of thick, fine black hair on her head. I kissed her stubby nose, her strong chin. I wiggled her wooden ear-ring plugs. I ran my hands over her square shoulders and short, straight back. I explored her spatulate toes and the built-in, platform-soles of callouses on her feet. I felt her round calves and I undid the single strand of tight vine-bonding beneath each battered knee. I kissed the old scars and newish cuts. I ran my tongue, for several night-times, up the long, soft insides of her thighs, devoid, as far as I could see, of even the downiest hairs. It seemed a sensible idea, too, at the time, the Yanomami idea, that sperm comes straight from the lower abdomen, has nothing to do with the testicles, and that, in order to enjoy a week or a month of uninterrupted erections, all you have to do is constantly replenish the reservoir by eating equivalent amounts of well-chewed meat between each bout of love-making.

'Matchstick girl,' I wanted very much to say to her, 'I know I am old and hairy, and that, unlike you, I sweat and I smell horrible and I happen to be filthy, whereas you are clean, and used to all this, and know what to do and, anyway, have the most beautiful brown eyes of all the Siapateri, but just supposing we slipped outside together . . .?'

I was suddenly grabbed from behind. I tried to shake myself free, but could not. The hands pinioning my arms were large and powerful. I looked up. An enormous stomach seemed to curve away above me into the far dark of the roof.

'Get up,' said Chimo, 'it's time to go.'

The matchstick girl grinned. She had seen it all before.

'Holy mother, Reymono,' said Chimo, when he had got me outside, 'you were about to kill the lot of us without even trying. The Yanomami have always killed the Curipaco and the Bare and they kill each other, too. We are afraid of them.

We cannot help it. And you, also—you should be afraid of them. Did you know you were staring at Jarivanau's woman *for several hours*?'

'It is revolting,' Juan said, joining in, 'you look at everything like a man in a drink.'

I was thinking of Simon, and for the first time I felt sorry for him, knowing that at this moment he would be at a cool, dry table in a London restaurant free of mosquitoes, half-way through a jeroboam of claret.

SALMAN RUSHDIE

EATING THE

EGGS OF LOVE

I first read Omar Cabezas's book, *Fire from the Mountain*, on the plane from London to Managua. (The English title is much less evocative, though shorter, than the Spanish, which translates literally as *The Mountain is something more than a great expanse of green*.) Now, on the road to Matagalpa, travelling towards the mountains about which he'd written, I dipped into it again. Even in English, without any of the 'Nica' slang that had helped make it the most successful book in the new Nicaragua (its sales were close to 70,000 copies), it was an enjoyable and evocative memoir of 'Skinny' Cabezas's recruitment by the FSLN, his early work for the Frente in León, and his journey up into the mountains to become one of the early guerrillas. Cabezas managed to communicate the terrible difficulty of life in the mountains, which were a hell of mud, jungle and disease (although one of his fans, a young Nicaraguan soldier, thought he had failed to make it sound bad enough because he had made it too funny). But for Cabezas the mountains were something more than a great expanse of unpleasantness. He turned them into a mythic, archetypal force, The Mountain, because during the Somoza period hope lay there. The Mountain was where the Frente guerrillas were; it was the source from which, one day, the revolution would come. And it did.

Nowadays, when it was the Contra that emerged from The Mountain to terrorize the *campesinos*, it must have felt like a violation; like, perhaps, the desecration of a shrine.

Forested mesas flanked the road to Matagalpa; ahead, the multiform mountains, conical, twisted, sinuous, closed the horizon. Cattle and dogs shared the road with cars, refusing to acknowledge the supremacy of the automobile. When the trucks came, however, everybody got out of the way fast.

Tall cacti by the roadside. Women in fatigues carried rifles over their shoulders, holding them by the barrels. Moss hung in clumps from the trees and even from the telephone wires. Children pushed wooden wheelbarrows full of wood. And then, as we neared Matagalpa, we came upon a sombre procession carrying a distressingly small box: a child's funeral. I saw three in the next two days.

It had begun to rain.

Salman Rushdie

I was pleased to be getting out of Managua again. Matagalpa felt like a real town, with its church-dominated squares, its town centre. It was like returning to normal, but normality here was of a violent, exceptional type. The buildings were full of bullet-holes left over from the insurrection years, and dominating the town was a high, ugly tower which was all that remained of the National Guard's hated command post. After the revolution, the people had demolished the Guardia's fearsome redoubt.

The ice-cream shop had no ice-cream because of the shortages. In the toy shop the evidence of poverty was everywhere; the best toys on display were primitive 'cars' made out of a couple of bits of wood nailed together and painted, with Coca-Cola bottle tops for hub-caps. There were, interestingly, a number of mixed-business stores known as 'Egyptian shops', boasting such names as 'Armando Mustafa' or 'Manolo Saleh', selling haberdashery, a few clothes, some toiletries, a variety of basic household items—shampoo, buckets, safety-pins, mirrors, balls. I remembered the Street of Turks in *One Hundred Years of Solitude*. In Matagalpa, Macondo did not seem so very far away.

The faces in the Egyptian shops didn't look particularly Egyptian but then neither did the Orientally-named Moisès Hassan, mayor of Managua. In the cafés, I met some more familiar faces. Posters of the Pope and of Cardinal Obando y Bravo were everywhere, the Cardinal's scarlet robes rendered pale pink by the passage of time. Sandinistas, unconcerned about the company they were keeping, drank hideously sweetened fruit squashes, including the bright purple *pitaya*, and munched on the glutinous kiwi-like *mamón*, beneath the watching Cardinal. I talked to Carlos Paladino, who worked in the office of the *delegado* or governor of Matagalpa province, about the regional resettlement policy.

Large areas of the mountainous and densely jungled war zone in the north-eastern part of Jinotega province had been evacuated, and the population relocated in southern Jinotega, and Matagalpa province, too. It had been a 'military decision'—that is, compulsory. The army had been having trouble fighting the Contra because the scattered civilian population kept getting in the way. The people were also in danger from the Contra, who regularly kidnapped *campesinos*, or forced them to grow food for the counter-revolutionary soldiers,

58

or killed them. But wasn't it also true, I asked, that many people in those areas sympathized with the Contra? Yes, Paladino replied, some men had gone to join them, leaving many women with children behind. The large number of one-parent families of this type had become quite a problem. But in many cases the men would return, disillusioned, after a time. The government offered a complete amnesty for any *campesino* who returned in this way. 'We don't hold them responsible,' Paladino said. 'We know how much pressure the Contra can exert.'

Resettlement brought problems. Apart from the single-parent issue—how were these women to be involved in production when they had to look after their children?—the resettled northerners were people who were utterly unfamiliar with living in communities. They had led isolated lives in jungle clearings. Now they were being put into clusters of houses built close together. Their animals strayed into their neighbours' yards. Their children fought. They hated it. Many of them were racially different from the local *mestizos*: they were Amerindians, Miskito or Sumo, with their own languages, their own culture, and they felt colonized. 'We made many mistakes,' Carlos Paladino admitted.

The plan was to have child-care centres at each co-operative settlement, but so far they had only been able to put in eleven such centres in over fifty communities. They had also managed to build some schools, some health-care facilities; but there was still a lot of resentment in the air.

The lack of resources (and, no doubt, the haste with which the operation had been carried out) had meant that in some places the authorities had been unable to provide the resettled families with completed houses. The 'roof only policy,' as it was called, offered the uprooted families exactly what its name suggested: a roof. They had to build the walls out of whatever materials they could find. It was not a policy calculated to win hearts and minds. But, Paladino insisted, the state was doing its best, and international volunteer brigades and relief agencies were helping, too. There were even some unexpected individual initiatives. 'A few days after the mine blew up and killed the thirty-two bus passengers,' he told me, 'a tall, fair-haired man appeared in the area, a foreigner, with fifteen hundred dollars to give away. He was just carrying it in his pockets, and looking for the

families of the thirty-two, to hand over the money. It was his savings.'
Progress remained slow. 'It isn't easy,' Carlos said. 'Eight new
communities have been destroyed by the Contra in the last six
months. Hundreds of *campesinos* die in the attacks every year.'
Our best defence is the people in arms. 'The people are more and
more able to undertake their own defence. In November 1985 at
Santa Rosa hundreds of Contra were killed. Since then, in the attacks
on the new co-operatives, hundreds more.'

But the Contra were doing damage, all right. For a country in
Nicaragua's position, the loss of an estimated forty percent of the
harvest was a crippling blow.

When Carlos Paladino came to work in Matagalpa, he was
highly critical of the way the revolution had handled the
resettlements, and won the approval of the regional *delegado*, Carlos
Zamora, for his new approach. He went into the jungle with his staff,
and lived with the peasants for months, to learn about their way of life
and their needs before attempting any resettlement. This altered the
layout of the new settlements, and greatly increased the officials'
sensitivity to the people's wishes. Paladino became an expert on
Miskito Indian culture, and had started writing about it. In his spare
time (!) he was doing a history degree. Not for the first time, I felt
awed by the amount people were willing to take on in Nicaragua.

After I'd been talking to him for more than an hour, I discovered
that Paladino had been in hospital twenty-four hours earlier, having a
.22 bullet removed from his lung. It had been there since before the
'triumph', the result of an accident: he had been shot in training by a
careless cadet. He opened his shirt, after I had bullied him into it, and
showed me the scar. It was an inch away from his heart.

I stayed in a wooden chalet in the mountains high above Matagalpa,
and that night the *delegado*, Carlos Zamora, and his deputy,
Manuel Salvatierra, dropped by to inspect the *escritor hindú*.
Zamora was small, slight, moustachioed; Salvatierra of much bigger
build. They were old college friends. We sat down to a dinner of beef
in hot pepper sauce, squash with melted cheese, and banana chips.

The week before on the seventh anniversary of the revolution,
Zamora volunteered, the Contra had moved a thousand men into
Jinotega province. Their plan had been to attack one of the two

hydro-electric stations and cut the power cable. They had also intended to ambush *campesinos* on their way to Estelí. 'They failed completely,' he said with satisfaction. 'Our intelligence was good enough. But 700 of them are still in the region, still in Nicaragua. The rest have returned to Honduras.'

Salvatierra stressed the Contra's morale problem. 'They're scared of us,' he said. 'Dollars won't help that.'

I changed the subject. Was it true that it cost six head of cattle to get your car serviced?

They laughed. 'Or ten hectares of maize,' said Carlos Zamora.

So, then, I said, if prices are that high, tell me about corruption.

They looked embarrassed, not unexpectedly, but they didn't refuse to answer. Yes, Zamora said, there was, er, some. 'About the car service,' he said. 'You see, a mechanic will tell you that a certain part is unavailable, or can be ordered for crazy money, but he just happens to have one at home, for a price.'

The black market accounted for maybe forty percent of the country's liquid assets. 'Anything that can be bought can be sold down the road for more,' Salvatierra said. 'There is an old woman who hitch-hikes from Matagalpa to León every day, with a suitcase full of beans, mangoes and rice. She earns 5,000 cordobas a day. I earn around 3,000.'

Zamora and Salvatierra had been 'bad students' in Managua when the FSLN recruited them. Zamora's father was a garage mechanic. (I had accidentally hit on the right subject when I talked about servicing motor cars.) 'He wasn't against the revolution, but he wasn't for it, either.' I said that it seemed at times that the revolution had been a struggle between the generations—the Frente's *muchachos*, kids, against the older generation of Somocistas and cautious, conservative *campesinos*. No, no, they both hastened to correct me. But the impression stuck.

'How old are you?' I asked them. They giggled prettily.

'Thirty,' Carlos Zamora said. He had fought a revolution and was governor of a province, and he was nine years younger than me.

Later, when a little Flor de Caña Extra Seco had loosened things up, the old stories came out again: of the battle of Pancasán in 1974, at which the Sandinistas suffered a bloody defeat, but after which, for the first time, the *campesinos* came to the Frente and asked for arms, so that the defeat was a victory after all, the moment at which the *muchachos* and the peasants united; and of the local boy, Carlos Fonseca, who was born in Matagalpa. Sandino and Fonseca were both illegitimate, they told me.

'So what's the connection between bastards and revolutions?' I asked, but they only laughed nervously. It wasn't done to joke about the saints.

I tried to get them to open up about the period in the seventies during which the Frente had split into three 'tendencies', after a bitter dispute about the correct path for the revolution. (The 'Proletarian faction', led by Jaime Wheelock, believed that a long period of work with the *campesinos*, to politicize and mobilize them, was the way forward, even if it took years. The faction that favoured a prolonged guerrilla war, and based itself in the mountains, included Carlos Fonseca himself; and the third faction, the *terceristas*, which believed in winning the support of the middle classes and proceeding by a strategy of large-scale urban insurrection, was led by Daniel Ortega and his brother. The factions united, in December 1978, for the final push to victory, and it was the *tercerista* plan that carried the day.)

Zamora and Salvatierra denied that there had been any internal power struggles, claiming that the division had been tactical and not a real split.

'I've never heard of a revolution without a power struggle in the leadership,' I said. 'Wasn't it true that Jaime Wheelock was accused of being responsible for the split? Wasn't it true that Daniel Ortega became President because the *tercerista* faction won the internal fight?'

No, they said, anxiously. Not at all. 'The directorate has always been very united.'

That simply wasn't true. Where had they spent the insurrection years, I asked them.

'I was in the cities,' Zamora replied, and Salvatierra nodded. So they had belonged to the urban-insurrectionist, *tercerista* faction, the winning team. They didn't want to seem to be gloating over the victory.

To stir things up, I said that the case of Edén Pastora suggested that the divisions were deeper than they cared to admit. After all, Pastora had been a *tercerista* himself, he had been the famous

'Commander Zero', glamorous and dashing, who had led the sensational attack on the Palácio Nacional, taken the entire Somocista Chamber of Deputies hostage, and obtained the release of fifty jailed Sandinistas plus a half-million dollar ransom; and there he was today, in exile in Costa Rica, having tried to lead a counter-revolutionary army of his own... He had been defeated by the Sandinistas, but surely his break with the revolution he helped to bring about was significant?

There were grins and embarrassed laughs from the *delegado* and his deputy. 'Edén Pastora wanted personal glory,' Salvatierra said. 'He joined the wrong army in the first place.'

The next day I drove up into the north. I knew that the road I was on, the one that went up past Jinotega and headed for Bocay, was the one on which the Contra mine had exploded, killing 'the thirty-two', and even though that had happened a good deal further north than I was going, I felt extremely fearless as we went over the bumps. 'How do you protect the roads?' I asked the army officer who was accompanying me.

'It's impossible to guarantee total safety,' he replied.

'I see,' I said. 'Yes. By the way, how do you know when there's a mine in the road?'

'There's a big bang,' came the straight-faced reply.

My breakfast of rice and beans—*gallo pinto*, it was called, painted rooster—began to crow noisily in my stomach.

There were vultures sitting by the roadsides. Low clouds sat among the mountains. The road-signs were punctured by bullet-holes. In the jeep, the driver, Danilo, had a radio, or rather a 'REALISTIC' sixteen-band scanner, on which he picked up Contra transmissions. We passed co-operatives with resolutely optimistic names: *La Esperanza. La Paz.* The mountains thickened and closed: walls of tree and cloud. There was a flash of electric-blue wings; then, suddenly, a peasant shack surrounded by trees and hedges clipped into cones, domes, rectangles, spheres, all manner of geometric shapes. To be a topiarist in a jungle, I reflected, was to be a truly stubborn human being.

Then there was a tree lying across the road, blocking our way. Was this it? Was this where Contra fiends with machetes between

63

their teeth would burst from the foliage, and goodbye *escritor hindú*? It was just a tree across the road.

The Enrique Acuña co-operative was named after a local martyr, who had been murdered by a wealthy local landowner after Somoza's fall. (The killer got away, fleeing the country before he could be arrested.) It was a CAS, a Cooperativa Agricola Sandinista, that is, a proper co-op, with all the land held and farmed collectively. Elsewhere, in areas where there had been resistance to the co-operative idea, the government had evolved the CCS, the Co-operative of Credits and Services. In a CCS the land was owned and farmed by individuals, and the government's role was limited to supplying them with power, water, health care and distribution facilities. There was no doubt that the *campesinos* were encouraged to adopt the CAS structure, but the existence of the alternative was an indication of the authorities' flexibility; this was not, surely, the way a doctrinaire commune-ist regime would go about its business.

The houses were built on the 'mini-skirt' principle: metal roofs stood over walls that were made of concrete up to a height of three feet, and of wood above that height. This had become the *campesinos*' favourite building method. The Contra couldn't set fire to the roofs, or shoot the occupants through the walls while they lay sleeping. The houses were arranged around wide avenues, with plenty of space between them. Pigs were snoozing in the shade. There was a tap with running water, and even a shower. In a ramshackle shed, a play school was in progress: clapping games and songs. In the next room, there was a baby care centre with instructions for the care and diagnosis of diarrhoea pinned up on the wall, written out and illustrated by the children themselves. The disease was the main child-killer in the rural areas.

All around the co-operative's residential area was a system of trenches. The *campesinos* did guard duty on a rota basis, and many of the men were familiar with the workings of the AK-47 automatic rifle. They were also geniuses with the machete. The *campesino* who had hacked to pieces the tree that had held us up could have shaved you without breaking your skin. Alternatively, he could have sliced you like a loaf.

Last November, the Contra had attacked the Acuña co-operative, by daylight and in force: around 400 of them against thirty-two armed defenders. Arturo, the burly young man who was in charge of the defence committee, told me proudly that they had held out for three hours until help arrived from a neighbouring co-operative. In the end the Contra were beaten off, with thirteen dead and around forty wounded. 'We lost nobody,' Arturo boasted. Since then, the Contra had been seen in the neighbourhood twice, but had not attacked.

A thought occurred to me: if the opposition were correct, and the Sandinistas were so unpopular, how was it that they could hand out all these guns to the people, and be confident that the weapons would not be turned against them? There wasn't another regime in Central America that would dare to do the same: not El Salvador, not Guatemala, not Honduras, not Costa Rica. While in Nicaragua, which the US was calling tyrannical, 'Stalinist', the government armed the peasantry, and they in turn pointed the guns, every one of them, against the counter-revolutionary forces.

Could this mean something?

I got talking to a group of five *campesinos* during their lunch break. They parked their machetes by hacking them into a tree-stump, but brought their AKs along. Did they know anyone who had joined the Contra? They knew of kidnaps, they said. But how about someone who had joined voluntarily? No, they didn't. The people were afraid of the Contra.

One of the *campesinos*, Humberto, a small man with a big-toothed smile, was an *indígena*, but he wasn't sure what sort. He wasn't Miskito or Sumo, he knew that. 'I'm trying to find out what I am.' He had lived in the north, in the area now evacuated. The Contra, he said, had kidnapped him, threatened to kill him, but he had escaped. A while later he heard that they were still after him, and intended to recapture him. 'This time they'd have killed me for sure.' So he was delighted to be resettled. 'It was hard at first, but for me it was a blessing.' He sat close to a matchstick-thin man with wiry black hair sticking out sideways from beneath his peaked cap.

'The same happened to me,' this man, Rigoberto, said. 'Just the same story. Me, too.'

Another of the quintet came from a coastal fishing community, where there had been no possibility of getting any land. The other two were locals. 'So do you think of this as your home now?' I asked. 'Or does it seem like just some temporary place?'

Arturo, the defence organiser, answered. 'What do you mean? We've put our sweat into this earth, we've risked our lives for it. We're making our lives here. What do you mean? Of course it's home.'

'It's our first home,' the fisherman said, the oldest of the five at around fifty. He was called Horacio, and as I listened to him, the penny dropped. What he had said, and what the *indígena* Humberto had told me—'I'm trying to find out what I am'—were both connected to an idea I had heard before in Managua: that one's own country can be a place of exile, can be Egypt, or Babylon. That in fact Somocista Nicaragua had literally *not been* these people's country, and that the revolution had really been an act of migration, for the locals as well as the resettled men. They were inventing their country, and, more than that, themselves. It was by belonging here that Humberto might actually discover what he was.

I said: 'You're lucky.' The idea of home had never stopped being a problem for me. They didn't understand that, though, and why should they? Nobody was shooting at me.

The co-operative's day began at five a.m., when the workers assembled to hear the day's work rota from the representatives of the various (annually elected) committees. Then they went home, breakfasted on tortillas and beans, and were in the fields (coffee, rice) at six, working for around eight hours. After work there were adult education classes. Three of the five men I spoke to had learned to write since arriving here—Humberto, he confessed, 'not very well.' The classes went up to the fourth grade.

What did they do for fun? Cock-fighting, cards, guitar music, the occasional social call at the neighbouring co-op, the odd trip into Jinotega or Matagalpa, and of course the various fiestas. But they seemed awkward talking about fun. 'In spite of the men lost to the war effort'—Arturo insisted on getting the conversation back to the serious stuff—'we have kept up our levels of production.'

With the generosity of the poor, they treated me to a delicacy at lunch. I was given an egg and bean soup, the point being that these eggs were the best-tasting, because they had been fertilized. Such eggs were known as 'the eggs of love'. When people had so little, a fertilized hen's egg became a treat.

As I ate my love-eggs, which really did taste good, there were children playing in the shack next door to the kitchen hut. Their playing-cards were made out of rectangles of paper cut out of an old Uncle Scrooge comic book. *Waak! My money! You dratted...* Pieces of Huey, Dewey and Louie fled from the rage of the billionaire American duck. While on a radio, I promise, Bruce Springsteen sang 'Born in the USA'.

The Germán Pomares field hospital, on the road back to Jinotega, was named after the FSLN leader who had been killed in May 1979, just two months before the 'triumph'. Pomares had been a great influence on Daniel Ortega, and one of the most popular Sandinista leaders.

'He was so loved,' my interpreter told me, 'that his death wasn't even announced on the news for six months.' I added this to my collection of depressing sentences, alongside the one about the 'cosmetic' nature of press freedom, the justification offered me earlier in Managua to explain the recent closing of *La Prensa*, the only opposition paper.

At the sentry-box at the hospital gate everybody was supposed to hand in their weapons, but our driver, Danilo, hid his pistol under a sweatshirt I'd taken off as the day grew hotter. Stripping in the heat was one thing, but he would have felt under-dressed, he agreed when I discovered his deception, without some sort of gun.

The hospital was just two years old. 'We have had to develop it quickly,' said the director, Caldera, an Indian-looking man with a shell-picture of Che on his office wall. 'Never in the history of our nation have we had so many wounded.' The specialist staff were all Cubans. Nicaraguan doctors were gradually being trained to take over, but at present simply didn't have the skills required for this kind of surgery.

The average age of the patients was twenty-one. Ten percent of them were regular soldiers, thirty percent came from the peasant militias, and no less than sixty percent were youngsters doing their military service.

67

'That's astonishing,' I said. 'Why so many military service casualties?'

The reason, Caldera said, was that these kids were the main components of the BLI forces, the small commando units that would pursue the Contra deep into the jungle, into the Mountain. Military service in Nicaragua was no joy-ride.

In recent months, many of the hospital's patients had been mine-blast victims, and almost all of these had died. Otherwise the main injuries were from bullet wounds. 'Eighty-three percent heal completely,' said director Caldera, who knew his statistics. 'Six to seven percent survive with disabilities.' That left ten percent. I didn't ask what happened to them.

By chance, I visited the Pomares hospital when there were quite a few empty beds, and very few amputees. Usually, Caldera said, things were different. 'If it was always this way I could write poetry.' Another poet. There was no escape from the fellows.

I asked if they had to import blood. No, he said, the national blood donation programme provided enough. That struck me as fairly remarkable. It was a small country, and it had been losing a lot of blood.

The young men in the wards were all gung-ho, all volubly starry-eyed about the revolution—'Since my injury,' one teenager told me, 'I love this revolutionary process even more' —and all super-keen to return to the fray. I met a nineteen-year-old youth who had been fighting for six years. I met a shamefaced seventeen-year-old who had shot himself accidentally in the foot. I met an eighteen-year-old with wounds all over his body. 'First I was hit in the leg,' he said, 'but I could keep firing. Then the shrapnel, here'—he indicated his bandaged forehead—'and my vision blurred. I passed out, but only for a moment.' I asked about the alarming gash above his right knee. 'I don't know,' he said. It looked too large to have arrived without being noticed, but he shook his head. 'It's funny, but I just don't know how I got it.'

They were all very young, yet already so familiar with death that they had lost respect for it. That worried me. Then, as I was leaving, I met a young woman in a wheelchair. She had been shot in the groin, and her face was glassy, expressionless. Unlike the boy soldiers, this was someone who knew she'd been shot, and was upset about it. 'And what do you think about the revolution?' I asked her. 'I've got no time for that junk,' she replied. 'Are you against it?' 'Who cares?' she shrugged. 'Maybe. Yes.' So there were people for whom the violence was too much, and not worth it. But it also mattered that she had been entirely unafraid. She had been in the presence of several officers of the state, and it hadn't bothered her a bit.

W hen I was back in my chalet, the mountains looked so peaceful in the evening light that it was hard to believe in the danger they contained. Beauty, in Nicaragua, often contained the beast.

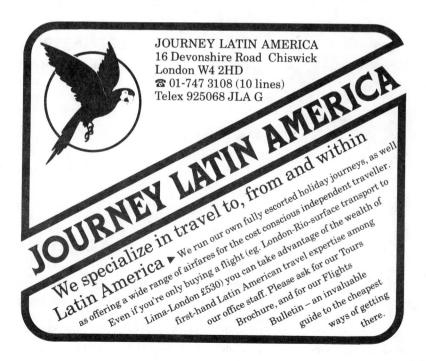

COLIN THUBRON
A FAMILY IN
NANJING

Colin Thubron

Weigi, a Chinese acquaintance, was separated by his job from his wife and parents, and had asked me to visit them when I travelled to Nanjing. So one evening, carrying his gift of clothes for them, I groped down a dark street in a district of shabby blocks of flats. I felt vaguely misused and prepared myself for an evening of courtesies.

Weigi's parents lived in rooms of a kind by now familiar to me: bare-floored, crudely furnished, and stark with the signs of modest privilege—a television, a refrigerator. A huge, fragmentary family had assembled to meet me: children of absent aunts, wives of husbands still at work. I could not sort them all out. They massed across the sitting-room in a wavering crowd of hesitating hands and smiles and greetings, sabotaged by an undertow of yelling babies.

The old couple were formal and reticent. They had joined the Revolution from Nanjing in the mid-1940s, and had now entered a decent retirement, cushioned by six children. Of their two daughters-in-law, one was a pert-faced girl from Suzhou, a city famous for its women's beauty. Her delicately-lashed eyes looked as if they had been surgically widened, and she chattered with steely brightness.

But the second woman, Weigi's wife Hua, was extraordinary. Whereas the others were dressed in workaday shirts and trousers, she wore an evening dress, flamboyant white, and her neck dangled a quartz pendant-watch. She was darkly imposing. She intentionally eclipsed them all—seemed not to notice them. She clasped my hand and stared at me with a face not beautiful but oddly arresting: a feral power about the heavy slope of her cheeks and bow-shaped mouth. In another society she would have been a sexual predator. Here she emanated a black charge of frustration and contempt. She seized the parcel I had brought from her husband to his parents, pulled it open, then tossed it derisively onto a sofa. 'Just men's things.'

The old people had prepared a banquet for me—an extravagant spread of cold meats and dumplings which we ate with the prestige television blaring, and nobody watching it. I had always thought of the Chinese family as a stereotype of unity and closeness, but here mother-in-law and daughter-in-law were soon waging war in iron silences. Compared to the old couple—conservative peasants—Hua was the daughter of a once-discredited bourgeoisie: voluble, raw, overbearing.

72

The Suzhou girl was different again. She could scarcely bear the sight of her three-year-old son, an electric urchin with a sprout of chimney-brush hair. 'I think he's mad. He never stops. Not even at night. I don't think he sleeps. He just wears me to death.' Her pretty face never smiled as he sprawled yelling across her knees. She pushed him away. He came back. She pushed him away again. 'Do you have a word for this in English?'

'Hyperactive, I think.'

She thought about this word, and said softly 'Hypercti,' as if it held some solution.

'Hypercti! Hypercti!' the boy screamed. He dashed the chopsticks out of her hands. She pushed him away. He thrust a fist into her rice. She elbowed him back.

At last, he reached into his pants—which with Chinese children are conventionally slit for excreting—discovered his penis, plucked it out and waved it derisively round the table. For a few seconds everybody pretended not to notice. The old couple developed an important conversation together. The women's gaze shuddered into their laps, and the foreigner concentrated on his dumplings. The cabaret ended only with a furious slap from the boy's mother—the first and last time that I saw a child hit in China—and a volley of laughter from Hua.

I turned tactfully away. On my other side sat a shrimpy, thirteen-year-old girl with long, hoydenish legs and plaits, who promised to be beautiful. She wormed against me and started practising her English. Hua tried to shut her up, but she only said loudly: 'I like *Weigi*. He's nice.'

I asked: 'Is the little boy your brother?'

'No. I'm Yulong. My parents aren't here. I haven't got any brothers or sisters, and I'm glad.' She rotated her bony shoulders. 'It means I get all the love.'

Around me, then, were a mother who hated her son, a niece who despised her aunt and a bullying daughter-in-law. Almost everybody was competing for my attention. I felt amused but uneasy. Hua tried to monopolize me with a sexual tyranny which seemed second nature to her. 'I'm a singer,' she said. 'I sing for factory workers. But I'm studying Western opera too.' Her head tilted back in a silent High C. 'You'll come to my home afterwards and I'll sing for you.'

Her home, in this confused family, turned out to be that of an absent sister, a divorcee whose daughter was the skinny nymphet Yulong. It was still early when the three of us wandered there along a muddy lane. In their tenth-storey flat the signs of prerogative multiplied—a Hitachi cassette-player, an electric fan, an old Chinese-made piano, central heating—but when I mentioned hot water they laughed.

Over this eyrie presided Hua's mother. She had been half paralysed by a series of strokes a decade before, and she looked even older than her eighty-eight years. Her hand, when I took it, was a cold hook. Her hair was coiled in a grey pigtail, clipped to the back of her head by a huge iron paper-clip, and her nose sank so flat that its bridge completely vanished, and seemed to place her eyes on collision course. Almost immobile, she navigated the tiny rooms by premeditated shuffles, often clutching the shoulder of a daughter or granddaughter in front, and heaved one dead leg after her like a club.

'I can't grip,' she said, staring at her hand in disgust. 'I'm sorry. Often . . . often I can't speak either. There are days . . . when I can't say anything at all. My voice goes. But today I can . . . say things.' The fingers of her live hand circled her throat. 'I should talk Russian with you. I used to teach Russian in . . . in Harbin. But I can't speak it now. All those consonants . . . I can't express anything any more . . .'

She settled watchfully on the sofa, smoking out of a box of two hundred cigarettes, while Hua sat at the piano in her astonishing dress as if this were a concert hall. Her voice was so good, she said, that her academy teacher had hoped she might represent China at international festivals, and she had rehearsed six show arias for over a year. She longed to go abroad; she craved Western dresses and make-up, which she called the good things of life. But the factories had refused to release her.

She turned back the lid of the piano. 'Shall I play "I love you, China"?'

Her voice was a deep contralto: astonishingly strong and sure, harshly expressive, unlovely. It drowned the untuned piano and lingered sentimentally over selected phrases, with swooping portamenti. She sang on and on: Bach's 'Qui Sedes', the 'Habanera' from *Carmen*, Strauss's 'Zueignung'. After each one she would ask: 'You like it? Really? *Really*?' She was exultant that I knew these songs. And all the time her voice grew louder and fuller. She trilled at the bare wall in front of her as if a vast auditorium lay beyond. I wondered what the neighbours thought. And now the cramped bareness of the room and the crippled woman hunched in the dim light had ceased to exist for her. Her face was burning with self-love. She was creating a first-night audience, an ocean of idolaters applauding her arpeggios or legatos, her shimmering white dress, her fierce, momentary, masculine beauty—a clapping Festspielhaus, a cheering Carnegie Hall, a whole Scala. But her shoes on the pedals were caked with suburban mud; one of the piano ivories had gone dead, and her old mother was suddenly, uncontrollably laughing. She rocked up and down on the sofa with short, guttural, mocking coughs.

'When I laugh I can't stop ... I don't know why.' She massaged her throat. 'I just can't stop.'

Hua took no notice. She launched into *Les Huguenots*. The nymphet came in from the bedroom looking wronged and defiant, and flung out again with a groan. The old woman's laughter guttered into coughing. The last coloratura bars of 'Nobles Seigneurs' rolled dreamily from Hua's lips, and for a few seconds, while the badly-tuned piano's notes survived her own, she went on gazing at the wall plaster. Then: 'You liked it? *Really*? You really did?' She was darkly radiant, touching, preposterous. 'My husband hates my singing.'

The old woman spluttered like a fire-cracker.

Hua said: 'Do you want to see the clothes I'm going to sing in? You'll tell me what you think.' She vanished into the bedroom and reappeared with an olive-green jacket. 'I sing in this for the workers. What do you think?'

I said it was smart, a bit stiff perhaps.

'I hate it. I long to get rid of it. I want to dress as a woman!' She disappeared back into the bedroom.

I sat down by her mother, and in the sudden quiet we started to talk.

The old lady was bitter. Her parents had been educated people from Harbin university in Manchuria, she said. They'd spoken Russian, and she'd become a teacher. But Hua, she implied, had married into a family of village farmers, and that class—in post-

Mao China—carried no dignity on the old lady's lips.

'Do you know what sort of clothes Weigi sent with you? Hua told me. Just men's clothes. Poor quality shirts. Cheap ones.' She cracked into laughter, then abruptly stopped. 'He sent things for his parents, but nothing for anyone else. I suppose he hasn't any money.'

Hua emerged suddenly from the bedroom in a black *cheongsam* garnished with a brooch of artificial pearls. 'How does it look?' She twisted her hips outrageously. Her fingers trickled over her breasts and down her thighs. Her raven hair and black eyes shone above the black curves below. My own gaze was drawn irresistibly down to her broad hips and up again to her cheeks and mouth. 'You really like it? You do?'

Her mother went on ignoring her, trickling cigarette-ash on to the floor with the ceaseless tapping of her liver-spotted hand. Hua vanished again.

'I don't like living here,' the old woman said. 'Yulong is always weeping and complaining. I hate her.' The people she hated were many. Her eldest daughter had divorced, and this had rankled for years. It was proof that the world was rotting. 'Such things weren't done by my generation. That man still comes to visit me at the New Year Festival, I don't know why.' She stared bitterly at the window. 'I hate him.'

Most of the time she sat gazing in front of her, brooding in the narcotic halo of her smoke, but then she would suddenly turn her face to me and I would see a kaleidoscope of slyness, humour and cynicism. These expressions alternated unpredictably, so I lost confidence that I was reading them right, and I did not always understand why she laughed or why the ancient eyes, undivided in their plain of noseless flesh, should sometimes narrow into theatrical distrust. 'I hate Hua.' She lit a new cigarette from another barely started. 'She's got a pile of money but she never shares it.' She added: 'I shouldn't have had daughters.'

In 1938, during the Japanese invasion, she said, she and her husband had retreated with the Nationalists to Chongqing, the temporary capital, and there she'd borne her children. 'My husband died when the youngest was three.'

'In an accident?'

'No. I think he was just tired out with so many children. I think he just gave up.'

'So you brought them up yourself?'

'It was very hard. Those times.'

'You must be proud of them.'

'No,' she said stubbornly, angrily. 'I'm not proud. They're all monkeys. Just a lot of monkeys. They have no education. None of them. They don't know a thing. And none of them is pretty.'

At this moment Hua reappeared in wine-red velvet. 'Yes? No? What do you think?'

'Just monkeys,' the old woman said.

Hua spun round. She drew the cloth in tighter at the waist, letting her hips fall into languorous disequilibrium.

'My children keep going away. They're nearly all gone. I had one son and five daughters, but two died in Chongqing as tiny girls.' The old woman wedged her dwindling cigarette between the fingers of her dead hand, and pulled a sprig of dirty grapes out of her pocket. 'They all leave me on my own. And now Hua wants to leave me too. She wants to go to Beijing—'

Hua was grimacing down at her dress. Its faint shimmer dissatisfied her. 'It spoils everything. Look, look!' She plucked at the material, setting off a rippling sheen. Once or twice she grasped my hand to emphasize some point. Our fingers twined. The old lady was stuffing grapes into her mouth. Hua said: 'Weigi doesn't care about my dresses. Sometimes he's like a peasant.'

'—She just wants to get away to Beijing,' the old woman said. 'A week after Weigi went she realized she was pregnant, so what does she do? She goes to the doctor and gets it aborted. She doesn't want to have a baby here. Not here.' She bolted down the last grapes. 'Not with her old mother.'

They asked me to stay the night with them. The buses had stopped and it was starting to rain in light, scuttling gusts. Hua ushered me into the bedroom. 'You'll sleep here,' she said.

But nobody slept yet. I became the object of an obscure, half-conscious duel. On the dressing-table were Hua's music sheets and cassette-recorder, on which she played me operatic arias. Her cultural isolation was formidable. She owned four classical cassettes, acquired at random: she had never heard of Callas or Sutherland.

Then Yulong barged into the room, and Hua flounced out.

Yulong had changed into a black, bare-shouldered night-dress dotted with pink flowers and her hair was loosed down her back in a glossy torrent. She stretched out on my bed in delectation, coddling a Japanese cassette-player and a pair of earphones. She sang tunelessly to herself.

'Have I taken your bed?' I asked. 'Is this your room?'

'Yes,' she said resentfully. 'But it's Hua's now. It *used* to be mine.' She clipped her earphones gently over my head. I was surprised to hear a tinny Beethoven piano sonata. 'That's what I like,' she said. She edged closer to me, spreading her homework possessively over Hua's dressing-table, and opened an English exercise book. I read: 'Mary likes to go to lessons every week...'

But now Hua was back. 'I'd like you to help me with my French diction.' She lowered the score of 'Claire de lune' on my knee, displacing Yulong's book. 'Listen. Is this right? Listen:

Votre âme est un paysage choisi
Que vont charmants masques...'

The words whispered and fluted through her pouts. 'We can't afford proper English tuition, you see. Weigi's so poor. We've been married seven years, and look!' She extended empty fingers. 'No ring! He can't even afford that. So poor, but always working. Even when he's here he comes home late, and it's work, work, work. We never talk. No time any more. Not any more. *Au calme claire de lune triste et beau...*'

Before the evening was out she had metamorphosed twice more—first into a crimson ball gown and finally into an unbecoming mini-skirt in which she eventually went to bed. She could only have acquired such clothes in the privileged Friendship Stores, but there was no opportunity for her to wear them, except in secret. Hers, I felt, was the narcissism of the emotionally deprived, an enforcement of self.

I slept in the bedroom, alone, while the three women lay in the sitting-room on sofas and camp-beds. Outside, the rain steadied, thickened. I fell into a dream haunted by the wife of Mao Zedong's ex-president, Liu Shaoqi: the Red Guards had attempted to break her by decking her out in the trappings of a grotesque femininity—a necklace of ping-pong balls.

By dawn the verandahs of the blocks of flats opposite were a commotion of hanging birds cages and onions and suspended bedrolls violently swinging. Potted plants were rolling along the balustrades. I woke to rain and wind beating through the mosquito meshing of my window, its flimsy curtains billowing. When I peered into the sitting-room, only Yulong was awake; she lay indolently with her dress thrown up above her thighs, staring at the ceiling. Half an hour later Hua lumbered out of her camp-bed. The glow of the night before had gone. She looked heavy and ordinary.

The old woman was sitting at the piano. 'Years ago I had another piano,' she said, 'better than this one. I bought it by scraping together a few *kwai* from my salary over years. But it was smashed in the Cultural Revolution, so my children wasted money by buying me this one.' Her face had softened. She lifted her dead hand fruitlessly onto the keys. 'Wasted.'

For all I knew, she was proud of her children, or even loved them.

Photographs by Laurie Sparham

Literary Review

Now edited by Auberon Waugh and Kate Kellaway, the *Literary Review* covers the entire world of books, including reprints and paperbacks. With lively gossip columns, prose and poetry competitions, general articles and arts coverage and reviews by an impressive list of star writers, it is essential reading for all who wish to stay in touch.

Recent contributors have included Peter Levi, Paul Foot, Keith Waterhouse, Margaret Forster, Edmund White, Hermione Lee, Paul Theroux, Richard Cobb, Michael Foot, Marina Warner, John Lahr, Malcolm Bradbury, Angela Carter, Penelope Lively, Elizabeth Jennings, George Melly, A N Wilson and Anthony Burgess.

It costs only £10.00 a year for twelve issues.

I wish to subscribe to the Literary Review and enclose a cheque/postal order for £10.00 (UK)/£15.00 (Europe)/£25.00 (Airmail outside Europe)

Please debit my Access/VISA/American Express card number

Signature_____Date card expires_____

Name_____

Address_____

_____

_____ Post Code_____

Literary Review 51 Beak Street London W1R 3LF.

The £10.00 gift that lasts all year and will change the life of the recipient.

TIMOTHY
GARTON ASH
UNDER EASTERN
EYES

'Flüchte du, im reinen Osten
Patriarchenluft zu kosten'
—Goethe, *West-Östlicher Divan*

Prague

'Karel is out,' she says. 'You know he works during the day. I mean
of course'—she blushes—'he does his real work at night.' Work:
bricklaying. Real work: writing. 'You know, if you earn your living
by writing, it's regarded as quite suspicious, and, well, almost
unworthy.'

Now here is a room full of writers, few of whom do anything
so . . . unworthy. They sit around, feet in slippers, drinking
wine and swapping jokes about Chernobyl. They have just
produced the best journal of new writing in Czechoslovakia. It took
about twenty minutes.

This is how it's done. Once a month they meet for a small
'party' at somebody's flat. Instead of flowers or wine the guests bring
twenty copies of their latest text. (Most are carbon copies. It is a recognized fact that twelve is the largest number of legible copies
achievable at one typing. Twelve is therefore the *samizdat* unit of
reckoning—the writer's dozen.) The editorial meeting then has only
one task: to decide the order of texts and type the contents page,
also in twenty copies. This done, the texts are arranged in order in
twenty blank cardboard folders, with the contents page on top,
and—presto!—you have the Czech *Granta*. For the purposes of
literary criticism it is a journal called *Contents*. For the purposes of
police search or legal defence it is a miscellaneous collection of
typewritten papers in a blank folder. If students want to sit up half
the night typing further copies, that is their own business. (They
do.) If Czech exiles in the West want to re-issue *Contents* in print
(they do), how can the writers prevent them? And if people want to
bring these printed copies back to Prague, what on earth can the
poor writers do?

89

The old Jewish cemetery. The famous tomb of Rabbi Loew, its pale grey-pink coping decorated with beautiful Hebrew script.

'Rabbi Loew,' says the guide to a party of German tourists, 'is reputed to be able to grant your wishes. Just write your wish on a piece of paper and tuck it into that corner of the tomb.' She points to a crack beneath the coping, already stuffed with wish papers. Their faces look blank, bored, not even embarrassed. (Germans, Jewish cemetery . . .).

'Don't you have a wish?' says a fat-faced *Hausfrau* to a muscular young man with an artificial sun-tan.

'No,' says the young man sadly, 'he couldn't grant *my* great wish.'

'What's that?'

'To change places with my boss.'

The Olšany cemetery. Here, every year in January, young Czechs light candles and lay wreaths with the simple message 'We Remember' on one modest grave. The headstone declares this to be the grave of Marie Jedličkova. Who was Marie Jedličkova? I don't know. Her mourners don't either. All they know is that seventeen years ago a young man was buried in this grave. His name was Jan Palach and he immolated himself to bear witness against Soviet occupation. To extinguish his memory the Husák regime subsequently had his remains removed to a country churchyard, and put the unknown Marie J. in his place. But Palach's mourners will not be cheated. So, every year on the anniversary, they light candles before the tombstone of an unknown stranger.

Early evening. A cellar beneath a ponderous red-brick, nineteenth-century office building, now part of the Ministry of Culture. The cellar contains a grimy strip of carpet, two easy chairs (one with springs), an old office desk, a camp-bed, a tin percolator, a typewriter and a piano which looks as if it first saw service at the Café Europa in 1896. On the walls, a newspaper portrait of Stalin surrounded by his adoring subjects, circa 1951, and a black wire silhouette of a girl, circa 1963, with breasts that can only be described as proud. A dirty T-shirt hangs from one nipple. Through a small sky-light I see the rain splashing off the cobbles on the street outside, but in here it is dry and very warm, thanks to the huge coal-fired boiler in the next room.

My host, courteously ushering me to the chair with springs, starts to discuss the philosophy of Hayek. At one point he says: 'You know—but this is a *private* conversation, isn't it? You won't tell my friends?

'No, of course not.'

'Well, you know, I have to say that I myself don't entirely reject *all* elements of socialism.'

When he left university he knew there was no chance of pursuing an academic career in his subject, and remaining honest. So he decided to become a stoker. It gives him time for his real work— philosophy. Income: small. Prospects: none. Spirit: unbroken.

'Now, would you like to hear my rags?' he asks, after two hours' quiet argument. He sits down at the old piano and starts to pound out 'The Entertainer'. Then 'Bohemia','our national rag'. I notice how, against the white keys, his fingernails are broken and black from shovelling coal. He's not really a good player—wouldn't pass muster in any jazz club in New York City—but endless practice has brought him up to an impressive tempo, and his playing, here, is somehow electrifying. It has a kind of defiant ferocity. I see the music leap out of the basement sky-light, like an escaping genie, force its way up through the pouring rain, giving a two-finger salute to the Ministry of Culture as it passes, and then up, up, high above the sodden city, above the smoke from his boiler's chimney, above the rain-clouds, the two fingers turn the other way now, proclaiming V for Victory.

When you've spent a few days in this world turned upside-down, among the writers-turned-bricklayer or -window-cleaner, between the philosopher-stoker and the poet-dustman, you inevitably start playing the 'If-game'. Philip Roth does it in his novella, *The Prague Orgy*: 'I imagine Styron washing glasses in a Penn Station bar-room, Susan Sontag wrapping buns at a Broadway bakery, Gore Vidal bicycling salamis to school luncheons in Queens—I look at the filthy floor and see myself sweeping it.' Anyone can play. Just insert your own favourite characters; end up with yourself. 'Me? Oh, I'd be cleaning lavatories. Sure. I wouldn't last five minutes under a dictatorship. Fascist or communist, they'd never publish *me*.' But what makes you so sure?

Timothy Garton Ash

Maybe they would and maybe you (we, I) wouldn't. Maybe you
(we, I) would still be (perish the thought) published writers. And
then, what about all these official publishers and literary journals?
Their former editors are all working as window-cleaners, or in exile.
But who edits them now? Somebody must. Window-cleaners? It
would be more fun if they did. But the answer is: writers, journalists, men of letters. Second- or third-rate, semi-literate and corrupt writers, to be sure, but are there none such in our own literary
establishments?

Here's the other half of the If-game, the half we leave out
because it's not so pretty. It would be invidious to name names.
Let's be invidious: 'I imagine ———— editing the New York
Review of Books, ———— taking over at the TLS, ————
getting a rave review from ————, and ———— being published
after making his self-criticism on television.' And why not, 'I look at
this bookshop, and see my books adorning its front window'?

What they all resent about Milan Kundera—and how!—is
not, I think, his extraordinary success (perhaps that a
little, too) but his stylized nightmare vision of a Prague
from which, by definition, no good thing can come. No, they say,
the Prague in which we live and work is *not* a 'Biafra of the spirit'.
One well-known writer (the gentlest of men) tells me Kundera has
to justify to himself 'the fact that he ran away' (but immediately
adds, 'No, these are not the right words; "ran away", that's too
strong'). And the self-justification, as for so many exiles, comes
through depicting what you have left behind as hell—and painting
how it was before as heaven. It wasn't heaven then. It isn't hell now.

I am determined to visit Václav Havel. It's not easy. He is staying
at his remote farmhouse in Northern Bohemia. It has no
telephone. I am told the police will try to prevent my visit. I set
off early in the morning in a hired car. After two hours' driving, as
I pass through a small town, there are suddenly three police cars in
front of me, lights flashing. I am guided on to the verge. *Damn*!
Three cars seems a little excessive. And how on earth did they
know? Then I notice that other cars are being waved down too. This
has nothing to do with me or Havel. We are all being stopped to
make way for a bicycle race. I watch as gaggles of prune-faced

youngsters come whizzing by. A *Tour de Bohème*. A banner in the window of the local toy shop says SOCIALISM—IS A CHILD'S SMILE.

Off again, winding up narrow lanes towards the Sudeten mountains, through the damp Bohemian pine woods; turn a corner, there is the house—and there are the police: a Lada estate parked right across the drive, two uniformed officers, one in plain clothes. Their eyes follow me as I drive past, inwardly cursing. Fortunately, however, I have about me my W.I.T.S, one of those marvels of Western technology that will confound the secret police and undermine the whole Soviet bloc. Activating my W.I.T.S, I become invisible, and re-materialize inside the inner courtyard of the farmhouse.

Havel is a short, stocky man with curly blond hair; his moustache and lower face remind me of a friendly walrus. He is dressed entirely in shades of damask—slippers, cord trousers and a T-shirt which declares TEMPTATION IS GREAT. (His latest play is called *Temptation*.) He is warm, intense, a concentration of nervous energy. He tells me the police turned up yesterday evening and have been there ever since. 'When this happens it's usually because there is a Western visitor in Prague. Genscher or somebody.' He has been listening to Radio Free Europe and the BBC, trying to discover who it might be.

He talks about the nervous strain of writing under these conditions, when at any moment the police might walk in and confiscate a year's work. How he has crept out into the woods at night and buried parts of his typescript in the bole of a tree. How as a manuscript piles up he writes faster and faster: the fear of a house-search concentrates the mind far more effectively than any publisher's deadline. Just yesterday he was writing about this nervous tension. Then his wife came in and said, 'The police are outside again. I'm afraid they aren't our usual ones.' And so he got nervous about writing about the nervous strain of writing when . . .

This is nothing compared with the conditions under which he had to write in prison. There, except for one letter a week to his wife—maximum four sides, and only about 'personal matters', as the prison regulations specify—he was not allowed to write at all. The letters were his only opportunity to express himself as a writer, over a period of almost four years. If any part of a letter was unacceptable, the whole letter would be confiscated. The commandant of the prison camp at Hermanice took a sadistic

93

delight in enforcing these instructions. This commandant was an old man, nearing retirement. His great days had been the 1950s, when he had more than a thousand political prisoners—bishops, professors, former government ministers—on whom to exercise his will. Things had never been as good since—worst of all in 1968, a little better after the invasion. But now, at last, he had some famous political prisoners to bully and abuse again: educated men, a writer, a journalist, a philosopher. His particular delight was censoring the writer's letters.

Havel started writing a 'cycle' of letters about his philosophical views. He mentioned the 'order of being'.

'The only order you can write about,' declared the commandant, 'is the prison order.' Then he decided Havel should not write about philosophy at all. 'Only about yourself.'

So Havel designed another cycle of letters on the subject of his moods: sixteen of them, two to each letter, one good, one bad, and he numbered them.

After eight, the commandant called him in: 'Stop numbering your moods!'

'No foreign words!' he ordered one week.

'No underlining!' the next. 'No exclamation marks!'

The book written under these conditions—for Havel conceived the series of letters to his wife as a book—is marvellous. Much of it consists of his philosophical reflections, and in Havel's conception these were perhaps the most important part of the book. Yet for me, and I suspect for most of his readers, they are actually the least compelling passages: partly because, since he was not allowed to keep copies of his earlier letters, there is a great deal of repetition and recapitulation; partly because in order to smuggle his *pensées* past the commandant he had to write in a fearfully convoluted and elliptical way. Instead of writing 'the regime', for example, he had to write something like 'the social-collective manifestation of the not-I.' Havel laughingly tells me that when he re-reads some of his deepest passages today, he hardly knows what he was talking about.

What makes this book so compelling is the incidental detail of prison life—the elaborate rituals that surround the drinking of tea, toasting the New Year in with a foaming glass of soluble aspirin—and the intense personal detail of his relationship with his wife: as a present, he makes her a piece of jewellery out of dried bread . . . 'I have tried to give it a touch of *Jugendstil*,' writes Havel.

Above all the book is a self-portrait of the writer. There is Havel setting himself tasks for his four years in prison: '. . . Three. To write at least four plays. Four. To improve my English. Five. To learn German at least as well as I currently know English. Six. To study all of the Bible thoroughly. . .' There is Havel fretting about his health, fretting about old friends outside. And sounding through it all, again and again, there is his overmastering determination to remain a *writer*, though he has only four pages a week and each word he chooses can endanger the whole work. 'Last week's letter did not come off,' he writes—meaning it was confiscated.

Early in his imprisonment, in 1979, Havel writes several times about a 'Faust' play that he is mentally re-working. This is the piece which, seven years later, has its premiere in Vienna under the title *Temptation*. As with most of his plays he has never seen it performed. He reads the reviews. Friends telephone from Vienna. And during rehearsals the actors call him with questions which show that they have not *exactly* understood the piece. In this case, they ring up a few days before opening and ask, 'Oh, by the way, is there really black magic in Czechoslovakia?' Yet this is what he regards as his real work: writing plays. His political activity, his essays, his letters from prison, his role as a moral and political authority for thousands of Czechs and Slovaks (and by no means only those actively engaged in opposition)—an authority which no writer in the West enjoys; all that is secondary.

Since, unlike Havel, I can travel to Vienna, I go to see *Temptation*. His fears about the limited understanding of the Viennese company are justified. The director of the academic institute in which Havel's Dr Faustka works, a deeply corrupt Party placeman, is played as if he was the manager of a department store in the Kärntnerstrasse. And yet, and yet . . . however much I make allowances for the Viennese factor, I still cannot avoid a deeper disappointment. The play, even as Havel has written it, is weak. And it is weak, it seems to me, for reasons directly related to his situation. For a start, the dramaturgy and the visual effects envisaged in his very detailed stage directions are stilted, and if not stilted, dated— all stroboscopes and smoke, c.1966. Not surprising, if you consider that he has been unable to work in a theatre for eighteen years. The dénouement is desperately predictable, and predictably political:

95

the Mephisto figure (called Fistula) turns out to be working for the secret police. Despite some grimly amusing dialogue, which survives even the Viennese production, most of the action is so carefully plotted, and so obviously pointed, as to be quite schematic. It feels like a plan for a play rather than the play itself. Not surprising again, when you consider that it was planned and re-planned through almost four years in prison.

So what of George Steiner's 'muse of censorship'? Here is a rather clear case, it seems to me, of an artist's work not enhanced but deformed and diminished by censorship and persecution. If he were a poet, it might be otherwise. But the playwright needs his theatre as a musician needs his instrument. Not merely the artist but the art has suffered. Yet at the same time, through that persecution and that censorship, or rather through his defiance of it, he has produced a volume of letters and a body of essays that will, I think, be read long after *Temptation* is forgotten. And what will then be known as his real work?

Paris

So here she comes, the fat whore, the tart, the harpy, flaunting her fancy clothes and waggling her bum. She has money. She has motor cars. She has sex. She has democracy. But she's lost her soul. She's deaf. She's blind. She doesn't know what she's got, nor how she's about to lose it. 'The West'? Mae West.

Today [writes Kazimierz Brandys in his *Warsaw Diary*], the West is emitting cries of horror; the intellectuals are grumbling; the consciousness of impotence is everywhere. They know already and are preparing themselves to be raped. All that matters now is that that rape not be a sexual murder but that it happen calmly, in some comfortable French bed. What should this upcoming state of affairs be called? Finlandization? Scandinavization? . . . But what if it's Czechoslovakization? In these preparations the French are, as always, in the intellectual vanguard. No one is able to spread their legs as aesthetically, to lie down for the act with such *esprit*,

as the French intellectuals. An old suspicion of mine:
how much money flows from the Soviet Embassy to
editorial offices in Paris?

Ah, there he blows: the Eastern prophet, the sage, the seer, righte-
ous eyes ablaze, arms raised to high heaven as he denounces the
whores of the rue de Babylone.

'You see it's really very simple,' says Sławomir Mrożek, looking out from his tranquil studio flat towards the Eiffel Tower. 'You
are a Pole, an intellectual. You think of yourself as supremely
Western and European: if only Poland were free, it would be a
Western country; if only it were Western, everything would be all
right. Meanwhile European values are preserved in the West, to
which you, unlike the Russians, indubitably belong. Then you come
to the West, and the West knows you not. So after a time you get up
on your hillock and rage, rage against the blindness of the West.
Inwardly you cry: "You may have your motor cars, your television,
your bestsellers. But you have lost your soul. Your *soul*. If you only
knew how great, how profound, how truly European I was, you
would print me in a million copies. Since you don't, you will be
eaten by the Russians."'

Part of this misunderstanding arises from what Mrożek calls the
'old-fashioned' idea of the moral value of culture and the role of the
writer, which still persists in Prague or Warsaw. Eastern Europe,
says Mrożek, is a very old-fashioned place, both materially (look at
the trams) and socially (respect for the old, religion). This is just one
more old-fashioned thing about it.

In the West there are no more *Dichter*. No writer is regarded as
a moral or spiritual leader, as Havel is in Czechoslovakia, or as
Miłosz and Herbert are in Poland. Quite a familiar remark, this. It
also comes as a question: 'Who was the last great intellectual
authority in Western Europe?' And the answer most often given—
Kundera's answer, in his essay on 'The Kidnapped West'—is . . .
Jean-Paul Sartre. Sartre, a moral authority! The author of *Les
Mains Sales*. Yes, all right, he changed his mind. But when I was
talking to Ivan Klíma in Prague about Western intellectuals' fatuous
envy of the persecuted (*Verfolgungsneid*), Klíma exclaimed. 'You
know, the man responsible for all this nonsense is Sartre.' Sartre, he

97

said, had come to Prague in the early sixties, looked around for a day or two, and then given a speech to Czech writers in which he told them how fortunate they were. 'You have real subjects,' he said. 'We in the West no longer have any real subjects'—and so on. Sartre!

Anyway, Mrożek continues, literature in the West has become just another 'line of business' (he uses the Polish word *'branża'*), alongside television, films, video and windsurfing. A line of business where public relations and promotion are more important than the product itself—'The book of the film', 'Now a major TV series', 'Winner of the ———— Prize.'

'I don't regret this,' says Mrożek. 'I don't like it, I don't dislike it: it's just the way the world has moved on.' (Modernity has its advantages: as we talk, the phone rings and he stands up to listen in to the caller speaking to his answering machine; sometimes he picks up; most often he just turns down the volume.) But as Mrożek talks on in his dry, sardonic way, it's obvious that he does regret it. He speaks about the television discussion programme, with its basic assumption that there are two sides to every question, as the characteristic intellectual form of our time. On my left the murderer, on my right the victim. Two points of view—and of course the murderer is often more *interesting*. Orwell, he says—'Or-vell'—was one of the few people to refute this fallacy. Orwell understood that there are some things which are not open to discussion: some questions have only one side. An East European, says Mrożek, knows this from personal experience. Orwell's achievement was to understand it without that experience.

Mrożek's own situation is almost a reverse-image of Havel's. Havel is deprived of theatrical experience—can never see his plays rehearsed or performed—but he still has what might be called *vernacular* experience: he lives in his own language. Mrożek has the theatrical experience but not the vernacular. He has lived abroad since 1963, in France since 1968. He can see his plays rehearsed and performed in English, French, German, Italian. But the Polish language of the street—changing slang, politics, contemporary allusions: all the essential stuff of most recent Polish writing—this he can absorb only at second or third hand. When his play *Ambassador* was (exceptionally) performed in Warsaw in the autumn of 1981, shortly before General Jaruzelski imposed martial law, the audience loudly applauded a scene in which the ambassador sits shivering beside a primitive coal stove. The Warsaw audience knew a political allusion when it saw one: who could not think of the bitter winter ahead, the shortage of heating fuel for which Solidarity blamed the government and the government Solidarity? Were not they, like the ambassador, besieged by a foreign power? Except that Mrożek had never intended any allusion. Sitting in Paris, he had not thought what the Warsaw audience would think.

Yet there are striking similarities between a Havel play and a Mrożek play. Both favour settings which have a Kafka-like non-specificity: neither Eastern nor Western, not Prague, not Paris. Both cleave to the theme of the individual seeking to defend himself—by heroism, by compromise or by humour—against the chicanery of impersonal powers. Both are fiercely intellectual: if you do not respond to the ideological argument in the dialogue, you have missed half the point. (As did the Viennese audience for Havel's *Temptation*. As did the audience for Mrożek's *Ambassador*, when I saw it in West Berlin. Shift this theatre just a couple of miles to the East, I thought, across the Wall into East Berlin, and the play would be understood.) Yet it would be a foolish critic who attributed all these shared qualities to the common East European background. Another, equally cogent, explanation comes in two words: Samuel Beckett.

The exile's dwelling. Two tiny bare rooms up a narrow uncarpeted staircase. A broom-cupboard of a kitchen. Stools for chairs. A camp-bed. And then the real essentials: cigarettes, tea, a telephone with a long flex, and books, books, books. Books to prop up the table, books to keep out the cold, books for food, books for drink, books for clothing.

Natalya Gorbanevskaya, whose dwelling I describe, is an extraordinary person. If you sat opposite her on the Metro you would probably take her for a student at the Sorbonne: a small, girlish figure in jeans and a chunky sweater, tousled hair, large spectacles, pulling at her cigarette with an air of distracted intensity. At second glance you might notice some hard-etched lines around the mouth and eyes, but you would never, never guess that she is in fact a fifty-year-old Russian poetess, let alone that she spent the years 1969 to 1972 in a prison psychiatric hospital in Kazan, being

99

treated for what Soviet psychiatry charmingly calls 'sluggish schizophrenia'— which is to say, being persecuted for her courage in political opposition. To enter a conversation with Natalya Gorbanevskaya is to feel yourself being seized by the hand and pulled helter-skelter down a steep, heavily wooded hillside—watch out for the Sinyavsky! jump over the Zinoviev!—screaming with a mixture of excitement and alarm, until you arrive, breathless but laughing, at a lake called Solzhenitsyn.

As we perch on our stools, eating the interesting omelette Natalya has volubly prepared in that tiny kitchen—cracking Kundera with one egg, tossing in Brandys with the next—her running commentary, delivered in fluent Polish, rapidly moves on to familiar ground. The trouble with Kundera is that he excludes Russia from his definition of European culture. The trouble with Zinoviev is that he reinforces the false Western identification of the Soviet Union with Russia—which was in fact the Soviets' first victim. Zinoviev simply has no idea about the immortal soul . . . And she talks, very movingly, about the unbroken courage and decency of some of the women she met in prison, about the faith of persecuted Christians, not only the Orthodox, but the Baptists and the Evangelical sects as well.

I ask what was the greatest shock of her arrival in the West (she left Russia in 1975, and has lived in Paris ever since). Natalya's answer is quite surprising: 'You know, one of the few things I really looked forward to in coming to the West was having the opportunity to join in a real, authentic Orthodox mass.' If Mrożek's cartoon-Pole hoped to find those true European values preserved in the West, she looked forward to finding the true spirit of Russian Orthodoxy, the exaltation and the mystery, preserved in the free world. But she too was bitterly disappointed. She found that Orthodox services here had become social rites: people came less to worship than to meet each other; to see and be seen.

In Paris, Natalya is now Deputy Editor of *Kontinent*, the Russian literary and political review with which Solzhenitsyn is most closely identified, and her views on the West also have that prophetic ring: 'It's such an effort for the West to begin to understand. And it's so important: we may have so little time.' A French journalist of her acquaintance recently returned from

Afghanistan, and he was so shocked to see what the Western press was writing about: Nicaragua. Nicaragua? 'Yes, that is the last battle, as it says in the "Internationale": the last battle against the evil empire.' People here just don't understand, she says, that this 'metaphysical evil' is spreading across the world: now in Afghanistan, now in Nicaragua. Yet the picture she draws in conversation is neither so solemn nor so starkly black-and-white as these lines in cold print might suggest.

Doesn't Solzhenitsyn, well, *exaggerate* a little? I ask. And what about his idealization of Tsarist Russia? *Ale oczywiście!* But of course he exaggerates! He has to, after sixty years during which the Russian people have been relentlessly drilled into believing the opposite; has to, if he's to make any impact at all. As for the West, the longer Natalya has been here, the more differentiated her picture has become. Even the French left has improved greatly in the last few years. They are quite stalwart, principled and outspoken when they are in opposition. But when they come to power it's a different story. Look at the French socialists. When they came into office they granted French citizenship to the exiled Leonid Plyusch, another victim of Soviet 'psychiatry'—and immediately stopped listening to what he had to say.

For Natalya, too, the one great exception among Westerners is Orwell. The East European knows some truths instinctively, she says, echoing Mrożek. He is born to them—'like the aristocracy'! An aristocracy of suffering. By comparison Westerners are, well, plebeians. 'But the plebeian who has become an aristocrat through his own exertions is the most admirable of all.' Thus are rewarded all the Old Etonian Blair's exertions to become a true plebeian—with a Russian patent of nobility.

My lasting impression of Natalya Gorbanevskaya is of a great warmth, a warmth that seems to insulate me even against the bitter January wind howling down the Avenue Gay Lussac as I walk back to the Metro. Here is a spirit permanently living at combustion point: exploding now into laughter, now into sympathy, now into anger—but if anger then always, to adapt Orwell's remark about Dickens, *generous* anger.

Party time. A farewell party for Seweryn Blumsztajn, a veteran from the Polish class of '68 and one of the best-known Solidarity figures in the West, who has now decided to return to Poland. An expansive, grand old apartment belonging to an expansive, grand old lady—an Ottoline Morrell of the Russian emigration. Parquet floors, high rooms, tables overflowing with *kanapki*, vodka and wine, Polish and Russian intellectuals mixing as they never could in Warsaw or Moscow. Who's that scintillating in the far corner? Why, of course—Pani Natalya! And scintillating in this corner is the editor of *Aneks*. And there's the editor of *Zeszyty Literackie*, also scintillating. And the editor of *Kontakt*. And someone from *Kultura*. And someone from *Arka*. There must be more editors per square yard in this apartment than there are lawyers in Lincoln's Inn. Plus all the accompanying feuds, rivalries, scandals and affairs, all raised to boiling-point by the pressures of exile.

For the first hour you might possibly recognize this as a literary party, as held in London or New York (or indeed Paris): the factional groups, the gossiping, this reviewer making up to that editor, more gossip, this editor making up to that author's wife, more gossip—except that here the volume, temperature and gestic range are already several points higher. But two hours later you couldn't possibly. For by now everyone is crowded into one room, and *singing*. The exiled *chansonnier* Jacek Kaczmarski has given an impromptu concert: sharp, contemporary political ballads sung in an angry, rough-edged voice, to his own accompaniment on the guitar—the nearest we get to this in England is a stage performance of Brecht-Weill songs, and it's not very near. Now Sewek Blumsztajn himself is sitting in the middle of the room, singing, in quick succession and apparently with equal delight, a Stalinist youth-movement song, violently anti-Church, and then the old religious-patriotic hymn, 'Rota'.

> We shall not yield our forebears' land
> Nor see our language muted
> Poles we are, our nation Polish
> By Piasts constituted.

A few, a very few, former comrades join in the first; everyone joins in the second.

Now play the If-game. Imagine, just try to imagine that at a certain point in your London literary party everyone stops standing around getting quietly drunk in little groups talking about the decline of the *TLS*, forgets about their own private interests, schemes, feuds and resentments. Instead, all crowd into one room, sitting on the floor, the piano, each other, anywhere, and start singing, very loudly:

Lilli bullero, lilli bullero bullen a la,
Lero lero, lilli bullero, lero lero bullen a la,
Lero lero, lilli bullero, lero lero bullen a la.

The film-maker Agnieszka Holland tells me that I must interview Blumsztajn about why he's returning to Poland, while she films us. I don't want to interview Blumsztajn. I want to go on enjoying this party. I hate doing interviews with a microphone to put people on their guard. I'm drunk, I have a stinking cold and a fever, and everybody in this room speaks better Polish than me. Why doesn't somebody else do it? No, she says, everyone else knows Sewek too well. They couldn't put the necessary, brutal, incomprehending questions. That's what journalists are for. Anyway, this film will be used to help win support in the West if, as seems probable, he is arrested and imprisoned on his return to Warsaw.

Impossible to resist the moral half-nelson. So here I am, at two o'clock in the morning, sitting amid the broken glass in the glare of the film-lights, with a head like a battered pumpkin, and asking feebly: 'Why are you returning to Poland?'

'Well,' says Blumsztajn, 'I am opposed to emigration.' All the crucial developments in Poland since the war have come from *inside* the country. It's still true today. That's why he feels he can be more useful there. And so on, in a well-rehearsed argument. I don't challenge it. I haven't the heart, let alone the head, to challenge it.

But the film-maker does. This is nonsense, she says. He can be much more use here than he can there. And why is he leaving his wife behind? Isn't it simply that he puts being with his friends before his work and his family?

And she said they couldn't ask the brutal questions.

After a bit more of this I begin to feel like an umpire trying to separate two boxers, and taking all the punches to the head. By the

103

end of round three the truth is plain, and indeed admitted with a sad smile. The guy's going back because he thinks he'll be happier there than here.

A few days later, Seweryn Blumsztajn did return to Poland. A great party of friends, Solidarity activists and sympathizers saw him off in Paris. At Orly airport he appeared at a press conference chaired by André Glucksmann. Another great party of friends, Solidarity activists and sympathizers awaited him at Warsaw airport. Everyone, in both places, was prepared to launch an instant volley of protest if he was arrested.

When he arrived at Warsaw airport he was immediately taken away by six policemen, who told him that his Polish passport was 'invalid' and had been 'misused', and then marched him straight back on to the Air France plane. The pilot was told that the plane would not be allowed to leave unless it had Blumsztajn on board. It left. He was on board.

I sometimes wonder what happened to that film.

MARTHA GELLHORN
CUBA REVISITED

The first morning in Havana, I stood by the sea-wall on the Malecon, feeling weepy with homesickness for this city. Like the exile returned; and ridiculous. I left Cuba forty-one years ago, never missed it and barely remembered it. A long amnesia, forgetting the light, the colour of the sea and sky, the people, the charm of the place.

The Malecon is a nineteenth-century jewel and joke. Above their arcade, the mini-mansions rise three storeys, each house exuberantly different from the next: windows garlanded with plaster roses, Moorish pointy windows of stained glass, caryatids, ornate ironwork balconies, huge nail-studded carved doors. The paint on the stone buildings is faded to pastel, a ghostly reminder of former brilliance: pink trimmed with purple, blue with yellow, green with cobalt. Whoever lived here, when Cuba was my home from 1939 to May 1944, had departed: fluttering laundry suggested that their rich private houses were now multiple dwellings.

A delightful little black kid bounced out of somewhere, in spotless white shirt and royal blue shorts. He smiled up at me with a look of true love and undying trust. '*Rusa?*' he asked. I was mortally offended. Russian women of a certain age, seen in Moscow, had bodies like tanks and legs like tree trunks.

'No,' I said crossly, '*Americana.*' I should have said '*Norteamericana.*' South of the US border, people do not accept Americans' exclusive ownership of the continent.

The loving smile did not change. '*Da me chicle,*' he said. Give me chewing-gum. Cuba does not manufacture chewing-gum. In due course, I gathered that kids admire gum chewing as seen in American movies, still the most popular.

The Prado is a stylish old street with a wide central promenade: live oak trees, big light globes on wrought iron lamp-posts, benches. The benches were occupied by old women knitting and gossiping, old men reading papers and gossiping, poor people by our standards, looking comfortable and content. Now in the lunch-hour, groups of school children—from gleaming black to golden blonde—romped about the promenade, healthy, merry and as clean as if emerged from a washing-machine. The little ones wear a uniform of maroon shorts or mini-skirts, short-sleeved white shirts and a light blue neckerchief; the secondary school children wear canary yellow long pants or mini-skirts and a red neckerchief. The neckerchiefs

107

show that they are Pioneers, blue for the babies, like Cubs and Scouts in my childhood.

Before, street boys would have drifted around here, selling lottery tickets or papers, collecting cigarette butts, offering to shine shoes, begging. They were funny and talkative, barefoot, dressed in dirty scraps, thin faces, thin bodies, nobody's concern. They did not attend school. Nor were they Afro-Cubans.

I had never thought of Cubans as blacks, and could only remember Juan, our pale mulatto chauffeur. Eventually I got that sorted out. A form of apartheid prevailed in central Havana, I don't know whether by edict or by landlords' decision not to rent to blacks. Presumably they could not get work either, unless as servants. But of course there were blacks in Cuba as everywhere else in the Caribbean, descendants of African slaves imported for the sugar-cane plantations. In my day, they must still have been concentrated in the eastern provinces, still cutting cane. Roughly one third of Cubans are of African or mixed blood, two thirds Caucasian.

Calle Obispo, formerly my beat for household supplies, had been turned into a pedestrian street. At one of the cross streets I saw the only cops I noticed in Havana, trying to disentangle a jam of trucks, motorcycles and hooting cars. The shops were a surprise: bikinis and cosmetics, fancy shoes, jewellery, a gift shop with china and glass ornaments. Not high fashion, but frivolous. And many bookstores, a real novelty; I remembered none. And a neighbourhood store-front clinic.

Faces looked remarkably cheerful, unlike most city faces, and the street was enveloped in babble and laughter. Men met women, kissed them on the cheek, talked, moved on. That public friendly cheek-kissing astonished me; I had never seen it in a Latin American country, and never here in my day. Most of the women wore trousers made of a stretch material called, I think, crimplene; and most women were amply built. Their form-hugging pants were lavender, scarlet, emerald green, yellow, topped by blouses of flowered nylon. The young, boys and girls, wore jeans and T-shirts. T-shirts printed with Mickey Mouse, a big heart and LUV, UNIVERSITY OF MICHIGAN. Presents from relatives in the US? Grown men wore proper trousers of lightweight grey or tan material and white shirts. These people were much better dressed than average Cubans before, and much better nourished.

At the top of this street, Salomon, a very small tubercular man of no definite age but great vitality, sold lottery tickets. Salomon was a communist and lived with the certainty of a glorious communist future, when everyone would eat a lot and earn their keep by useful work. I remembered him out of nowhere, and hoped with all my heart that he lived to see his dream come true, but doubted it; Salomon didn't look then as if he had the necessary fifteen years left.

I was staying at the Hotel Deauville, a post-war, pre-Revolución blight on the Malecon. It is a plum-coloured cement Bauhaus-style tower. I came to dote on the hideous Deauville because of the staff, jokey and friendly with each other and the guests. The Deauville is classed as three-star, not suitable for rich dollar tourists. My room with bath cost $26. Like all tourist hotels, the Deauville has its own Duty-Free Shop. Tourists of every nationality pay for everything in US dollars. You are given your change, down to nickels and dimes, in American money. For practical purposes one dollar equals one Cuban peso, a parallel economy for natives and tourists. President Reagan has tightened the permanent US economic embargo to include people. Cuba is off limits to American tourists. But that year, 1985, 200,000 capitalist tourists, from Canada, Europe, Mexico, South America, uninterested in or undaunted by communism, had caught on to the idea of the cheapest Caribbean holiday.

At the Deauville, I had my first view of the amusing and economical national mini-skirt: above-the-knee uniform for women employees, different colours for different occupations. And was also plunged into the national custom of calling everyone by first names, beginning with Fidel who is called nothing else. I was rather testy, to start, hearing 'Marta' from one and all and the intimate *tu* instead of *usted*, a disappearing formality. But I quickly adjusted and was soon addressing strangers as *compañero* or *compañera*. You cannot say comrad (American) or comraid (British) without feeling silly, but *compañero* has the cosy sound of companion.

I wanted to be on my way. I had not come to Cuba to study communism but to snorkel. At the Cuban Embassy in London, I found some tourist bumf, describing a new glamorous hotel at

Puerto Escondido, which included the magic word, snorkelling. I was going to Nicaragua, serious business, and meant to treat myself *en route* to two weeks mainly in the lovely turquoise shallows off the Cuban coast. A couple of days in Havana, to retrace my distant past; then sun, snorkelling, thrillers, rum drinks: my winter holiday.

You can go anywhere you want in Cuba, except to the American naval base at Guantanamo on the eastern tip of the island—an extraordinary piece of property which most foreigners do not know is held and operated by the United States. You can hire, with or without driver, a small Russian Lada sedan belonging to INTUR, the Ministry of Tourism. The Lada is as tough as a Land Rover, Third World model, with iron-hard upholstery and, judging by sensation, no springs. I asked INTUR for a car with driver, intending to look over the hotel at Puerto Escondido, the goal of my Cuban trip.

The driver, rightly named Amable, said that Puerto Escondido was half an hour from Havana; my introduction to Cuban optimism. 'No problem' might be the national motto; it is the one English phrase everyone can say. We drove through the tunnel under Havana harbour, new to me, and along the superhighway, adorned with billboards, very depressing: progress. The billboards are exhortations, not advertisements. A light bulb, with ENERGÍA in huge letters and a plea to save it. A bag of coins and a single-stroke dollar sign for the peso, recommending the public to bank their money at two-and-a-half percent interest. Many patriotic billboards: 'WE WOULD DIE BEFORE WE GIVE UP OUR PRINCIPLES.' Two hours from Havana found us bumping on a mud road through lush jungle scenery. A solitary soldier stopped us where the track ended. Puerto Escondido was not finished; it would be ready next year. More Cuban optimism. The soldier suggested a tourist resort at Jibacoa further on.

Amable managed to find Jibacoa—small brick houses, newly landscaped—and a bar and a restaurant. At the bar two Canadian girls, secretaries from Toronto who had arrived yesterday, were full of enthusiasm and information. They had a nice double room; the food was 'interesting'; rape was punished by shooting; Cubans were lovely people; and they looked forward to a night out at the Tropicana, Havana's answer to the Paris Lido. Goody, but what about snorkelling? A man in a wet-suit was coming up from the beach; the girls said he was Luis, in charge of water sports. Luis guaranteed that the snorkelling was fine and we both stared to the north where clouds like solid black smoke spread over the sky.

'*Un norte?*' I asked with dismay. I remembered only perfect winter weather.

'Yes, come back in a few days when it is passed.'

But it did not pass.

By morning, the sea was greenish black, matching the black sky. Waves smashed across the Malecon, closed to traffic, and drove sand and pebbles up the side streets. The wind was at gale force; it rained. A gigantic storm and worsening. I was cold and slumped into travel despair, an acute form of boredom. With no enthusiasm, I arranged to fill time, meeting people and seeing sights, until the storm ended.

The distinguished Afro-Cuban poet and I talked in the crowded lobby of the Hotel Nacional, an old four-star hotel. Suddenly she made a sound of disgust and said, 'I hate that stupid out-of-date stuff.' She spoke perfect American. The object of her disgust was a wedding party: bride in white with veil, groom in tuxedo, flower girls, bridesmaids, beaming parents and guests, headed for the wedding reception. I was pleased that the out-of-date could be freely practised by those who wanted it.

I had an important question to ask her but was very unsure of my ground. 'Something puzzles me,' I said. 'Fidel made a decree or whatever, as soon as the Revolución started, forbidding racism. I mean, he said it was over; there wouldn't be any more. And there isn't. Surely that is amazing?' It sure is. Even more amazing, it seems to work.

'Of course you can't change people's prejudices by law; you can't change what they feel in their hearts. But you can make any racist acts illegal and punish them. We hope that as we live together more and know each other better as human beings, the prejudices will disappear.'

We had no racist problem, she and I, just the wrong vibes. She thought me too light; I thought her too heavy.

I was interested in how writers earned their livings. Very few of the 600 members of the Writers' Union can live by books alone, like us. There are many publishing houses, state-owned but managed by distinct staffs for a varied public. You submit your manuscript; if accepted, you get sixty percent of the retail price of the first edition, whether the books are sold or not; then forty percent of further editions. Cubans love poetry, so poets abound and are widely read.

Feeling dull but dutiful, I went to look at Alamar—a big housing estate, white rectangular factories for living spread over the green land off the highway outside Havana.

'Marta, why do you say you do not like such a place? I have friends there. They have a very nice apartment.' Today's driver, called Achun, part Chinese, had served in Angola. He said he was truly sorry for those Africans; they were a hundred years behind Cuba.

I asked, 'How big?'

'Two bedrooms, three, four, depending on the number of the family.'

I told him about vandalism as we know it. Achun was dumbfounded.

'Why would people ruin their own homes?'

Close-up, Alamar was not bad; no graffiti on the white walls, no broken windows—on the contrary, shined and curtained—a skimpy fringe of flowers around each building, and thin new trees. The buildings are four storeys high, widely separated by lawn.

'The cinema is behind those buildings,' Achun said.

Here the bus stopped; a few weary people were piling out. The forty-minute ride to and from Havana in the always overcrowded buses has to be a trial. (Havana is about to get a needed metro system.) This central shopping area reduced me to instant gloom. I thought at first it was filthy. The impression of grime was not due to dirt but to unpainted cement. Of course Cuba is poor and needs many things more vital than paint, yet it distresses me that these people, who adore bright colour, must be denied it.

The bookstore was attractive because of the gaudy book covers. A soldier and a child were the only customers in the middle of a chilly grey weekday afternoon. A corner of the room had been set aside for children's books. The paper is coarse, the covers thin, but books cost from forty-five to seventy-five cents.

'Every year we have a quota,' said the middle-aged saleslady. 'And every year we exceed it.'

'How can you have a quota? You can't force people to buy books, can you?'

'Oh no, it is not like that. Every year we are sent a quota of books and every year we must ask for more, because they are sold. All ages buy books. Fidel said "Everything basic to the people must be cheap. Books are basic."'

'What is most popular?'

'Detectives and romantic novels.'

I drove around Havana, sightseeing, half-curious, and wholly sick of the miserable weather. I chatted in the dingy main market where the toy counter and meat and poultry counter were the busiest. I asked about fares at the jammed railroad station, learning that the best fast train to the other end of the island costs $10.50. I cruised through the stylish section of Vedado with the big hotels, airline offices, shops, restaurants, movies and the large Edwardian houses. I peered at the Miramar mansions. The rich departed Cubans left a bountiful gift to the Revolución, all their grand homes and classy apartment buildings. The big houses are clinics, kindergartens, clubs for trade unions, and whatever has no public use is portioned off for private living space.

Then I decided I needed some action and barged into a secondary school, announcing that I was a foreign journalist and would like to sit in on a class and see how they taught their students. This caused extreme confusion. (As it probably would if I barged into the Chepstow comprehensive.) The school sent me to the local Poder Popular office where I met the very cornerstone of bureaucracy: the woman at the door. Behind a desk/table/counter in every government office is a woman, preferably middle-aged; her job is to keep people out. Poder Popular sent me to the Ministry of Education. There the woman at the door said that Public Relations at INTUR, the Ministry of Tourism, must write to Public Relations at the Ministry of Education. I reported this to INTUR, decrying it as an absurd fuss about nothing. INTUR promised that a school visit would be arranged. 'Be patient, Marta,' said Rosa, an INTUR director. 'Everything is done through organizations here.'

Martha Gellhorn

To their credit, the Ministry of Education sent me to a very modest school in a poor suburb. The Secondary School of the Martyrs of Guanabacoa. The driver could not find it. We were twenty minutes late. I got out of the Lada and saw school kids in canary yellow lined up along the path to the front door and a greeting committee of adults. I apologized unhappily for keeping everyone waiting and walked past the honour guard, feeling absurd. Instead of a twenty-one-gun salute, I got a shouted slogan. On the school steps a little Afro-Cuban girl stepped from the ranks, shouted something and behind her the official chorus shouted an answer. This went on for several minutes but I could not decipher a single shouted word. I was then presented with a sheaf of gladioli and lilies in cellophane and began to feel as if I were the Queen Mother.

The man in charge, whose position I never understood, presented the school principal, a large shy Afro-Cuban woman in dark blue crimplene trousers and white blouse. I was shown the school bulletin board with its smiling photographs of the 'martyrs'— handsome girls and boys, not much older than the children here, killed by Batista's police for their clandestine work in the Revolución. Asked what I would like to visit, I said the English class. The school was unpainted cement inside and out, built on the cheap in 1979.

The English teacher was nervous and nice and desperately eager for his class to perform well. Each child read aloud a sentence from their textbook, dealing with Millie's birthday party. Offhand, I could not think of a deadlier subject. '"Toothbrush" and "toothpaste"' (Millie's birthday presents!) 'are very hard for them to say; also "room."' His own accent was odd; the kids were choked with stage fright, rivalling mine.

A bell blessedly rang. Here, the children stay in one room, the teachers move. It was the history hour in another classroom. The children—the top form, aged fifteen—rose to their feet and shouted a slogan, led by the elected class prefect who was always a girl. Hard to understand, but it sounded like promising Fidel to study and be worthy of the Revolución. Each class devised its own slogan, a new one every month, and five times a day, at the start of their class periods, they shouted this at the teacher. The history teacher was a thin intense shabbily-dressed young man who described the sugar

114

crisis of 1921, when prices fell and the people suffered despair and starvation though their work had enriched the bourgeoisie and the American capitalists. I wanted to say that American workers suffered too in times of depression and unemployment, but didn't feel that speech-making was part of my new role.

Biology was taught by a stout mulata compañera in lavender pants, and taught brilliantly. The subject for the day was the renal system, up to that moment a total mystery to me. All the kids raised their hands, competing to answer. This subject—their bodies— clearly interested them much more than history or English. After class, the teacher explained that by the end of the term they would have studied the sexual organs, the nine months of pregnancy and birth. To finish, they would discuss 'the human couple, and the need for them to be equals and share the same ideals and interests.' She showed me their laboratory, a small room with a few bunsen bur- ners. Her only teaching-aid was a plaster human torso, open at the front, with all the brightly-coloured alarming organs in place.

There were 579 children, more caucasian than Afro-Cuban, and fifty teachers, about equally divided as to colour and sex. School is compulsory through the ninth grade, age fifteen. After that, children can choose to continue for three years in pre-univer- sity studies or technical schools, according to their grades. At eigh- teen, the boys do military service, but university students are exempt since Cuba needs all the professionals it can train.

Snacks had been laid out in the principal's office. I looked at these poorly-dressed men and women and grieved to think of them chipping in for this party. They were so excited about me because the school had never received a visitor before, no Cuban personage, let alone a foreigner. They spoke of their students with pride; it must feel good to teach such lively and willing children. Never mind that they had no library, no workshop, no gym, no proper laboratory in this bleak building. The staff invented substitutes and got on with the job. I asked to meet the Head Prefect, elected by her peers. She was a lovely tall slim girl, almost inaudible from shyness, blonde with grey eyes. She said that the entire school went on two camping weekends a year and for a week to Varadero, Cuba's fam- ous beach. The top student (this girl) joined all the other secondary school top-graders for a whole summer month at Varadero. Fun and sport as a reward for work. I remember winning a school prize,

115

a richly-bound uninteresting book.

I liked everyone and told them they had a fine school, meaning it, and thanked them for the visit. In the Lada, returning to Havana, I gave my character a shake and became again a normal, not a Very Important, person.

That night, on the thirteenth floor of the Deauville, I listened to the howling wind. The storm had renewed itself with spiteful vigour and would never end. Snorkelling was a dead dream. I gave up. I had no choice; there was nothing left to do except cramp myself into a Lada, drive around the country and get a general idea of how communism works in Cuba.

For transport on this journey to the Cuban hinterland, I went to Rosa at INTUR, my sole contact with the Cuban government. She is small, brunette, very pretty, very bright and kind and patient above and beyond the call of duty. My manners to her were abominable and in no way deserved. I was rudely determined that nobody was going to show or tell me anything; I would see and question for myself. Rosa assigned Rafael as my driver. Rafael is grey-haired, mid-forties, overweight, racked by a cigarette cough, intelligent, good and a charmer. We drank a lot of delicious ice-cold Cuban beer and he laughed at my disrespectful jokes.

Rafael's story is one example of how the Revolución has changed lives. His wife works as an accountant in some ministry. Rafael is an official of the drivers' trade union, bargaining on his members' behalf with another ministry. 'Whoever gets home first cooks the dinner.' One son is reading English at Havana University. Another, having failed his exams, is doing military service and expects a place in medical school afterwards. Rafael pays thirty-five dollars monthly rent for an apartment in Vedado, formerly the chic section of Havana, and soon will own it. Rents pile up like down payments year after year, until the sale price of the flat is reached, whereupon bingo, you become an old-fashioned capitalist owner. Mrs Thatcher's vision of a home-owners' society coming true in communist Cuba.

Rafael left me strictly alone whenever we stopped. I stayed in several sumptuous hotels; these were the Mafia's legacy to Cuban tourism, built with Mafia money because they included casinos, now closed. It was all new to me; I had never bothered to travel in Cuba when I lived here and had no sense of its size—730 miles long by an average of fifty miles wide—or of the variety of the towns and the landscape. We drove without any previously arranged plan—wherever I felt like going—and covered 1,500 miles in the back-breaking Lada, a partial look at about a third of the country. Our first stop was Trinidad.

Trinidad is a beauty; Cubans are very proud of it. It is an unspoiled colonial town, most of it late eighteenth- and early nineteenth-century, but inhabited from the sixteenth century. The streets are cobbled, the houses one storey high, with vast, hand-some wood doors, wide enough for a carriage, and bowed iron grille-work on the front windows. Every house is painted, and paint makes the difference—pale green, pink, blue, yellow. The Cathed-ral, at the top of the town, is yellow trimmed in white, and fronts a flowery square that descends in steps to the houses.

The Museo Historico was the home of a nineteenth-century sugar baron. The enchanting girl in charge, aged around twenty, with blonde hair in a pony tail, wore the museum uniform, immacu-late white shirt, dark blue jacket and mini-skirt. 'He had thirty slaves,' she said. '*Thirty*. They lived in that one big room at the back.' The idea of slaves horrified her. Earlier, when she had col-lected my entry centavos, she said, 'Cuba was under Spanish domi-nation for three centuries, until 1899. After that, it was under American domination until 1959.' It had sounded pat and off-put-ting, straight Party line, until I thought it over and decided it was true, no matter how it sounded.

The US actually ruled Cuba twice, and the Marines had been around in the usual Monroe Doctrine way. Until 1934, the United States government had the right by law to interfere in internal Cuban affairs. But American domination was mainly felt through its support of whatever useless Cuban government protected Ameri-can investments. In my time, no one ever talked politics or bothered to notice which gang was in office and robbing the till. I cannot remember any elections, though I think the government did change, perhaps by palace coup. One day driving in to Havana, I heard shooting and Salomon or the street boys advised me to settle in the Floridita and drink frozen daiquiris until it was over; the noise was farther down towards the harbour. This was taken lightly as a joke:

117

who cared which crooks got in, the results would be the same. The poor would stay poor; the rich would stay rich; a different bunch of politicians would grow richer. After World War Two, during the Batista dictatorship, apart from the standard horrors of such rule— arrest, torture, executions—corruption must have been out of control, thanks to Batista's faithful friends, the Mafia.

At the Museo Romantico, said to be the former home of a Count, a bunch of noisy young people was clattering up the stairs to the salons and bedrooms. In the hall, a white-garbed nun waited, saying that she had seen it before. 'If you have lived in Spain,' said the little dark Spanish nun, 'there is nothing to look at in this country.' She seemed about thirty years old and had a sharp, severe face. She had come to Trinidad from Cienfuegos with the young people to attend the cathedral wedding of two of them, tomorrow. Her order has two houses, in Cienfuegos and Havana. There are eight Spanish, three Mexican and three Cuban nuns in all.

'People must be very brave to go to Mass,' she told me. 'We do not go out in the street with the young for fear of compromising them. There is much fear.'

'Fear? You mean fear of prison, fear for their lives?'

'No, no,' she said impatiently. 'Fear of losing their jobs or not getting a good one, if they are seen to be practising Catholics.' Mass is celebrated here in the Cathedral and in another church 'down there,' twice on Sundays and that is all. She felt outraged by this. 'No, nuns are not molested in any way but we are not allowed to do our pastoral work in the streets.' As far as I was concerned, that was great: I don't want anyone of any religion, secular or spiritual, haranguing me in the streets. 'Still, people do talk to us.'

I pointed out that she had come here with these young people, a whole band of them, to take part in a church wedding.

'Yes, they are very loyal,' she said.

The stern Afro-Cuban museum lady, the ticket collector, stared at us with plain dislike. The nun remarked on it. 'She does not want me to talk to you.' Even so, it did not stop the nun from talking to me, an obvious foreigner.

Cuba is awash with museums. Museums for everything, past and present. The museums are scantily furnished—no great art treasures—and are visited with interest by all kinds of Cubans, young and old. I don't think I've ever raced through so many anywhere and I think I understand them. This is consciousness-raising on a national scale. The mass of Cubans had no education and no real sense of identity. Being Cuban meant being somebody else's underling, a subordinate people. I knew a few upper-class Cuban sportsmen; they spoke perfect English, had been educated abroad, and were considered honorary Americans or Europeans, not in words, nor even in thought, but instinctively: they were felt to be too superior to be Cubans. Now, through these innumerable museums, Cubans are being shown their history, how their ruling class lived and how the people lived, the revolts against Spanish 'domination', and everything about the Revolución. They are being told that they have been here a long time: they are a nation and they can be proud to be Cubans.

Between Trinidad and Sancti Spiritus, the country looked like Africa: hump-backed, bony cattle, like Masai cattle; palms and ceibas, the handsomer Cuban form of the African baobab tree; jungle-green hills; brown plains; but where were we going to sleep? We had been turned away at two hotels, full up with Cubans, who travel joyfully and constantly. We set out again, hunting for rooms.

Suddenly loud horns and sirens. Motorcycle cops pushed the traffic to the roadside. Ten first-class buses flashed past, filled with excited kids, singing, shouting, waving. 'Pioneers,' Rafael said. They were primary school children, the baby Pioneers of the light-blue neckerchief. 'They are going to camp at Ismaela. They go for a week with their teachers and continue with their lessons.'

Not that bunch, far too elated for lessons.

'Fidel started the idea of camping,' Rafael went on. 'Nobody in Cuba ever did that, live in a tent, cook over a fire. Now everybody does it. It is very popular.' Cubans have two paid vacations a year, two weeks each, and alternate full weekends. Besides camping, many new beach resorts dot the coasts. These resorts are simple, rudimentary—I don't want to give the impression of places like luscious photos in travel brochures—and so inexpensive that most Cubans must be able to afford them. And there are town parks with children's playgrounds, swimming pools, sports grounds. I like the government's decision in favour of pleasure: Cuba's Revolución is not puritanical. Outlawing drugs, gambling and prostitution eradicated crime as big business, hardly a bad idea. But there remain the delicious beer and rum, flowing freely, and cigarettes and cigars, since Cubans haven't yet heard of the horrors of smoking. But I think that the main cause of a different, open, pleasurable life-style is the change in women. The old Hispanic and Catholic custom of the women at home—isolated, the daughter guarded, the stiffness of that relation between men and women—is truly gone. Women are on their own at work, feeling equal to men, and showing this new confidence. Girls are educated equally with boys and chaperonage is dead. There is a feeling that men and women, girls and boys are having a good time together, in a way unknown before.

Bayamo, said the tourist map, offered historical sights; the church where the national anthem was first sung and other episodes of heroism against the Spanish overlords. I was not interested; I was interested in food. The food is ghastly, apart from breakfast. If Cuba means to earn millions of tourist dollars, it will have to make a culinary Revolución. On a corner of the main square, I saw an ice-cream parlour and bought a huge helping of delicious chocolate ice-cream.

I was enjoying this feast at an outside table when a boy came up, said his name was Pépé, shook hands, sat down and asked my name and where I came from. I thought he was eighteen; he was twenty-four, good-looking with light brown hair, blue eyes and a summery smile. He wanted to buy a pack of my cigarettes, Kools from a hotel Duty-Free; I said he could share mine. He wanted to see what a dollar looked like; I showed him. He wanted to know the price of cigarettes, gas lighters, dark glasses and trousers in England. He then brought out of his wallet a small colour print of a beautiful little bejewelled and bedecked doll, the Virgen de la Caridad de Cobre, patron of Cuba. He handed me this as if he were giving me a family photo.

A young Afro-Cuban in a dark business suit lurked nearby, listening. I said, 'Why do you stand there with a look of suspicion? Sit with us.' His presence at first annoyed Pépé, then he ignored the newcomer.

Pépé wished to talk about religion, absolutely not my subject.

'Are you a believer? Do you go to Mass? Do you believe in Jesus Christ?' By now we had another member of the seminar—an older Afro-Cuban—and slowly the waitresses pulled up chairs around our table.

Hoping to bring an end to this topic, I said, 'In our country, people are Protestants.' Easy misinformation.

'What religion is that?' said Pépé. *'Protestante?'*

'They are not loyal to the Pope,' the older Afro-Cuban said.

'But you believe?' Pépé insisted.

As an untroubled unbeliever, I could not go into a long thing about Jesus as a man and a teacher, so I said, *'De vez en cuando'*—which comes out as 'sometimes' and satisfied Pépé.

'There are churches in Bayamo?' I asked.

'Four,' they said in unison.

'People go to Mass?'

In unison, 'Yes.'

'They have trouble if they go to Mass?'

Again in unison, 'No.'

'I want to see a capitalist country,' Pépé said. 'I want to go to France. I met some Frenchmen here.'

'You want to leave?' the business suit asked, scandalized.

'No, not leave,' Pépé said. 'Visit. To see. But they will never give me a passport. Only to the socialist countries.'

The older Afro-Cuban said, 'Artists can go. Musicians, people like that.'

I didn't want Pépé to cherish hopeless golden dreams and could imagine the Frenchmen talking about France as the French do. 'You know, Pépé, everything is not perfect in our capitalist countries. We are not all rich and happy. We have great unemployment. There is also much crime.'

'There is no crime here,' said both Pépé and the business suit.

'No unemployment,' said the others.

Cubans believe that there is no crime in Cuba. They feel safe in their homes and on their streets. You see very small unaccompanied children going about their business in Havana, and women walking alone at night wherever they wish to go. No one fears mugging. Rape is too unimaginable to think about. But of course there are crimes since there are gaols for common criminals.

121

We were now talking about education and the main members of the seminar, Pépé and the business suit, agreed that education was very good here. 'And free,' Pépé added, 'everything is free, even universities.'

Business suit, who was a serious young man employed as health inspector for hotel and restaurant kitchens, now departed: end of the lunch-hour. The rest of the seminar drifted back to work.

Pépé, it developed, was a night-watchman at a cement factory, scarcely a demanding job, and had only completed two years of secondary school. I began to realize that he was twenty-four going on sixteen, but no less sweet and interesting for that. 'Do people have servants in England? Not here, there are no servants here. Could I come to England and be your servant, chauffeur or something? I wouldn't want any money.' How he longed to see the mysterious capitalist world. 'If I was going about in France, just looking, doing nothing wrong, would they give me difficulties?' Cuban police are notably absent everywhere, and as Pépé had talked openly in front of his compatriots, strangers to him, he must have picked up some ominous news about police in the free world.

By now we were great friends and he said confidentially, 'I don't like dark girls.' I thought: gentlemen prefer blondes. But no. 'I only like girls with light skin.' He now produced two photographs from his wallet, almost identical Caucasian Cubans with a lot of brunette hair.

'Two *novias*, Pépé, isn't that one too many?'

He grinned, then said in a low voice, 'I have a brother who is a racist. He told me.'

I imagined an older brother and said, 'There is nothing much he can do about it, is there? You don't have to marry a dark girl. You aren't obliged to make any friends you don't want, are you?'

'No. Clearly no.'

'Well then. How old is your brother?' I disliked this tedious dummy brother, a bad example for young Pépé, and remembered the Afro-Cuban poet and the prejudices of the heart.

'Thirteen,' said Pépé. I shouted with laughter. At first he was bewildered; racism is no joke, an offence in law; then gradually he understood and the summery smile appeared.

I wandered into the square: live oaks, Ali Baba flower jars, benches of bright patterned tile, a design in the paving bricks—the Cubans had luck, architecturally, to be colonized by Spain. No sign of Rafael, so I sat on a bench in the shade, and an elderly lady sat beside me. She wore a neat, rather prissy cotton dress and a hat, unheard-of, a proper lady's hat; I felt she should have gloves. She said her husband had gone to the 'office' to speak about their pension. 'We are retired. Our pension is fifty-two pesos monthly. What can you do with that? Some people get seventy pesos. If you have children, they could help. Or else you must do work at home, little work.' She was very worried and indignant. 'Ridiculous,' she said. 'Impossible. I hope they listen to my husband.'

In the car I asked Rafael about this. He said that pensions depended on how long you had worked. His mother got sixty pesos a month, from his dead father's pension. I pointed out that his brother lived in the same village and would help her and so would he. 'Surely it is a bad system, Rafael, if people must depend on their children for money in their old age. It would be a reason to have as many children as possible.'

'But people do not want many children; they want few and to give them more. People do not have big families now. Every woman, girl, can get birth control assistance, whether married or not. There is no sense in big families.'

I abandoned pensions.

'Stop, Rafael. I want to take a photo.' This was a picture of rural poverty. Everywhere, in the villages, along the roads, the sign of new private prosperity was paint. If they could afford no more, people painted their door a brilliant colour and painted a band to outline their windows. Here three small, crumbling, unpainted wood houses stood on bare treeless ground in the middle of nowhere. They were typical peasants' homes; painted, beflowered, they would be picturesque cottages. They are box-shape, one room wide, with a porch on wood pillars. If very poor, the roof is palm thatch, less poor, it is corrugated tin. I chose the worst of the three.

'Did you see that?' Rafael pointed.

I had not. Each of the houses had a TV aerial.

Martha Gellhorn

'Marta,' Rafael said, 'have you seen anyone without shoes?'
'No.'
'You say everyone is too fat. When you lived here, how did the *campesinos* look?'
How did the *campesinos*, the peasants, look; how did everyone look? They looked abjectly poor or just everyday poor. Except for us, the narrow top layer. You could live in princely comfort on very little money in Cuba.
There was a farmhouse, barely visible beyond our land, east of the driveway. It was a bit larger than these houses, with peeling paint. The farmer was a bone-thin, unsmiling man; he kept chickens. If I saw him I said good morning. That is all I knew about him; I don't even know if the cook bought eggs there. The village below our place was a small cluster of houses like these; I knew nothing about the village except that it had a post office. The children waved when I drove by, I waved back, lots of smiles. They were in rags, barefoot, and everyone was unnaturally thin.
I did not say to myself: it isn't my country, what can I do? I didn't think about Cuba at all. Everything I cared about with passion was happening in Europe. I listened to the radio, bought American newspapers in Havana, waited anxiously for letters from abroad. I wrote books, and the minute I could break free, I went back to the real world, the world at war. Rafael had asked the wrong question. The right question would be: who looked at the *campesinos*? Who cared? Nobody, as far as I knew; including me.
'I know, Rafael. They were hungry and miserable.'
'Those people own their houses and prefer to stay there, not move themselves to a new co-operative building which is like an apartment block.'
'So would I.'
'Good, if they prefer television to making their houses beautiful, that is their business. When they get more money, maybe they will improve their homes. My mama lives in a house like that. I was born in a house like that. Clearly it is better repaired.'

'What is that thing, Rafael?'
He slowed the car.
'Back there, a sort of monument.'
It looked like a little cement obelisk, standing by the empty road
124

among the hills, not a house in sight. I got out to read the inscription. MARTYR OF THE REVOLUCIÓN. TEACHER. KILLED IN 1960. All those who were killed in the years of rebellion against Batista are called Martyrs of the Revolución.

'How can this be, Rafael? The Revolución won in 1959.'

'He would have been a volunteer teacher in the literacy campaign. Killed by the *campesinos* who had crazy ideas, maybe from propaganda by the priests. The *campesinos* thought the literacy campaign would take their daughters away and ruin them. Many young volunteers were killed at that time. It is very sad, very stupid.'

We were on a winding road, in pleasing green tree-covered hill country, that led down to a hotel by the sea. This hotel was post-Revolución, built for Cubans and lesser tourists. The site, on a bay surrounded by mountains, was lovely and the architects merit high marks. Otherwise, it had little to recommend it. The manager was always absent at Party meetings. They ran out of bread, and never had butter; when I ate the fish, I knew I was doomed. The bath towels had been washed to fragility. The front fell off the unwanted air-conditioning and barely missed my Russian vodka, the only booze I had left.

I settled grumpily at the snack bar which had nothing to offer except Cuban soft drinks, far too sweet, and had a heart-to-heart with the Afro-Cuban lady in charge. We shouted at each other over the din of the whiney-sugary anti-music that Cubans love. She was thirty with three children, divorced. The oldest, aged fourteen, was at school in Havana with his father, the others at school here. 'Oh compañera, life has changed much, much. We have things we never had before. Furniture, frigidaire, television, and the right to work which women never had. We work, we have our own money.' And the pay? 'Women are paid equal to men, *igual, igual.*'

At lunch, a group of Polish tourists murmured to each other in whisper voices. They were the only non-capitalist tourists I saw. They looked bemused and pitiful, dressed in shades of grey, a non-colour, with grey skin. Lunch finished, their guide-nanny, a young, pretty Cuban woman, came to talk to them in Polish, no doubt the day's agenda; she raised a timid laugh. She had well cut and well set black shoulder-length hair and wore tight yellow pants, a brilliant poncho, big gold loop ear-rings, and lots of make-up. What on earth could these sad Poles think of communism, Cuban-style?

125

A man was watching TV in the hall; Fidel on the box. At this time, Fidel had been giving one of his marathon interviews to the *Washington Post* and it was broadcast like a serial on TV. The front desk receptionist beckoned to me. 'You should talk to him, Marta, the doctor on horseback.'

A fair-haired young man, with specs and a beard, tweed jacket, jeans, was telephoning. I waited and latched on to him. He had just finished his medical training, six years, and was now stationed in the mountains. 'They asked for volunteers, for two years. It is very dynamic work.' He lives alone in the Sierra Maestra and visits patients on horseback if they cannot come to his *consultorio*, a room in his three-room house. He is in charge of 117 families. This is a new idea, a doctor who stays in close touch with the same families over years, urban as well as rural preventive medicine. 'The main complaint is high blood pressure; maybe too much salt, maybe overweight. There is no tuberculosis, no cancer, no diabetes. Sometimes parasites. My work is to teach hygiene.' The people raise coffee and cattle in the mountains. The children go to primary school up there and come down to rural boarding schools for secondary education. I had seen a few of these, large buildings planted in the fields.

'Older women had as many as twelve children. Now women have two or three at most. There is every form of birth control, it is the physician's task to find what is best for each woman.'

'Don't you think the women are much too fat?'

'Yes, but it is the custom of the country and men like women to be fat. It is slow education, to teach them to eat less starch and sweets. They enjoy eating; you know, to be fat here was a sign of wealth. No, I am not lonely. I have many books and I like the people very much.'

Fidel announced somewhere, sometime, that he wished Cuba to be 'the greatest medical power in the world.' I dislike the form of words but applaud the ambition. The rule-of-thumb gauge of public health is the nation's infant mortality rate. I am using the figures given in the World Health Organisation Statistics Annual for 1985. These figures are their estimates, arguably more accurate than the figures supplied by the nations concerned, and more recent. In 1985, Cuba's infant mortality rate was 19 per 1,000 live births. (Great Britain's was 11 per 1,000 live births.) No other country in

Latin America compares with Cuba by this standard: Mexico, 47; Guatemala, 57; Argentina, 32; El Salvador, 60; Chile, 36. For a population of almost ten million, there are 260 hospitals, of which fifty-four are rural. Public health depends on preventive medicine and quick early care, so they have 396 polyclinics—an outpatient service. General practitioners, neurologists, gynaecologists and paediatricians work in polyclinics, with X-ray machines and laboratory facilities in the building. There are 158 rural medical stations (the type I had seen in the villages) and 143 dental clinics. Most of the doctors and dentists, middle-class professionals, emigrated after the Revolución, but the number of physicians had tripled from 1958 to 1983 (increasing every year), the number of dentists quadrupled and nursing staff, less than a thousand in 1958, numbered over 30,000 in 1983.

Apart from the grandiose hospital in Havana, which is Fidel's monument, hospitals and clinics are basic like everything else, but they are there, fully and willingly manned. They have eradicated malaria, polio and diphtheria; no deaths from tuberculosis since 1979 and the incidence of the disease in 1983 down to 0.7 per 100,000 population. Maybe they have finished it off by now. Tuberculosis, a poverty disease, is endemic in this part of the world. In health, as a single indicator of progress, Cuba is unique in Latin America. Ordinary people, which means the vast majority, from Mexico south to Tierra del Fuego, would weep with joy to have the medical care that is free and routine for Cubans. Millions of North Americans would feel the same.

For a quarter of a century, everybody has heard how communism works in Cuba from successive American administrations. I do not believe anything that any governments say. Judge them by their deeds, by results, by what you can observe yourself and learn from other unofficial observers. Apart from Jimmy Carter, all American presidents have hated Fidel Castro as if he were a personal enemy. They have done their varied powerful best to destroy him, and failed. Since it was politically impossible to accept that the monster Castro might be popular, even loved by his people, he had to be oppressing ten million cowed Cubans.

127

Whatever it is, Cuba is not a police state ruled by fear. You can sense fear at once, anywhere, whether the police are communist or fascist, to use the simplified terms. Fear marks the faces and manners of the people. It makes them suspicious, especially of strangers. And it is catching; fear infects the visitor. I know, for I have never been more frightened than in El Salvador, and I was shaking with relief to be safe inside the airplane leaving Moscow. No government could decree or enforce the cheerfulness and friendliness I found around me in Cuba. I haven't space to describe all the people I met in all the places but this is what matters: none of them was afraid to talk to a foreigner, to answer my questions, and they spoke their minds without hesitation.

The undeniable shame of the Cuban government is political prisoners. Sources that I trust estimate about one hundred men in jail for political reasons. The trials were secret, neither charges nor evidence published. The sentences, dating back to the early years of the Revolución, were crushing, twenty years and more. These prisoners call themselves *plantados*, firmly and forever planted in their loathing of Castro communism. They refuse to wear prison uniforms or be 're-educated' politically. Defiant to the end of their tremendous jail terms, released *plantados*—now abroad—have reported atrocious prison conditions, brutality from jailers, denial of family visits and mail, appalling malnutrition, periods of solitary confinement and barbarous medical neglect. These are terrible accusations and there is no reason to doubt them.

A book called *Against All Hope* by a former *plantado*, Armando Valladares, has recently appeared. Valladares served twenty-two years in prison and is now happily alive and well in Madrid. His charges against the Cuban prison regime are frightful, including torture, biological experiments, lightless cells and murder. The book should be studied with dispassionate care, especially by medical experts. The immediate question is: why did none of the many freed *plantados*—among them writers—provide such information earlier?

Amnesty has this year adopted five Cuban prisoners of conscience. Apparently four are long-term prisoners and one, a teacher of adult education, was arrested in 1981. Three of them are dissident Marxists; I don't know about the others. Amnesty is absolutely reliable. But whatever the remaining political prisoners are, I cannot understand why Fidel Castro does not release them all and allow them to go abroad. Or publish the charges and evidence that would justify the sentences. The secrecy about the *plantados* and the conditions of their imprisonment damage Cuba irreparably in world opinion. And, in the end, the *plantados* are released anyway. So what is the point? What is the Cuban government's need for this self-multilation? The Revolución has triumphed. It has gone far beyond the threatened inexperienced violent early years. It has made an admirable record in social reform, in education, in public health; and, in its own way, it is an upwardly-mobile society where anyone can better his life through individual ability. Why spoil that record, why disgrace the Revolución by holding political prisoners?

You can name in minutes the few governments which hold no political prisoners. This ugly fact does not condone Cuba but puts it into perspective. My sources did not suggest that political arrests were a continuing frequent process in Cuba. But a small country existing under a relentless state of siege, persecuted by the strongest nation on earth, is not in the best shape for flourishing freedom. If any American administration truly cared about Cuban political prisoners and Cuban civil liberties, it would let up on Cuba, leave Cuba alone, give Cuba a chance to breathe for a while and feel secure enough to afford more and more freedom. I hope for the arrival, one day, of a sensible US administration which will come to sensible live-and-let-live terms with Cuba. I hope this for the sake of both America and Cuba.

I returned to Havana from Santiago de Cuba by air; the Lada had destroyed me. As I was about to leave Cuba, the sky cleared. On a sunny morning I collected Gregorio and we went to visit my former home, the Finca Vigía, fifteen miles outside Havana, now a museum or indeed a shrine. Gregorio is eighty-seven years old, the only link to my Cuban past and the only Cuban repository of Hemingway lore, as he was the sailor-guardian of Hemingway's boat, the *Pilar,* for twenty-three years. People come from far and wide to hear his verbatim memories, which he quotes like Scripture. Hemingway and he were the same age. His devotion to his patron-hero is genuine and time has added lustre to that devotion. The

Pilar years were surely the best for Gregorio. He is a tall thin weather-beaten man, with calm natural dignity. He was liked and respected—thought, typically, to have the finest qualities of a Spaniard. Not that anybody troubled about his separate existence; I had never seen his house.

The Museo Hemingway, temporarily closed to the public for repairs, is wildly popular with Cubans. They come again and again, bringing picnics to spend the day, after a respectful tour of the house. The long driveway is flanked by towering royal palms and sumptuous jacaranda trees. I couldn't believe my eyes; I remembered nothing so imposing. The driveway curved to show the house, now glaring white and naked. 'It looks like a sanatorium,' I said. 'What did they do to the ceiba?'

Forty-six years ago, I found this house through an advertisement and rented it, for one hundred dollars a month, indifferent to its sloppiness, because of the giant ceiba growing from the wide front steps. Any house with such a tree was perfect in my eyes. Besides, the terrace beyond the steps was covered by a trellis roof of brilliant bougainvillaea. Flowering vines climbed up the wall behind the ceiba; orchids grew from its trunk. All around the house were acres of high grass, hiding caches of empty gin bottles, and rusty tins, and trees. The house was almost invisible but painted an unappetizing yellow; I had it painted a dusty pale pink; the Museo changed it to glaring white. The great tree was always the glory of the finca.

'The roots were pulling up the floor of the house. The Museo had to cut it down,' Gregorio said.

'They should have pulled down the house instead.'

I never saw a ceiba like it, anywhere. The enormous trunk, the colour and texture of elephant hide, usually dwarfs the branches of a ceiba. But this one had branches thick as other tree trunks, spreading in wide graceful loops; it was probably several hundred years old. The house is a pleasant old one-storey affair of no special style; the six rooms are large and well proportioned, full of light.

The members of the museum staff have their office in the former garage; they are earnest, devout keepers of the shrine. I recognized all the furniture I had ordered from the local carpenter, and lapsed into giggles over the later addition of stuffed animal heads and horns on every wall. In the master's bedroom, the biggest buffalo head I had ever seen, including hundreds on the hoof, glowered over the desk. True, I had never been so close to any buffalo, living or dead. 'He did not write here,' said one of the staff. He wrote *For Whom The Bell Tolls* at this desk, but that was pre-buffalo.

The house depressed me; I hurried through it, eager to get back to the trees. How had I taken for granted this richness? Then it struck me: time, the years of my life at last made real. The trees had been growing in splendour for forty-one years—the immense mangoes and flamboyantes and palms and jacarandas and avocates were all here before, but young then like me.

I had definitely forgotten the size and the elegant shape of the swimming-pool. Gregorio was interested in two large cement cradles, placed where the tennis court used to be. The *Pilar* was his inheritance, he had cared for it and given it to the state, and it was to be brought here and placed on these cradles.

'Like the *Granma*,' I said, and everyone looked slightly shocked at the irreverence. The *Granma* is the large cabin cruiser that bore Fidel and his followers from Mexico to Cuba in 1956: the transport of the Revolución. It is enshrined in a glass case in a small park in Old Havana. As an object of patriotic veneration, a lot jollier than Lenin embalmed. It seems that *Granma*, now the name of a province and of the major national newspaper, is simply a misspelling of Grandma, which is delightful.

The visit was as fast as I could make it—handshakes, compliments standing under a beautiful jacaranda by the garage—and we were off to Gregorio's house in the fishing village of Cojimar. The visit to the Museo had been a duty call; it was expected. I wanted to listen to Gregorio.

In the car, I began to have faintly turbulent emotions. I remembered with what gaiety I had come to this country and how I had left, frozen in distaste of a life that seemed to me hollow and boring to die. Looking after the finca ate my time, but was worth it because of the beauty. Then Cuba became worth nothing, a waste of time. Cuba now is immeasurably better than the mindless feudal Cuba I knew. But no place for a self-willed, opinionated loner, which is what I suppose I am. Never a team-player—though I wish this team, this people, well, and hope it improves, as it has, year by year.

'Gregorio, it is a comfort that nobody is hungry.'
Gregorio looked at me and smiled. 'You remember that?'
'Yes.'
'*Pues sí,* Marta, nobody is hungry now.'
Gregorio has owned his small cement house since 1936 and it is freshly painted, sky blue and white. Gregorio was still anxious about his wife, *mi señora* he calls her in the old way, who fell off a ladder weeks ago and broke her thigh. She was waiting for us indoors, in a chair, her leg in plaster. She kissed me, told me I was 'very well preserved', and they both recounted the saga of the leg. They have a telephone; the ambulance came at once; she was taken to hospital and operated on. '"A big operation," the doctor said.' Gregorio's turn: 'Very big. He said at our age the bones are like glass.' She stayed twenty days in hospital, then the ambulance brought her home. The doctor from the local polyclinic came every day to check her condition, now he only comes once a week. 'Not a cent, Marta, you understand. It did not cost even one centavo.'

Gregorio has a monthly pension of 170 pesos (call it pre-inflation dollars); actually a large pension, due to his long work years. Still, I thought this a skimpy sum until they told me the price system: six dollars a month flat for the telephone, which is a luxury; three dollars flat for electricity—and they have an electric fridge and cooker and water heater; the colour TV is bought on the never-never, at ten percent a month of salary or pension. The food ration is extremely cheap.

'Is it enough food?'

'Yes, yes, more than enough, but if you want different things you buy them. It costs more.' Clothes are also rationed and cheap; they would not need or want more than the yearly quota of shoes, shirts, underclothes etc. 'Young people care for clothes, they buy more off rations. And education is free too, Marta.'

His middle-aged daughter now arrived; she is volubly enthusiastic about the new Cuba. Then his grand-daughter appeared with a pink and white baby in her arms, Gregorio's great grandson, on her way to his weekly check-up at the polyclinic. Each generation owns its little house in this village.

I felt that Gregorio was getting a trifle restive among all these females so we moved to the front porch to smoke. He brought out a bottle of Cuban rum. 'As long as I have this,' he said, pouring me a hefty slug, 'and my cigars, I am content.' Now talking soberly he said, 'Marta, all the intelligentsia left, all of them.' I was baffled by that word: what would Gregorio know of intelligentsia? Then I guessed he meant the world he had known with Hemingway, the Sunday parties with the jai-alai players at the finca, parties at the Cojimar pub, the carefree company of the rich and privileged, the big-game fishermen, the members of the pigeon-shooting club, and though I had never seen the Country Club he meant that circle too, since the *Pilar* was berthed there in later years. He may have missed the glamour of a life he shared and did not share. But he had met Fidel. 'I think he is a good man,' Gregorio said. After Hemingway left in 1959, Gregorio returned to his old profession of fisherman, then retired and became unofficial adviser to the Museo Hemingway. 'I have never had any trouble with anyone.'

I asked about the few Cubans I could remember by name; they had all long decamped. I asked about the Basque jai-alai players, exiles from Franco's Spain, who had fought for their homeland and lost. I loved them, brave and high-spirited men who never spoke of the past, not expecting to see their country and families again.

'They left when Batista took power. They did not like dictatorship. There was much killing with Batista, in secret. I heard that Patchi died.'

'Patchi!' I was stunned. 'And Ermua?' Ermua was the great *pelotari* who moved like a panther and was the funniest, wildest of them all.

'Yes, he died too.'

'How could he? Why? So young?'

And suddenly I realized that Patchi was probably my age, Ermua maybe five years younger; they need not have died young.

'Gregorio, I am growing sad. Cuba makes me understand that I am old.'

'I too,' Gregorio laughed. *'Pues, no hay remedio.'*

My bag was packed, my bill paid and I had nothing to do until two a.m. when I took the plane to Nicaragua. I went back to Jibacoa where I had gone in hope of snorkelling on my first day. Now the weather was the way it ought to be, brilliantly blue cloudless sky, hot sun. I went to the Cuban resort, not the foreigners' tourist domain on the hill. There were dozens of small

133

cabins for two or four people, a boat-yard with rentable pleasure craft, an indoor recreation room, ping-pong and billiards, a snack bar to provide the usual foul American white bread sandwiches and a restaurant. The main feature was a beautiful long white sand beach, bracketed by stony headlands. Where there are rocks there are fish. I was loaned a cabin to change in and a towel: No, no, you pay nothing, you are not sleeping here. I could never decide whether I was treated with unfailing kindness because I was a foreigner or because of my age.

There were many people on the beach, looking happy in the lovely weather, all ages, sunbathing, swimming, picnicking. A young man offered me his deck-chair so that I could read and bake comfortably between swims. I put on my mask and plunged in, feeling the water cold after the storm, but bursting with joy to see familiar fish, special favourites being a shoal of pale blue ovoid fish with large smiles marked in black on their faces. In my old Cuban days, I wore motorcyclist's goggles; masks and snorkels had not been invented.

When I returned to my deck-chair at the far end of the beach, I found two small fat white bodies lying face down near me. After a while they worried me, and I warned them in Spanish that they were getting a dangerous burn. A grey-haired man sat up and said, 'Spik Engleesh?' They were 'Greek-Canadians' from the tourist resort above; they liked the place, they even liked the food. He said, 'They work slow. No, lady, I don't think it's the climate. But they're happy. The guy who looks after our group is doing double time. For that, he gets a month off.' He smiled, he shrugged.

From nine to five, the tour guide would be on hand to interpret if needed, to coddle the old if they wanted it, swim with the girls, play table tennis, eat, drink. Maybe he would take them on a day sight-seeing tour of Havana. And then, from five to one in the morning, if anyone was still awake, he would do the same, except he would drink more than swim, and dance with the girls to radio music in the bar, and of course escort them all on the big night out at the Tropicana. The Greek-Canadian's shrug and smile said clearly that he did not consider this to be hardship duty. Here was a small-scale capitalist deriding the easy life of communists. Soft communism, a comic turn-around from the dreaded American accusation: 'soft on communism.' I thought it the best joke yet.

AMITAV GHOSH
THE IMAM
AND THE INDIAN

Amitav Ghosh

I met the Imam of the village and Khamees the Rat at about the same time. I don't exactly remember now—it happened more than six years ago—but I think I met the Imam first.

But this is not quite accurate. I didn't really 'meet' the Imam: I inflicted myself upon him. Perhaps that explains what happened.

Still, there was nothing else I could have done. As the man who led the daily prayers in the mosque, he was a leading figure in the village, and since I, a foreigner, had come to live there, he may well for all I knew have been offended had I neglected to pay him a call. Besides, I wanted to meet him; I was intrigued by what I'd heard about him.

People didn't often talk about the Imam in the village, but when they did, they usually spoke of him somewhat dismissively, but also a little wistfully, as they might of some old, half-forgotten thing, like the annual flooding of the Nile. Listening to my friends speak of him, I had an inkling, long before I actually met him, that he already belonged, in a way, to the village's past. I thought I knew this for certain when I heard that apart from being an Imam he was also, by profession, a barber and a healer. People said he knew a great deal about herbs and poultices and the old kind of medicine. This interested me. This was Tradition: I knew that in rural Egypt Imams and other religious figures are often by custom associated with those two professions.

The trouble was that these accomplishments bought the Imam very little credit in the village. The villagers didn't any longer want an Imam who was also a barber and a healer. The older people wanted someone who had studied at al-Azhar and could quote from Jamal ad-Din Afghani and Mohammad Abduh as fluently as he could from the Hadith, and the younger men wanted a fierce, black-bearded orator, someone whose voice would thunder from the mimbar and reveal to them their destiny. No one had time for old-fashioned Imams who made themselves ridiculous by boiling herbs and cutting hair.

Yet Ustad Ahmed, who taught in the village's secondary school and was as well-read a man as I have ever met, often said—and this was not something he said of many people—that the old Imam read a lot. A lot of what? Politics, theology, even popular science . . . that kind of thing.

This made me all the more determined to meet him, and one evening, a few months after I first came to the village, I found my way to his house. He lived in the centre of the village, on the edge of the dusty open square which had the mosque in its middle. This was the oldest part of the village: a maze of low mud huts huddled together like confectionery on a tray, each hut crowned with a billowing, tousled head of straw.

When I knocked on the door the Imam opened it himself. He was a big man, with very bright brown eyes, set deep in a wrinkled, weather-beaten face. Like the room behind him, he was distinctly untidy: his blue jallabeyya was mud-stained and unwashed and his turban had been knotted anyhow around his head. But his beard, short and white and neatly trimmed, was everything a barber's beard should be. Age had been harsh on his face, but there was a certain energy in the way he arched his shoulders, in the clarity of his eyes and in the way he fidgeted constantly, was never still: it was plain that he was a vigorous, restive kind of person.

'Welcome,' he said, courteous but unsmiling, and stood aside and waved me in. It was a long dark room, with sloping walls and a very low ceiling. There was a bed in it and a couple of mats but little else, apart from a few, scattered books: everything bore that dull patina of grime which speaks of years of neglect. Later, I learned that the Imam had divorced his first wife and his second had left him, so that now he lived quite alone and had his meals with his son's family who lived across the square.

'Welcome,' he said again, formally.

'Welcome to you,' I said, giving him the formal response, and then we began on the long, reassuring litany of Arabic phrases of greeting.

'How are you?'

'How are you?'

'You have brought blessings?'

'May God bless you.'

'Welcome.'

'Welcome to you.'

'You have brought light.'

'The light is yours.'

'How are you?'

'How are you?'

He was very polite, very proper. In a moment he produced a kerosene stove and began to brew tea. But even in the performance of that little ritual there was something about him that was guarded, watchful.

'You're the *doktor al-Hindi*,' he said to me at last, 'aren't you? The Indian doctor?'

I nodded, for that was the name the village had given me. Then I told him that I wanted to talk to him about the methods of his system of medicine.

He looked very surprised and for a while he was silent. Then he put his right hand to his heart and began again on the ritual of greetings and responses, but in a markedly different way this time; one that I had learnt to recognize as a means of changing the subject.

'Welcome.'

'Welcome to you.'

'You have brought light.'

'The light is yours.'

And so on.

At the end of it I repeated what I had said.

'Why do you want to hear about *my* herbs?' he retorted. 'Why don't you go back to your country and find out about your own?'

'I will,' I said. 'Soon. But right now . . .'

'No, no,' he said restlessly. 'Forget about all that; I'm trying to forget about it myself.'

And then I knew that he would never talk to me about his craft, not just because he had taken a dislike to me for some reason of his own, but because his medicines were as discredited in his own eyes as they were in his clients'; because he knew as well as anybody else that the people who came to him now did so only because of old habits; because he bitterly regretted his inherited association with these relics of the past.

'Instead,' he said, 'let me tell you about what I have been learning over the last few years. Then you can go back to your country and tell them all about it.'

He jumped up, his eyes shining, reached under his bed and brought out a glistening new biscuit tin.

'Here!' he said, opening it. 'Look!'

Inside the box was a hypodermic syringe and a couple of glass phials. This is what he had been learning, he told me: the art of mixing and giving injections. And there was a huge market for it too, in the village: everybody wanted injections, for coughs, colds, fevers, whatever. There was a good living in it. He wanted to demonstrate his skill to me right there, on my arm, and when I protested that I wasn't ill, that I didn't need an injection just then, he was offended. 'All right,' he said curtly, standing up. 'I have to go to the mosque right now. Perhaps we can talk about this some other day.'

That was the end of my interview. I walked with him to the mosque and there, with an air of calculated finality, he took my hand in his, gave it a perfunctory shake and vanished up the stairs.

Khamees the Rat I met one morning when I was walking through the rice fields that lay behind the village, watching people transplant their seedlings. Everybody I met was cheerful and busy and the flooded rice fields were sparkling in the clear sunlight. If I shut my ears to the language, I thought, and stretch the date palms a bit and give them a few coconuts, I could easily be back somewhere in Bengal.

I was a long way from the village and not quite sure of my bearings, when I spotted a group of people who had finished their work and were sitting on the path, passing around a hookah.

'*Ahlan!*' a man in a brown jallabeyya called out to me. 'Hullo! Aren't you the Indian *doktor*?

'Yes,' I called back. 'And who're you?'

'He's a rat,' someone answered, raising a gale of laughter. 'Don't go anywhere near him.'

'Tell me *ya doktor*,' the Rat said, 'if I get on to my donkey and ride steadily for thirty days will I make it to India?'

'No,' I said. 'You wouldn't make it in thirty months.'

'Thirty months!' he said. 'You must have come a long way.'

'Yes.'

'As for me,' he declared, 'I've never even been as far as Alexandria and if I can help it I never will.'

I laughed: it did not occur to me to believe him.

139

When I first came to that quiet corner of the Nile Delta I had expected to find on that most ancient and most settled of soils a settled and restful people. I couldn't have been more wrong.

The men of the village had all the busy restlessness of airline passengers in a transit lounge. Many of them had worked and travelled in the sheikhdoms of the Persian Gulf, others had been in Libya and Jordan and Syria, some had been to the Yemen as soldiers, others to Saudi Arabia as pilgrims, a few had visited Europe: some of them had passports so thick they opened out like ink-blackened concertinas. And none of this was new: their grandparents and ancestors and relatives had travelled and migrated too, in much the same way as mine had, in the Indian sub-continent—because of wars, or for money and jobs, or perhaps simply because they got tired of living always in one place. You could read the history of this restlessness in the villagers' surnames: they had names which derived from cities in the Levant, from Turkey, from faraway towns in Nubia; it was as though people had drifted here from every corner of the Middle East. The wanderlust of its founders had been ploughed into the soil of the village: it seemed to me sometimes that every man in it was a traveller. Everyone, that is, except Khamees the Rat, and even his surname, as I discovered later, meant 'of Sudan'.

'Well, never mind *ya doktor*,' Khamees said to me now, 'since you're not going to make it back to your country by sundown anyway, why don't you come and sit with us for a while?'

He smiled and moved up to make room for me.

I liked him at once. He was about my age, in the early twenties, scrawny, with a thin, mobile face deeply scorched by the sun. He had that brightness of eye and the quick, slightly sardonic turn to his mouth that I associated with faces in the coffee-houses of universities in Delhi and Calcutta; he seemed to belong to a world of late-night rehearsals and black coffee and lecture rooms, even though, in fact, unlike most people in the village, he was completely illiterate. Later I learned that he was called the Rat—Khamees the Rat—because he was said to gnaw away at things with his tongue, like a rat did with its teeth. He laughed at everything, people said— at his father, the village's patron saint, the village elders, the Imam, everything.

That day he decided to laugh at me.

'All right *ya doktor*,' he said to me as soon as I had seated myself. 'Tell me, is it true what they say, that in your country you burn your dead?'

No sooner had he said it than the women of the group clasped their hands to their hearts and muttered in breathless horror: '*Haram! Haram!*'

My heart sank. This was a conversation I usually went through at least once a day and I was desperately tired of it. 'Yes,' I said, 'it's true; some people in my country burn their dead.'

'You mean,' said Khamees in mock horror, 'that you put them on heaps of wood and just light them up?'

'Yes,' I said, hoping that he would tire of this sport if I humoured him.

'Why?' he said. 'Is there a shortage of kindling in your country?'

'No,' I said helplessly, 'you don't understand.' Somewhere in the limitless riches of the Arabic language a word such as 'cremate' must exist, but if it does, I never succeeded in finding it. Instead, for lack of any other, I had to use the word 'burn'. That was unfortunate, for 'burn' was the word for what happened to wood and straw and the eternally damned.

Khamees the Rat turned to his spellbound listeners. 'I'll tell you why they do it,' he said. 'They do it so that their bodies can't be punished after the Day of Judgement.'

Everybody burst into wonderstruck laughter. 'Why, how clever,' cried one of the younger girls. 'What a good idea! We ought to start doing it ourselves. That way we can do exactly what we like and when we die and the Day of Judgement comes, there'll be nothing there to judge.'

Khamees had got his laugh. Now he gestured to them to be quiet again.

'All right then *ya doktor*,' he said. 'Tell me something else: is it true that you are a Magian? That in your country everybody worships cows? Is it true that the other day when you were walking through the fields you saw a man beating a cow and you were so upset that you burst into tears and ran back to your room?'

'No, it's not true,' I said, but without much hope: I had heard

141

this story before and knew that there was nothing I could say which would effectively give it the lie. 'You're wrong. In my country people beat their cows all the time; I promise you.'

I could see that no one believed me.

'Everything's upside-down in their country,' said a dark, aquiline young woman who, I was told later, was Khamees's wife. 'Tell us *ya doktor*: in your country, do you have crops and fields and canals like we do?'

'Yes,' I said, 'we have crops and fields, but we don't always have canals. In some parts of my country they aren't needed because it rains all the year around.'

'*Ya salám*,' she cried, striking her forehead with the heel of her palm. 'Do you hear that, oh you people? Oh, the Protector, oh, the Lord! It rains all the year round in his country.'

She had gone pale with amazement. 'So tell us then,' she demanded, 'do you have night and day like we do?'

'Shut up woman,' said Khamees. 'Of course they don't. It's day all the time over there, didn't you know? They arranged it like that so that they wouldn't have to spend any money on lamps.'

We all laughed, and then someone pointed to a baby lying in the shade of a tree swaddled in a sheet of cloth. 'That's Khamees's baby,' I was told. 'He was born last month.'

'That's wonderful,' I said. 'Khamees must be very happy.'

Khamees gave a cry of delight. 'The Indian knows I'm happy because I've had a son,' he said to the others. 'He understands that people are happy when they have children: he's not as upside-down as we thought.'

He slapped me on the knee and lit up the hookah and from that moment we were friends.

One evening, perhaps a month or so after I first met Khamees, he and his brothers and I were walking back to the village from the fields when he spotted the old Imam sitting on the steps that led to the mosque.

'Listen,' he said to me, 'you know the old Imam, don't you? I saw you talking to him once.'

'Yes,' I said. 'I talked to him once.'

'My wife's ill,' Khamees said. 'I want the Imam to come to my house to give her an injection. He won't come if I ask him, he doesn't like me. You go and ask.'

'He doesn't like me either,' I said.

'Never mind,' Khamees insisted. 'He'll come if you ask him— he knows you're a foreigner. He'll listen to you.'

While Khamees waited on the edge of the square with his brothers I went across to the Imam. I could tell that he had seen me—and Khamees—from a long way off, that he knew I was crossing the square to talk to him. But he would not look in my direction. Instead, he pretended to be deep in conversation with a man who was sitting beside him, an elderly and pious shopkeeper whom I knew slightly.

When I reached them I said 'Good evening' very pointedly to the Imam. He could not ignore me any longer then, but his response was short and curt, and he turned back at once to resume his conversation.

The old shopkeeper was embarrassed now, for he was a courteous, gracious man in the way that seemed to come so naturally to the elders of the village. 'Please sit down,' he said to me. 'Do sit. Shall we get you a chair?'

Then he turned to the Imam and said, slightly puzzled: 'You know the Indian *doktor*, don't you? He's come all the way from India to be a student at the University of Alexandria.'

'I know him,' said the Imam. 'He came around to ask me questions. But as for this student business, I don't know. What's *he* going to study? He doesn't even write in Arabic.'

'Well,' said the shopkeeper judiciously, 'that's true; but after all he writes his own languages and he knows English.'

'Oh those,' said the Imam. 'What's the use of *those* languages? They're the easiest languages in the world. Anyone can write those.'

He turned to face me for the first time. His eyes were very bright and his mouth was twitching with anger. 'Tell me,' he said, 'why do you worship cows?'

I was so taken aback that I began to stammer. The Imam ignored me. He turned to the old shopkeeper and said: 'That's what they do in his country—did you know?—they worship cows.'

He shot me a glance from the corner of his eyes. 'And shall I tell you what else they do?' he said to the shopkeeper.

143

He let the question hang for a moment. And then, very loudly, he hissed: 'They burn their dead.'

The shopkeeper recoiled as though he had been slapped. His hands flew to his mouth. 'Oh God!' he muttered. '*Ya Allah.*'

'That's what they do,' said the Imam. 'They burn their dead.'

Then suddenly he turned to me and said, very rapidly: 'Why do you allow it? Can't you see that it's a primitive and backward custom? Are you savages that you permit something like that? Look at you: you've had some kind of education; you should know better. How will your country ever progress if you carry on doing these things? You've even been to the West; you've seen how advanced they are. Now tell me: have you ever seen them burning their dead?'

The Imam was shouting now and a circle of young men and boys had gathered around us. Under the pressure of their interested eyes my tongue began to trip, even on syllables I thought I had mastered. I found myself growing angry—as much with my own incompetence as the Imam.

'Yes, they do burn their dead in the West,' I managed to say somehow. I raised my voice too now. 'They have special electric furnaces meant just for that.'

The Imam could see that he had stung me. He turned away and laughed. 'He's lying,' he said to the crowd. 'They don't burn their dead in the West. They're not an ignorant people. They're advanced, they're educated, they have science, they have guns and tanks and bombs.'

'We have them too!' I shouted back at him. I was as confused now as I was angry. 'In my country we have all those things too,' I said to the crowd. 'We have guns and tanks and bombs. And they're better than anything you have—we're way ahead of you.'

The Imam could no longer disguise his anger. 'I tell you, he's lying,' he said. 'Our guns and bombs are much better than theirs. Ours are second only to the West's.'

'It's you who's lying,' I said. 'You know nothing about this. Ours are much better. Why, in my country we've even had a nuclear explosion. You won't be able to match that in a hundred years.'

So there we were, the Imam and I, delegates from two superseded civilizations vying with each other to lay claim to the violence of the West.

At that moment, despite the vast gap that lay between us, we understood each other perfectly. We were both travelling, he and I: we were travelling in the West. The only difference was that I had actually been there, in person: I could have told him about the ancient English university I had won a scholarship to, about punk dons with safety pins in their mortar-boards, about superhighways and sex shops and Picasso. But none of it would have mattered. We would have known, both of us, that all that was mere fluff: at the bottom, for him as for me and millions and millions of people on the landmasses around us, the West meant only this—science and tanks and guns and bombs.

And we recognized too the inescapability of these things, their strength, their power—evident in nothing so much as this: that even for him, a man of God, and for me, a student of the 'humane' sciences, they had usurped the place of all other languages of argument. He knew, just as I did, that he could no longer say to me, as Ibn Battuta might have when he travelled to India in the fourteenth century: 'You should do this or that because it is right or good or because God wills it so.' He could not have said it because that language is dead: those things are no longer sayable; they sound absurd. Instead he had had, of necessity, to use that other language, so universal that it extended equally to him, an old-fashioned village Imam, and great leaders at SALT conferences: he had had to say to me: 'You ought not to do this because otherwise you will not have guns and tanks and bombs.'

Since he was a man of God his was the greater defeat.

For a moment then I was desperately envious. The Imam would not have said any of those things to me had I been a Westerner. He would not have dared. Whether I wanted it or not, I would have had around me the protective aura of an inherited expertise in the technology of violence. That aura would have surrounded me, I thought, with a sheet of clear glass, like a bullet-proof screen; or perhaps it would have worked as a talisman, like a press card, armed with which I could have gone off to what were said to be the most terrible places in the world that month, to gaze and wonder. And then perhaps I too would one day have had enough material for a book which would have had for its epigraph the line, *The horror! The horror!*—for the virtue of a sheet of glass is that it does not require one to look within.

But that still leaves Khamees the Rat waiting on the edge of the square.

In the end it was he and his brothers who led me away from the Imam. They took me home with them, and there, while Khamees's wife cooked dinner for us—she was not so ill after all—Khamees said to me: 'Do not be upset, *ya doktor*. Forget about all those guns and things. I'll tell you what: *I'll* come to visit you in your country, even though I've never been anywhere. I'll come all the way.'

He slipped a finger under his skull-cap and scratched his head, thinking hard.

Then he added: 'But if I die, you must bury me.'

HANIF KUREISHI
BRADFORD

Some time ago, I noticed that there was something unusual about the city of Bradford, something that distinguished it from other northern industrial cities.

To begin with, there was Ray Honeyford. Three years ago Honeyford, the headmaster of Bradford's Drummond Middle School, wrote a short, three-page article that was published in the *Salisbury Review*. The *Salisbury Review* has a circulation of about 1,000, but the impact of Honeyford's article was felt beyond the magazine's readership. It was discussed in the *Yorkshire Post* and reprinted in the local *Telegraph and Argus*. A parents' group demanded Honeyford's resignation. His school was then boycotted, and children, instructed by their parents not to attend classes, gathered outside, shouting abuse at the man who weeks before was their teacher. There were fights, sometimes physical brawls, between local leaders and politicians. The 'Honeyford Affair', as it became known, attracted so much attention that it became common every morning to come upon national journalists and television crews outside the school. And when it was finally resolved that Honeyford had to go, the Bradford district council had to pay him over £160,000 to get him to leave: ten times his annual salary.

But there were other things about Bradford. The Yorkshire Ripper was from Bradford. The prostitutes who came down to London on the train on 'cheap-day return' tickets were from Bradford. At a time when the game of soccer was threatened by so many troubles, Bradford seemed to have troubles of the most extreme kind. Days after the deaths in Brussels at the Heysel stadium, forty-seven Bradford football supporters were killed in one of the worst fires in the history of the sport. Eighteen months later, there was yet another fire, and a match stopped because of crowd violence.

There was more: there was unemployment in excess of twenty percent; there was a prominent branch of the National Front; there were regular racial attacks on taxi drivers; there were stories of forced emigration; there was a mayor from a village in Pakistan. Bradford, I felt, was a place I had to see for myself, because it seemed that so many important issues, of race, culture, nationalism,

This piece couldn't have been written without the help of Helen Jacobus.

and education, were evident in an extremely concentrated way in this medium-sized city of 400,000 people, situated between the much larger cities of Manchester and Leeds. These were issues that related to the whole notion of what it was to be British and what that would mean in the future. Bradford seemed to be a microcosm of a larger British society that was struggling to find a sense of itself, even as it was undergoing radical change. And it was a struggle not seen by the people governing the country, who, after all, had been brought up in a world far different from today's. In 1945, England ruled over six hundred million people. And there were few black faces on its streets.

The first thing you notice as you get on the Inter-City train to Bradford is that the first three carriages are first class. These are followed by the first-class restaurant car. Then you are free to sit down. But if the train is packed and you cannot find an empty seat, you have to stand. You stand for the whole journey, with other people lying on the floor around you, and you look through at the empty seats in the first-class carriages where men sit in their shirt-sleeves doing important work and not looking up. The ticket collector has to climb over us to get to them.

Like the porters on the station, the ticket collector was black, probably of West Indian origin. In other words, black British. Most of the men fixing the railway line, in their luminous orange jackets, with pickaxes over their shoulders, were also black. The guard on the train was Pakistani, or should I say another Briton, probably born here, and therefore 'black'.

When I got to Bradford I took a taxi. It was simple: Bradford is full of taxis. Raise an arm and three taxis rush at you. Like most taxi drivers in Bradford, the driver was Asian and his car had furry, bright purple seats, covered with the kind of material people in the suburbs sometimes put on the lids of their toilets. It smelled of perfume, and Indian music was playing. The taxi driver had a Bradford-Pakistani accent, a cross between the north of England and Lahore, which sounds odd the first few times you hear it. Mentioning the accent irritates people in Bradford. How else do you expect people to talk? they say. And they are right. But hearing it for the first time disconcerted me because I found that I associated northern accents with white faces, with people who eat puddings, with Geoffrey Boycott and Roy Hattersley.

We drove up a steep hill, which overlooked the city. In the distance there were modern buildings and among them the older mill chimneys and factories with boarded-up windows. We passed Priestley Road. J.B. Priestley was born in Bradford, and in the early sixties both John Braine and Alan Sillitoe set novels here. I wondered what the writing of the next fifteen years would be like. There were, I was to learn, stories in abundance to be told.

The previous day I had watched one of my favourite films, Keith Waterhouse and Willis Hall's *Billy Liar*, also written in the early sixties. Billy works for an undertaker and there is a scene in which Billy tries to seduce one of his old girlfriends in a graveyard. Now I passed that old graveyard. It was full of monstrous mausoleums, some with spires thirty feet high; others were works of architecture in themselves, with arches, urns and roofs. They dated from the late nineteenth century and contained the bones of the great mill barons and their families. In *The Waste Land* T.S. Eliot wrote of the 'silk hat on a Bradford millionaire'. Now the mills and the millionaires had nearly disappeared. In the cemetery there were some white youths on a Youth Opportunity Scheme, hacking unenthusiastically at the weeds, clearing a path. This was the only work that could be found for them, doing up the old cemetery.

I was staying in a house near the cemetery. The houses were of a good size, well-built with three bedrooms and lofts. Their front doors were open and the street was full of kids running in and out. Women constantly crossed the street and stood on each others' doorsteps, talking. An old man with a stick walked along slowly. He stopped to pat a child who was crying so much I thought she would explode. He carried on patting her head, and she carried on crying, until finally he decided to enter the house and fetched the child's young sister.

The houses were overcrowded—if you looked inside you would usually see five or six adults sitting in the front room—and there wasn't much furniture: often the linoleum on the floor was torn and curling, and a bare lightbulb hung from the ceiling. The wallpaper was peeling from the walls.

Each house had a concrete yard at the back, where women and young female children were always hanging out the washing: the cleaning of clothes never appeared to stop. There was one man—his house was especially run-down—who had recently acquired a new car. He walked round and round it; he was proud of his car, and occasionally caressed it.

It was everything I imagined a Bradford working-class community would be like, except that there was one difference. Everyone I'd seen since I arrived was Pakistani. I had yet to see a white face.

The women covered their heads. And while the older ones wore jumpers and overcoats, underneath they, like the young girls, wore *salwar kamiz*, the Pakistani long tops over baggy trousers. If I ignored the dark Victorian buildings around me, I could imagine that everyone was back in their village in Pakistan.

That evening, Jane—the friend I was staying with—and I decided to go out. We walked back down the hill and into the centre of town. It looked like many other town centres in Britain. The subways under the roundabouts stank of urine; graffiti defaced them and lakes of rain-water gathered at the bottom of the stairs. There was a massive shopping centre with unnatural lighting; some kids were rollerskating through it, pursued by three pink-faced security guards in paramilitary outfits. The shops were also the same: Rymans, Smiths, Dixons, the National Westminister Bank. I hadn't become accustomed to Bradford and found myself making simple comparisons with London. The clothes people wore were shabby and old; they looked as if they'd been bought in jumble sales or second-hand shops. And their faces had an unhealthy aspect: some were malnourished.

As we crossed the city, I could see that some parts looked old-fashioned. They reminded me of my English grandfather and the Britain of my childhood: pigeon-keeping, greyhound racing, roast beef eating and pianos in pubs. Outside the centre, there were shops you'd rarely see in London now: drapers, ironmongers, fish and chip shops that still used newspaper wrappers, barber's shops with photographs in the window of men with Everly Brothers haircuts. And here, among all this, I also saw the Islamic Library and the

Ambala Sweet Centre where you could buy spices: dhaniya, haldi,
garam masala, and dhal and ladies' fingers. There were Asian
video shops where you could buy tapes of the songs of Master Saj-
jad, Nayyara, Alamgir, Nazeen and M. Ali Shahaiky.

Jane and I went to a bar. It was a cross between a pub and a
night-club. At the entrance the bouncer laid his hands on my shoulders and told me I could not go in.

'Why not?' I asked.

'You're not wearing any trousers.'

I looked down at my legs in astonishment.

'Are you sure?' I asked.

'No trousers,' he said, 'no entry.'

Jeans, it seems, were not acceptable.

We walked on to another place. This time we got in. It too was
very smart and entirely white. The young men had dressed up in
open-necked shirts, Top Shop grey slacks and Ravel loafers. They
stood around quietly in groups. The young women had also gone to
a lot of trouble: some of them looked like models, in their extravagant dresses and high heels. But the women and the men were not
talking to each other. We had a drink and left. Jane said she wanted
me to see a working men's club.

The working men's club turned out to be near an estate, popu-
lated, like most Bradford estates, mostly by whites. The Asians
tended to own their homes. They had difficulty acquiring council
houses or flats, and were harassed and abused when they moved on
to white estates.

The estate was scruffy: some of the flats were boarded up, rubbish blew about; the balconies looked as if they were about to crash
off the side of the building. The club itself was in a large modern
building. We weren't members of course, but the man on the door
agreed to let us in.

There were three large rooms. One was like a pub; another was
a snooker room. In the largest room at least 150 people sat around
tables in families. At one end was a stage. A white man in evening
dress was banging furiously at a drum-kit. Another played the
organ. The noise was unbearable.

At the bar, it was mostly elderly men. They sat beside each
other. But they didn't talk. They had drawn, pale faces and thin,

narrow bodies that expanded dramatically at the stomach and then disappeared into the massive jutting band of their trousers. They had little legs. They wore suits, the men. They had dressed up for the evening.

Here there were no Asians either, and I wanted to go to an Asian bar, but it was getting late and the bars were closing, at ten-thirty as they do outside London. We got a taxi and drove across town. The streets got rougher and rougher. We left the main road and suddenly were in a leafy, almost suburban area. The houses here were large, occupied I imagined by clerks, insurance salesmen, business people. We stopped outside a detached three-storey house that seemed to be surrounded by an extraordinary amount of darkness and shadow. There was one light on, in the kitchen, and the woman inside was Sonia Sutcliffe, the wife of the Yorkshire Ripper, an ex-schoolteacher. I thought of Peter Sutcliffe telling his wife he was the Yorkshire Ripper. He had wanted to tell her himself; he insisted on it. Many of his victims had come from the surrounding area.

The surrounding area was mostly an Asian district and here the pubs stayed open late, sometimes until two in the morning. There were no trouser rules.

During the day in this part of town the Asian kids would be playing in the streets. The women, most of them uneducated, illiterate, unable to speak English, would talk in doorways as they did where I was staying.

It was around midnight, and men were only now leaving their houses—the women remaining behind with the children—and walking down the street to the pub. Jane said it stayed open late with police permission. It gave the police an opportunity to find out what was going on: their spies and informers could keep an eye on people. Wherever you went in Bradford, people talked about spies and informers: who was and who wasn't. I'd never known anything like it, but then I'd never known any other city, except perhaps Karachi, in which politics was such a dominant part of daily life. Apparently there was money to be made working for the police and reporting what was going on: what the Asian militants were doing; what the racists were doing; who the journalists were talking to; what attacks or demonstrations were planned; what vigilante groups were being formed.

The pub was packed with Asian men and they still kept arriving. They knew each other and embraced enthusiastically. There were few women and all but three were white. Asian men and white women kissed in corners. As we squeezed in, Jane said she knew several white women who were having affairs with Asian men, affairs that had sometimes gone on for years. The men had married Pakistani women, often out of family pressure, and frequently the women were from the villages. The Asian women had a terrible time in Bradford.

The music was loud and some people were dancing, elbow to elbow, only able in the crush to shake their heads and shuffle their feet. There was a lot of very un-Islamic drinking. I noticed two Asian girls. They stood out, with their bright jewellery and pretty clothes. They were with Asian men. Their men looked inhibited and the girls left early. Jane, who was a journalist, recognized a number of prostitutes in the pub. She'd interviewed them at the time of the Ripper. One stood by Jane and kept pulling at her jumper. 'Where did you get that jumper? How much was it?' she kept saying. Jane said the prostitutes hadn't stopped work during the time of the Ripper. They couldn't afford to. Instead, they'd worked in pairs, one girl fucking the man, while the other stood by with a knife in her hand.

In 1933, when J.B. Priestley was preparing his *English Journey*, he found three Englands. There was guide-book England, of palaces and forests; nineteenth-century industrial England of factories and suburbs; and contemporary England of by-passes and suburbs. Now, half a century later, there is another England as well: the inner city.

In front of me, in this pub, there were five or six gay men and two lesbian couples. Three white kids wore black leather jackets and had mohicans: their mauve, red and yellow hair stood up straight for a good twelve inches and curved across their heads like a feather glued on its thin edge to a billiard ball. And there were the Asians. This was not one large solid community with a shared outlook, common beliefs and an established form of life; not Orwell's 'one family with the wrong members in control.' It was diverse, disparate, strikingly various.

Jane introduced me to a young Asian man, an activist and local political star from his time of being on trial as one of the Bradford

155

Twelve. I was pleased to meet him. In 1981, a group of twelve
youths, fearing a racial attack in the aftermath of the terrible
assault on Asians by skinheads in Southall in London, had made a
number of petrol bombs. But they were caught and charged under
the Explosives Act with conspiracy—a charge normally intended
for urban terrorists. It was eleven months before they were acquit-
ted.

I greeted him enthusiastically. He, with less enthusiasm, asked
me if I'd written a film called *My Beautiful Laundrette*. I said yes, I
had, and he started to curse me: I was a fascist, a reactionary. He
was shouting. Then he seemed to run out of words and pulled back
to hit me. But just as he raised his fist, his companions grabbed his
arm and dragged him away.

I said to Jane that I thought the next day we should do something less exhausting. We could visit a school.

I had heard that there was to be a ceremony for a new school that
was opening, the Zakariya Girls School. The large community
hall was already packed with three hundred Asian men
when I arrived. Then someone took my arm, to eject me, I thought.
But instead I was led to the front row, where I found myself sitting
next to three white policemen and assorted white dignitaries, both
women and men, in smart Sunday-school clothes.

On the high stage sat local councillors, a white Muslim in white
turban and robes, and various Asian men. A white man was addressing the audience, the MP for Scarborough, Sir Michael Shaw. 'You
have come into our community,' he was saying, 'and you must
become part of that community. All branches must lead to one
trunk, which is the British way of life. We mustn't retire to our own
communities and shut ourselves out. Yet you have felt you needed
schools of your own . . .'

The MP was followed by a man who appeared to be a homegrown Batley citizen. 'As a practising Roman Catholic, I sym-
pathize with you, having had a Catholic education myself,' he said,
and went on to say how good he thought the Islamic school would
be.

Finally the man from the local mosque read some verses from
the Koran. The local policemen cupped their hands and lowered

their heads in true multi-cultural fashion. The other whites near me, frantically looking around at each other, quickly followed suit. Then Indian sweets were brought round, which the polite English ladies picked politely at.

I left the hall and walked up the hill towards the school. The policeman followed me, holding the hands of the six or seven Asian children that surrounded him.

Batley is outside Bradford, on the way to Leeds. It is a small town surrounded by countryside and hills. The view from the hill into the valley and then up into the hills was exquisite. In the town there was a large Asian community. The Zakariya Girls School had actually been started two years ago as a 'pirate' school, not having received approval from the Department of Education until an extension was built. Now it was finished. And today it became the first high school of its kind—an Islamic school for girls—to be officially registered under the Education Act. As a pirate school it had been a large, overcrowded old house on the top of a hill. Now, outside, was a new two-storey building. It was spacious, clean, modern.

I went in and looked around. Most of the books were on the Koran or Islam, on prayer or on the prophet Mohammed. The walls were covered with verses from the Koran. And despite its being a girls school there were no girls there and no Asian women, just the men and lots of little boys in green, blue and brown caps, running about.

The idea for the school had been the pop star Cat Stevens's, and he had raised most of the money for it privately, it was said, from Saudi Arabia. Stevens, who had changed his name to Yusaf Islam, was quoted as saying that he had tried everything, running the gamut of international novelties to find spiritual satisfaction: materialism, sex, drugs, Buddhism, Christianity and finally Islam. I wondered if it was entirely arbitrary that he'd ended with Islam or whether perhaps today, the circumstances being slightly different, we could as easily have been at the opening of a Buddhist school.

Yusaf Islam was not at the school but his assistant, Ibrahim, was. Ibrahim was the white Muslim in the white robes with the white turban who spoke earlier. There was supposed to be a press conference, but nothing was happening; everything was disorganized. Ibrahim came and sat beside me. I asked him if he'd talk about the school. He was, he said, very keen; the school had been the result of so much effort and organization, so much goodness. I looked at him. He seemed preternaturally good and calm.

Ibrahim was from Newcastle, and had a long ginger beard. (I remembered someone saying to me in Pakistan that the only growth industry in Islamic countries was in human hair on the face.) Ibrahim's epiphany had occurred on a trip to South Africa. There, seeing black and white men praying together in a mosque, he decided to convert to Islam.

He told me about the way the school worked. The human face, for instance, or the face of any animate being, could not be represented at the school. And dancing would not be encouraged, nor the playing of musical instruments. Surely, he said, looking at me, his face full of conviction, the human voice was expressive enough? When I said this would probably rule out the possibility of the girls taking either art or music O-Levels, he nodded sadly and admitted that it would.

And modern literature? I asked.

He nodded sadly again and said it would be studied 'in a critical light.'

I said I was glad to hear it. But what about science?

That was to be studied in a critical light too, since—and here he took a deep breath—he didn't accept Darwinism or any theory of evolution because, well, because the presence of monkeys who hadn't changed into men disproved it all.

I took another close look at him. He obviously believed these things. But why was he being so apologetic?

As I walked back down the hill I thought about the issues raised by the Zakariya Girls School. There were times, I thought, when to be accommodating you had to bend over backwards so far that you fell over. Since the mid-sixties the English liberal has seen the traditional hierarchies and divisions of British life challenged, if not destroyed. Assumptions of irrevocable, useful and moral differences—between classes, men and women, gays and straights, older and younger people, developed and underdeveloped societies—had changed for good. The commonly made distinction between 'higher' and 'lower' cultures had become suspect.

It had become questionable philosophically to apply criteria of judgement available in one society to events in another: there could not be any independent or bridging method of evaluation. And it followed that we should be able, as a broad, humane and pluralistic society, to sustain a wide range of disparate groups living in their own way. And if one of these groups wanted *halal* meat, Islamic schools, anti-Darwinism and an intimate knowledge of the Koran for its girls, so be it. As it was, there had been Catholic schools and Jewish schools for years.

But Islamic schools like the one in Batley appeared to violate the principles of a liberal education, and the very ideas to which the school owed its existence. And because of the community's religious beliefs, so important to its members, the future prospects for the girls were reduced. Was that the choice they had made? Did the Asian community really want this kind of separate education anyway? And if it did, how many wanted it? Or was it only a few earnest and repressed believers, all men, frightened of England and their daughters' sexuality?

The house Delius was born in, in Bradford, was now the Council of Mosques, which looked after the interests of the Bradford Muslims. There are 60,000 Muslims and thirty Muslim organizations in Bradford. Chowdhury Khan, the President of the Council, told me about the relations between men and women in Islam and the problem of girls' schools.

He said there were no women in the Council because 'we respect them too much.' I mentioned that I found this a little perplexing, but he ignored me, adding that this is also why women were not encouraged to have jobs or careers.

'Women's interests,' he said confidently, 'are being looked after.'

And the girls'?

After the age of twelve, he said, women should not mix with men. That was why more single-sex schools were required in Bradford. The local council had agreed that this was desirable and would provide more single-sex schools when resources were available. He added that despite the Labour Party Manifesto, Neil Kinnock approved of this.

159

I said I doubted this.

Anyway, he continued, the local Labour Party was lobbying for more single-sex schools after having tried, in the sixties, to provide mixed-sex schools. But—and this he emphasized—the Council of Mosques wanted single-sex schools *not* Islamic ones or racially segregated schools. He banged on his desk, No, no, no! No apartheid!

He wanted the state to understand that, while Muslim children would inevitably become westernized—they were reconciled to that—they still wanted their children to learn about Islam at school, to learn subcontinental languages and be taught the history, politics and geography of India, Pakistan and Bangladesh. Surely, he added, the white British would be interested in this too. After all, the relations between England and the subcontinent had always been closer than those between Britain and France, say.

I found Chowdhury Khan to be a difficult and sometimes strange man. But his values, and the values of the Council he represented, are fairly straightforward. He believes in the pre-eminent value of the family and, for example, the importance of religion in establishing morality. He also believes in the innately inferior position of women. He dislikes liberalism in all its forms, and is an advocate of severe and vengeful retribution against law-breakers.

These are extremely conservative and traditional views. But they are also, isolated from the specifics of their subcontinental context, the values championed by Ray Honeyford, among others. There were a number of interesting ironies developing.

I sought out the younger, more militant section of the community. How did its members see their place in Britain?

When I was in my teens, in the mid-sixties, there was much talk of the 'problems' that kids of my colour and generation faced in Britain because of our racial mix or because our parents were immigrants. We didn't know where we belonged, it was said; we were neither fish nor fowl. I remember reading that kind of thing in the newspaper. We were frequently referred to as 'second-generation immigrants' just so there was no mistake about our not really belonging in Britain. We were 'Britain's children without a home'. The phrase 'caught between two

cultures' was a favourite. It was a little too triumphant for me. Anyway, this view was wrong. It has been easier for us than for our
parents. For them Britain really had been a strange land and it must
have been hard to feel part of a society if you had spent a good deal of
your life elsewhere and intended to return: most immigrants from
the Indian subcontinent came to Britain to make money and then go
home. Most of the Pakistanis in Bradford had come from one
specific district, Mirpur, because that was where the Bradford mill-
owners happened to look for cheap labour twenty-five years ago.
And many, once here, stayed for good; it was not possible to go
back. Yet when they got older the immigrants found they hadn't
really made a place for themselves in Britain. They missed the old
country. They'd always thought of Britain as a kind of long stop-
over rather than the final resting place it would turn out to be.

But for me and the others of my generation born here, Britain
was always where we belonged, even when we were told—often in
terms of racial abuse—that this was not so. Far from being a conflict
of cultures, our lives seemed to synthesize disparate elements: the
pub, the mosque, two or three languages, rock 'n' roll, Indian films.
Our extended family and our British individuality co-mingled.

Tariq was twenty-two. His office was bare in the modern style:
there was a desk; there was a computer. The building was
paid for by the EEC and Bradford Council. His job was to
advise on the setting-up of businesses and on related legal matters.
He also advised the Labour Party on its economic policy. In fact,
although so young, Tariq had been active in politics for a number of
years: at the age of sixteen, he had been chairman of the Asian
Youth Movement, which was founded in 1978 after the National
Front began marching on Bradford. But few of the other young men
I'd met in Bradford had Tariq's sense of direction or ambition,
including the young activists known as the Bradford Twelve. Five
years after their acquittal, most of them were, like Tariq, very
active—fighting deportations, monitoring racist organizations,
advising on multi-cultural education—but, like other young people
in Bradford, they were unemployed. They hung around the pubs;
their politics were obscure; they were 'anti-fascist' but it was difficult to know what they were for. Unlike their parents, who'd come

here for a specific purpose, to make a life in the affluent west away from poverty and lack of opportunity, they, born here, had inherited only pointlessness and emptiness. The emptiness, that is, derived not from racial concerns but economic ones.

Tariq took me to a Pakistani café. Bradford was full of them. They were like English working men's cafés, except the food was Pakistani, you ate with your fingers and there was always water on the table. The waiter spoke to us in Punjabi and Tariq replied. Then the waiter looked at me and asked a question. I looked vague, nodded stupidly and felt ashamed. Tariq realized I could only speak English.

How many languages did he speak?

Four: English, Malay, Urdu and Punjabi.

I told him about the school I'd visited.

Tariq was against Islamic schools. He thought they made it harder for Asian kids in Britain to get qualifications than in ordinary, mixed-race, mixed-sex schools. He said the people who wanted such schools were not representative; they just made a lot of noise and made the community look like it was made up of separatists, which it was not.

He wasn't a separatist, he said. He wanted the integration of all into the society. But for him the problem of integration was adjacent to the problem of being poor in Britain: how could people feel themselves to be active participants in the life of a society when they were suffering all the wretchedness of bad housing, poor insulation and the indignity of having their gas and electricity disconnected; or when they were turning to loan sharks to pay their bills; or when they felt themselves being dissipated by unemployment; and when they weren't being properly educated, because the resources for a proper education didn't exist.

There was one Asian in Bradford it was crucial to talk to. He'd had political power. For a year he'd been mayor, and as Britain's first Asian or black mayor he received much attention. He'd also had a terrible time.

I talked to Mohammed Ajeeb in the nineteenth-century town hall. The town hall was a monument to Bradford's long-gone splendour and pride. Later I ran into him at Bradford's superb Museum of Film, Television and Photography, where a huge photo of him and his wife was unveiled. Ajeeb is a tall, modest man, sincere, sometimes openly uncertain and highly regarded for his tenacity by the Labour leader Neil Kinnock. Ajeeb is careful in his conversation. He lacks the confident politician's polish: from him, I heard no well-articulated banalities. He is from a small village in the Punjab. When we met at the Museum, we talked about the differences between us, and he admitted that it had been quite a feat for someone like him to have got so far in Britain. In Pakistan, with its petrified feudal system, he would never have been able to transcend his background.

During his time in office, a stand at the Valley Parade football ground had burned down, killing fifty-six people and injuring 300 others. There was the Honeyford affair, about which he had been notoriously outspoken ('I cannot see,' he said in a speech that contributed to Honeyford's removal, 'the unity of our great city being destroyed by one man'). As mayor, Ajeeb moved through areas of Bradford society to which he never had access before, and the racism he experienced, both explicit and covert, was of a viciousness he hadn't anticipated. And it was relentless. His house was attacked, and he, as mayor, was forced to move; and at Grimsby Town football ground, when he presented a cheque to the families of those killed in the fire, the crowd abused him with racist slogans; finally, several thousand football supporters started chanting Honeyford's name so loudly that Ajeeb was unable to complete his speech. He received sackfuls of hate mail and few letters of support.

Ajeeb said that no culture could remain static, neither British nor Pakistani. And while groups liked to cling to the old ways and there would be conflict, eventually different groups would intermingle. For him the important thing was that minorities secure political power for themselves. At the same time, he said that, although he wanted to become a Parliamentary candidate, no one would offer him a constituency where he could stand. This was, he thought, because he was Asian and the Labour Party feared that the white working class wouldn't vote for him. He could stand as Parliamentary candidate only in a black area, which seemed fine to him for the time being; he was prepared to do that.

There were others who weren't prepared to put up with the

racism in the trade union movement and in the Labour Party itself in the way Ajeeb had. I met a middle-aged Indian man, a tax inspector, who had been in the Labour Party for at least ten years. He had offered to help canvas during the local council elections—on a white council estate. He was told that it wouldn't be to the party's advantage for him to help in a white area. He was so offended that he offered his services to the Tories. Although he hated Margaret Thatcher, he found the Tories welcomed him. He started to lecture on the subject of Asians in Britain to various Tory groups and Rotary Club dinners, until he found himself talking at the Wakefield Police College. At the Wakefield Police College he encountered the worst racists he had ever seen in his life.

He did not need to go into details. Only a few months before, at an anti-apartheid demonstration outside South Africa House in London, I'd been standing by a police line when a policeman started to talk to me. He spoke in a low voice, as if he were telling me about the traffic in Piccadilly. 'You bastards,' he said. 'We hate you, we don't want you here. Everything would be all right, there'd be none of this, if you pissed off home.' And he went on like that, fixing me with a stare. 'You wogs, you coons, you blacks, we hate you all.'

Ajeeb said that if there was anything he clung to when things became unbearable, it was the knowledge that the British electorate always rejected the far Right. They had never voted in significant numbers for neo-fascist groups like the National Front and the British National Party. Even the so-called New Right, a prominent and noisy group of journalists, lecturers and intellectuals, had no great popular following. People knew what viciousness underlay their ideas, he said.

Some of the views of the New Right, Ajeeb believed, had much in common with proletarian far-right organizations like the National Front: its members held to the notion of white racial superiority, they believed in repatriation and they argued that the mixing of cultures would lead to the degeneration of British culture. Ajeeb argued that they used the rhetoric of 'culture' and 'religion' and 'nationhood' as a fig-leaf; in the end they wished to defend a mythical idea of white culture. Honeyford was associated with the New Right, and what he and people like him wanted, Ajeeb said, was for Asians to behave exactly like the whites. And if they didn't do this, they should leave.

This movement known as the New Right is grouped around the Conservative Philosophy Group and the *Salisbury Review*, the magazine that published Honeyford's article. The group is a loose affiliation of individuals with similar views. A number of them are graduates of Peterhouse, Cambridge. These include John Vincent, Professor of History at Bristol University, who writes a weekly column for the *Sun*; Colin Welch, a columnist for the *Spectator*.

Like a lot of people in Bradford, Ajeeb became agitated on the subject of the New Right and Honeyford's relationship with it. But how important was it? What did the views of a few extremists really matter? So what if they wrote for influential papers? At least they weren't on the street wearing boots. But the ideas expressed by Honeyford had split Bradford apart. These ideas were alive and active in the city, entering into arguments about education, housing, citizenship, health, food and politics. Bradford was a city in which ideas carried knives.

Ray Honeyford went to Bradford's Drummond Middle School as Headmaster in January 1980. The children were aged between nine and thirteen. At the time the school was fifty percent Asian. When he left last spring it was ninety-five percent.

Honeyford is from a working-class background. He failed his exams for grammar school, and from the age of fifteen worked for ten years for a company that makes dessicated coconut. In his late twenties, he attended a two-year teacher-training course at Didsbury College, and later got further degrees from the universities of Lancaster and Manchester. He described himself as a marxist, and was a member of the Labour Party. But all that changed when he began teaching at a mixed-race school. He submitted an unsolicited article to the *Salisbury Review,* and the article, entitled 'Education and Race—An Alternative View', was accepted.

The article is a polemic. It argues that the multi-racial policies endorsed by various members of the teaching establishment are damaging the English way of life, and that proper English people

Hanif Kureishi

should resist these assaults on the 'British traditions of understate-
ment, civilized discourse and respect for reason.' It wasn't too surprising that a polemic of this sort written by the headmaster of a
school made up almost entirely of Asian children was seen to be
controversial.

But the real problem wasn't the polemic but the rhetorical
asides and parentheticals. Honeyford mentions the 'hysterical
political temperament of the Indian subcontinent', and describes
Asians as 'these people' (in an earlier article, they are 'settler
children'). A Sikh is 'half-educated and volatile', and black
intellectuals are 'aggressive'. Honeyford then goes on to attack
Pakistan itself, which in a curious non-sequitur seems to be
responsible for British drug problems:

> Pakistan is a country which cannot cope with
> democracy; under martial law since 1977, it is ruled by a
> military tyrant who, in the opinion of at least half his
> countrymen, had his predecessor judicially murdered. A
> country, moreover, which despite disproportionate
> western aid because of its important strategic position,
> remains for most of its people obstinately backward.
> Corruption at every level combines with unspeakable
> treatment not only of criminals, but of those who dare to
> question Islamic orthodoxy as interpreted by a despot.
> Even as I write, wounded dissidents are chained to
> hospital beds awaiting their fate. Pakistan, too, is the
> heroin capital of the world. (A fact which is now
> reflected in the drug problems of English cities with
> Asian populations.)

It is perhaps not unreasonable that some people felt the article
was expressing more than merely an alternative view on matters of
education.

Honeyford wrote a second piece for the *Salisbury Review,*
equally 'tolerant', 'reasonable' and 'civilized', but this one was
noticed by someone in Bradford's education department, and then
the trouble started—the protests, the boycott, the enormous public-
ity. A little research revealed that Honeyford's asides were a feature
of most of his freelance journalism, his most noteworthy being his

166

reference in the *Times Educational Supplement* to an Asian parent who visited him wanting to talk about his child's education: his accent, it seems, was 'like that of Peter Sellers's Indian doctor on an off day.'

The difficulty about the 'Honeyford Affair' was that it did not involve only Honeyford. His views are related to the much larger issue of what it is to be British, and what Britain should be in the future. And these views are, again, most clearly stated by the New Right, with which Honeyford closely identified himself. 'He is,' Honeyford said of Roger Scruton, the high Tory editor of the *Salisbury Review,* 'the most brilliant man I have ever met.'

It would be easy to exaggerate the influence of the New Right. It would be equally easy to dismiss it. But it is worth bearing in mind that shortly after Honeyford was dismissed, he was invited to 10 Downing Street to help advise Margaret Thatcher on Tory education policy. Thatcher has also attended New Right 'think tanks', organized by the Conservative Philosophy Group. So too have Paul Johnson, Tom Stoppard, Hugh Trevor-Roper and Enoch Powell.

The essential tenet of the New Right is expressed in the editorial of the first issue of the *Salisbury Review*: 'the consciousness of nationhood is the highest form of political consciousness.' For Maurice Cowling, Scruton's tutor at Peterhouse in Cambridge, the consciousness of nationhood requires 'a unity of national sentiment'. Honeyford's less elegant phrase is the 'unity notion of culture'. The real sense underlying these rather abstract phrases is expressed in the view the New Right holds of people who are British but not white: as Ajeeb pointed out, Asians are acceptable as long as they behave like whites; if not, they should leave. This explains why anti-racism and multi-racial policies in education are, for the New Right, so inflammatory: they erode the 'consciousness of nationhood'. For Scruton, anti-racism is virtually treason. In 1985, he wrote that

> Those who are concerned about racism in Britain, that call British society 'racist', have no genuine attachment to British customs and institutions, or any genuine allegiance to the Crown.

The implications are fascinating to contemplate. John Casey is a Fellow of Caius College, Cambridge, and co-founded the Conservative Philosophy Group with Scruton. Four years ago, in a talk entitled 'One Nation—The Politics of Race', delivered to the same Conservative Philosophy Group attended by the Prime Minister, Casey proposed that the legal status of Britain's black community be altered retroactively, 'so that its members became guest workers . . . who would eventually, over a period of years, return to their countries of origin.' 'The great majority of people,' Casey added, dissociating himself from the argument, 'are actually or potentially hostile to the multi-racial society which all decent persons are supposed to accept.'

This 'great majority' excludes, I suppose, those who brought over the Afro-Carribean and Asian workers—encouraged by the British government—to work in the mills, on the railways and in the hospitals. These are the same workers who, along with their children, are now part of the 'immigrant and immigrant-descended population' which, according to Casey, should be repatriated. It is strange how the meaning of the word 'immigrant' has changed. Americans, Australians, Italians, and Irish are not immigrants. It isn't Rupert Murdoch, Clive James or Kiri Te Kanawa who will be on their way: it is black people.

There is a word you hear in Bradford all the time, in pubs, shops, discos, schools and on the streets. The word is 'culture'. It is a word often used by the New Right, who frequently cite T.S. Eliot: that culture is a whole way of life, manifesting itself in the individual, in the group and in the society. It is everything we do and the particular way in which we do it. For Eliot culture 'includes all the characteristic activities of the people: Derby Day, Henley regatta, Cowes, the Twelfth of August, a cup final, the dog races, the pin-table, Wensleydale cheese, boiled cabbage cut into sections, beetroot in vinegar, nineteenth-century gothic churches and the music of Elgar.'

If one were compiling such a list today there would have to be numerous additions to the characteristic activities of the British people. They would include: yoga exercises, going to Indian restaurants, the music of Bob Marley, the novels of Salman

Rushdie, Zen Buddhism, the Hare Krishna Temple, as well as the films of Sylvester Stallone, therapy, hamburgers, visits to gay bars, the dole office and the taking of drugs.

Merely by putting these two, rather arbitrary, lists side by side, it is possible to see the kinds of changes that have occurred in Britain since the end of the war. It is the first list, Eliot's list, that represents the New Right's vision of England. And for them unity can only be maintained by opposing those seen to be outside the culture. In an Oxbridge common-room, there is order, tradition, a settled way of doing things. Outside there is chaos: there are the barbarians and philistines.

Among all the talk of unity on the New Right, there is no sense of the vast differences in attitude, life-style and belief, or in class, race and sexual preference, that *already* exist in British society: the differences between those in work and those out of it; between those who have families and those who don't; and, importantly, between those who live in the North and those in the South. Sometimes, especially in the poor white areas of Bradford where there is so much squalor, poverty and manifest desperation, I could have been in another country. This was not anything like the south of England.

And of course from the New Right's talk of unity, we get no sense of the racism all black people face in Britain: the violence, abuse and discrimination in jobs, housing, policing and political life. In 1985 in Bradford there were 111 recorded incidents of racist attacks on Asians, and in the first three months of 1986 there were seventy-nine.

But how cold they are, these words: 'in the first three months of 1986 there were seventy-nine.' They describe an Asian man being slashed in a pub by a white gang. Or they describe a Friday evening last April when a taxi company known to employ Asian drivers received a 'block booking' for six cabs to collect passengers at the Jack and Jill Nightclub. Mohammed Saeed was the first to arrive. He remembers nothing from then on until he woke seven hours later in the intensive care ward of the hospital. This is because when he arrived, his windscreen and side window were smashed and he drove into a wall. And because he was then dragged from the car, kicked and beaten on the head with iron bars, and left on the pavement unconscious. He was left there because by then the second taxi had arrived, but Mohammed Suleiman, seeing what lay ahead, reversed his car at high speed: but not before the twenty or thirty whites rushing towards him had succeeded in smashing his windows with chair legs and bats. His radio call, warning the other drivers, was received too late by Javed Iqbal. 'I was,' he told the *Guardian* later, 'bedridden for nearly a fortnight and I've still got double vision. I can't go out on my own.'

NORMAN LEWIS
THE SHAMAN OF
CHICHICASTENANGO

W hen I met Ernestina again she had lived in Guatemala City for six years, and now a great divide of time and unshared experience separated us. She was living, in Guatemalan colonial fashion, in a house with five patios, the first occupied by the owner, Doña Elvira, and the rest shared by family members, visiting relatives and friends, servants and permanent hangers-on. Ernestina was the companion of this elderly, powerful widow, whose natural genius was slowly being invaded and consumed by the cancer concealed in great inherited wealth.

Doña Elvira claimed to be a member of the 'fourteen families' élite, who could prove their descent from one of the mass murderers sent by Spain to conquer the country, but like so many of her kind she had been ensnared in habits of indolence, spending too much of her day seated in a throne-like chair on a wide balcony over the street. Here she waited for the president—preceded, flanked and followed by his numerous escort—to roar past on his Harley-Davidson. Sooner or later he usually did. Doña Elvira studied the way the president crouched over the handlebars of his machine or sat confidently bolt upright, convinced of being able to pick up valuable hints from these minutiae of behaviour. In the changing membership of his cortège she would identify shifts in political power. It was an activity that epitomized the watchful lethargy of the country. The preoccupation of the City, as ever, was with the possibility of this or any other regime coming to a peaceful or violent end, and with the improvements to be fought for, or, in the case of the privileged ladies with whom Doña Elvira played canasta most evenings, the deprivations to be endured.

This process of looking-on, the torpor, the eternal canasta, the incessant parties organized in celebration of trivial events, the ritual of over-eating (Doña Elvira consumed five meals a day), the ever-present sensation of lives drifting towards a bloodbath: all this took its toll in Guatemala. Life expectation among the ruling classes, despite their high standard of living, was relatively short. The nervous and indolent five percent at the top of the social pyramid were the victims of heart, liver and stomach diseases reaching almost epidemic proportions.

In addition they were prey to numerous other ailments, less easily diagnosable, which were seemingly fostered by the intellectual and emotional climate in which these people passed their lives. In a single week, for example, Doña Elvira had complained to Ernestina of pounding headaches, a persistent itch in an inconvenient place, a tendency to burst into unreasoning and uncontrollable laughter, tingling in the extremities, reduction of the field of vision, the feeling that she was 'somebody else', and a lunatic urge when in the most straight-laced company to shout out the word *cojones!* (Balls!)

Ernestina herself, in the former years robustly devoid of neurotic symptoms, had been unable to escape the contagion of her surroundings. She was troubled by a mysterious constriction of the throat that made it difficult to swallow, and within a few days of my arrival came up with the remarkable suggestion that I should take her to the small town of Chichicastenango, some hundred miles away in the mountains, for treatment by an Indian shaman.

The Guatemalans had become devotees of fringe-medicine, of acupuncture, homeopathic remedies, faith-healing and the like, and now after the centuries of contempt the Indians, long suspected of being experts in this field, were in the public eye. Many Guatemalans claimed to have experienced almost miraculous cures at the hands of the shamans, and the pilgrimages to Chichicastenango had begun.

We hired a car and set out northwards through a landscape copied from China: bamboos brushed in on mist; the grey lace of precipices hung from mountain outlines in the sky; Indians dressed in coolie straw under the slant of rain; a stork in silhouette transfixed in a swamp; soft, melancholic, water-washed colours.

In Chichicastenango a big church had been built on top of a great pile of masonry with a flight of steps up to its doors. Its echoes of the Mayan pyramids of old, it was hoped, would attract the Indians. Otherwise the town was a rigmarole of low rain-stained houses, general stores selling candles and rope, and slatternly cantinas where it was possible to get drunk and stay drunk indefinitely on very little indeed. Behind the face of Christianity the Indians remained stolidly pagan, but a comfortable arrangement had been reached some twenty or thirty years before with the priest

173

of the church of Santo Tomás: before entering the church they were permitted to build their altars, burn incense and invoke their gods on the steps; thereafter they would go through roughly the same devotional procedures in favour of the Christian god and the saints. Almost within memory of the oldest grandfather the Indians had been forcibly baptized, compelled to live in houses without windows, debarred on pain of death from riding a horse, forbidden the use of their twenty-day calendar, prohibited from taking astronomical measurements to work out the dates for sowing their crops, and flogged publicly in the square for failing to produce a child within a year of marriage. Yet now the ancient civilization of the Maya-Quiché, buried in secret in the mountains for nearly five centuries, had stealthily re-emerged, and there were aloof and dignified men in their Indian finery in the streets of the town: the *Regidores* and *Principales* of the old pre-Columbian hierarchy, to whom more than a shadow authority had returned.

The shamans were to be contacted in a slightly shamefaced way through an Indian on the staff of the Mayan Inn, the town's one hotel. We explained to him what was wanted, then settled down for a wait of uncertain length. The powerful and mysterious figures who were the repositories of the ancient culture were extremely poor and obliged therefore to live by raising crops in tiny and remote mountain clearings. From these they returned with ceremony— having let off rockets to announce their imminent arrival—after absences often lasting a week. The hotel go-between promised to enlist the services of a shaman regarded by the Indians as an incarnation of the god Zoltáca, Mayan guardian of the dead—poorest, he assured us with some pride, and most prestigious of them all.

B eyond the spectacular rites performed on the church steps, Chichicastenango offered little by way of entertainment. Indian groups from all over the mountains came here to conduct their special ceremonies. They wore long indigo capes, sometimes great winged hats modelled on those of the Spanish alguazils of the sixteenth century, and were otherwise clad in garments woven with symbols proclaiming not only the social, religious and marital status but also the sexual potency of the wearer. They capered in pious frenzy to the music of drums and flutes, burned copal incense, swung their censers, let off firecrackers and banished the lurking spirits of evil with furious gestures—oblivious of the tourists, who little suspected that according to local Indian conviction they were no more than ghosts who had succeeded in taking possession of the world.

In the evening a tiny flea-pit of a cinema functioned in a haphazard fashion, invariably showing some instalment of the old B-movie series *Crime Does Not Pay*. The cinema could only operate when two policemen were available to control the audience. Among it there were always a few for whom this was a first-time experience, and they were prone to violent intervention, in the belief that what they were viewing was an episode from real life. Whenever the policemen were called away to deal with some emergency the cinema closed until their return.

After the adventure of the flea-pit, the evening's last option was a visit to a cantina called 'I Await My Beloved', which was dark and full of charcoal smoke and insanely drunk Indians, and whose decor attempted to attract custom with a vast collection of dried snakes—some of extraordinary length—dangling from the rafters. Whites up from the City, attacked by boredom and *nostalgie de la boue*, would sometimes slip in here to try the sinister and legendary *boj*. This, brewed illegally by the mountain Indians, and originally sipped only by the officiating priesthood on sacred occasions, was sold here at some risk, since its possession or sale was punishable by a stiff spell in gaol. The *boj,* frothing and bubbling, released a faintly animal smell, and was kept in a great earthenware pan in a cavern haunted by hairy spiders at the back of the cantina, into which a customer practically had to crawl to be served. It was made from sugar-cane juice fermented with certain pounded-up roots; and although the first mouthfuls tasted no better than slightly sour beer it filled the body with fire and the mind with benign visions, and fostered in the drinker the impulse to give his property away. It was for this latter reason that labour recruiters hung about Indian mountain villages—on the lookout for happy soaks who, having handed over their possessions to anyone who seemed to be in need of them, could easily be cajoled into putting their mark on a contract committing them to three months' labour on a plantation for a dollar a week.

B y a curious accident the mission house, run by a fervent American evangelist, was next door: a simple and straight-forward man, Mr Fernley must have been one of the few inhabitants of Chichicastenango who had no idea what was going on in the cantina practically under his nose. Nor did he realize that he had *boj* to thank for the regular evening attendance of a handful of softly smiling Indians, who reeled in to the mission from the cantina in search of a quiet place to sleep—which, if left alone, they were able to do in almost any posture.

Mr Fernley's presence in the town was not viewed with enthusiasm by the local authorities, or by the management of the Mayan Inn Hotel, which depended heavily for its revenues upon American tourists for whom the Indians were a prime attraction. The missionary furiously disagreed with the local Catholic Church's policy of 'doing a deal with the devil', as he was said to have described it. He had no power to put an end to the pagan cere-monies that set so many shutters clicking, or the spectacular and dangerous performance of the *Palo Volador,* in which the Indians attached themselves to ropes at the top of a revolving pole and were then swung out centrifugally in mid-air. Nevertheless, he set out to disrupt such entertainments in every way he could—often with some success. Mr Fernley's scouts kept him informed of fiestas when such things occurred, and he would hurry to the spot carrying a movie camera on a stand, and start close-up filming. This was often enough to frighten the performers into taking to their heels. He had not the slightest hesitation about discussing the mission's motives in such interventions. Whatever Don Martín Herrera, the priest of the Church of Santo Tomás might claim, he said, the Mis-sion would not accept that the souls of these Indians had been saved. Nor *would* they be saved until every vestige of the customs linking them to a hopeless pre-Christian past—including their dances, music and dramatic entertainments—had been abolished.

T he missionary was both ingenious and persevering. He had opened the first tourist shop outside Guatemala City, displaying in its window the finest collection of huipils—the blouses worn by the Indian women—that Ernestina had ever seen. These were of a classic design, now hardly obtainable, woven from cotton threads dipped in dye obtained from molluscs, snails, the bark of trees, insects and the excrement of certain birds, and at best they were examples of pure Mayan art surviving only here in Guatemala. Now they were rapidly disappearing, or suffering degradation through the introduction of trade textiles and aniline dyes. Mr Fernley's collection, woven with symbols providing biographical information about the wearer and sometimes a potted history of her tribe, was impossible for collectors to resist. Ernestina, not knowing at that time with whom she was dealing, asked to be allowed to go through the stock, and Mr Fernley smilingly agreed.

'All these wonderful things are disappearing,' she told him, and he nodded in sympathy.

She was on the look-out for a Tzutuhil huipil from Lake Atitlán for her collection, but Mr Fernley shook his head. He had obtained several, he said, but the designs included 'representations of horses', by which he meant horses copulating. These, Ernestina was stunned to hear, he had destroyed. Most of his customers, he mentioned, were Americans or museums of Indian art, and he found the ones with horses too ugly to offer for their approval.

In removing from circulation these masterpieces of Mayan art, Ernestina admitted, Mr Fernley was doing no more than accelerating a process that had been going on for years. Parties of women from the city went out into the mountains, equipped with ordinary good-quality blouses and skirts and a reserve of new dollar coins. Whenever they spotted a woman wearing an exceptional huipil they would force five dollars into her hands and persuade her to change clothes on the spot. Either from fear or not wishing to appear ill-mannered, the Indians rarely refused. Mr Fernley agreed that it was the method his own agents adopted, except that instead of paying cash they were instructed to offer a metal bowl as part of a barter arrangement, in the hope that these would eventually come to replace gourds decorated with figures from the pre-Columbian legends, which he found repellent. As we later discovered, Mr Fernley had gone a step further than the enthusiastic collectors from Guatemala City, for on the blouses he gave in exchange for huipils the symbols of old had been replaced by Disney ducks, mice and rabbits. Women wearing these were beginning to appear in the streets of Chichicastenango.

The town's season of Indian pageantry and festivals occurred in December, immediately preceding the winter solstice, and at the time of our visit nothing much was happening. At all times Guatemalans from the city were rare enough, and it was reasonable to suppose that Mr Fernley suspected such visits as ours of having something to do with the new approach in the capital to problems of health—and that this was what provoked him to call at our hotel.

For the first time I was confronted with a missionary, and he was not what I expected. I imagined an unsmiling presence; a man charged with sternness and censure. Of these Mr Fernley showed no signs. He was about forty years of age, a native of Minnesota, mild in manner, and with a soft, reassuring voice. The talk was at first of homely problems. There was a whiff of cheerfully-endured domesticity about him. He did the jobs about the house and the shopping, his wife (who was engaged in the translation of biblical stories into Maya-Quiché) being of delicate physique. He apologized twice for calling upon us before coming to the point, which was to inquire what we were doing in Chichicastenango. 'I felt obliged to come in the hope you would talk with me,' he said. 'You'll have heard of our work here. There are two of us against so many. So far we're holding the line, but it's quite hard.'

I told him we were there to see a shaman, and he nodded understandingly. 'We discussed the trip with our doctor and he had nothing against it,' I said. 'He hadn't been able to help, and he took the civilized view that there was nothing to be lost.'

'Yes,' he said. 'Yes. I suppose that's a point of view.' He sighed. 'Could you not bring yourself to give the doctor one more trial?'

'I don't think it matters so much as all that to either of us. The doctor has a very up-to-date attitude and he's probably quite happy to be associated with what he sees as an experiment. There's no doubt at all that the Maya have a great inheritance of medical knowledge, much of which we've never bothered to investigate. There was a recent article in *La Prensa* claiming they're able to cure cancer.'

Mr Fernley smiled with ineffaceable patience. 'Whatever they may do here is without God's sanction,' he said.

The next day a small boy arrived at the hotel to say that the shaman was back, and to summon us to his presence. He took us to a shack in the lane at the back of the town, and just as we arrived a shining black Cadillac swung away from its door. Ernestina recognized the man at the wheel as one of the country's great landowners, with a finca in Totonicapán so vast that only recently an unknown tribe of Indians had been discovered there living in some caves. Like Doña Elvira, this man suffered from a sense of lost identity.

A slatternly Indian woman let us in and we found ourselves in a single room divided by a curtain, behind which a fairly large family busied itself with domestic routine. In the foreground the shaman awaited us, providing yet another of Guatemala's many surprises. We had been prepared for an encounter with a dignitary in full regalia, of the kind one saw so often on the steps of Santo Tomás, but instead the incarnation of Zoltáca was a small barefooted peasant in frayed trousers and shirt, with stained, deep-set eyes, fine hairs at each corner of the mouth, and an expression that could have been sullen, and was at best indifferent. Here there was no altar smoking with incense, no magic figures chalked in white on the floor, no prancing image of Tzijolach, messenger of the gods, no candles, no coloured tapes to keep the spirits in their places. Children scuffled and mewed behind the curtain; a parrot squawked; a hairless dog invaded the shaman's privacy, then backed hastily away. Smoke from an open fire beyond the curtain drifted up and was trapped in a hole in the roof that was the only source of light. Strangely, although the day was warm, I felt as though a cold breeze was blowing through the room.

Ernestina described her symptoms and the shaman listened, eyes averted and with apparent lack of interest. Then he reached up, placed his forefinger and thumb on each side of her windpipe and squeezed with some force. *'No hay nada,'* he said, which could have meant, there's nothing there, or, there's nothing wrong with you.

'That's all, then?' Ernestina asked, and the shaman nodded.

Ernestina gave him the ritual present we had brought: five cheroots, five eggs and a bottle of aguardiente. These he took, and passed wordlessly behind the curtain.

Thus was the cure effected, for relief was instant and complete. Back in the City Ernestina wrote an account of her experience for the *Bulletin of the Indian Institute,* which aroused some interest. For a year or two people flocked to Chichicastenango to be cured of a variety of ailments. Then in 1954 the big Castillo Armas revolution took place, which gave everyone something else to think about other than their personal problems, and by the time things settled down again the shamans of Chichicastenango had been largely forgotten.

JONATHAN RABAN

Jonathan Raban's sail round Britain is by turns a very funny, very serious, very personal and very clear-sighted circumnavigation of the state of mind of its inhabitants. A brilliantly observed tragicomedy.

COASTING

From the reviews of Foreign Land:

'Quite beautifully written'
The Times

'A joy to read'
Guardian

'Raban's writing is a delight'
Mail On Sunday

£10.95   COLLINS HARVILL

Photographs of Chichicastenango by Alain Keler

RYSZARD
KAPUŚCIŃSKI
A TOUR OF
ANGOLA

For a long time now, I've been making expeditions to the general staff to secure a pass for the southern front. Moving around the country without a pass is impossible because check-points for the inspection of travel documents stand guard along the roads. There is usually a check-point on the way into each town and another one on the way out, but as you drive through villages you may also run across check-points thrown up by wary and vigilant peasants; at times a check-point spontaneously established by nomads grazing their herds nearby will appear in the middle of an open field or in the most untenanted bush.

On important routes where major check-points are found, the road is blocked by colourful barriers that can be seen from a distance. But since materials are scarce and improvisation is the rule, others do the best they can. Some stretch a cable at the height of a car's windshield, and if they don't have cable, they use a length of sisal rope. They stand empty gasoline drums in the road or erect obstacles of stones and volcanic boulders. They scatter glass and nails on the tarmac. They lay down dry thorn branches. They barricade the way with wreaths of stapelia or with cycad trunks. The most inventive people, it turns out, are the ones from the check-point at Mulando. From a roadside inn abandoned by the Portuguese, they dragged into the middle of the road a ceiling-high wardrobe built in the form of a huge triptych with a moveable crystal-glass mirror mounted on the central section. By manipulating this mirror so that it reflected the rays of the sun, they blinded drivers who, unable to proceed, stopped a good distance off and walked to the check-point to explain who they were and where they were going.

You have to learn how to live with the check-points and to respect their customs, if you want to travel without hindrance and reach your destination alive. You must bear in mind that the fate of your expedition, and even your lives, are in the hands of the sentries. These are people of diverse professions and ages. Rearguard soldiers, homegrown militia, boys caught up in the passion of war, and often simply children. The most varied armament: sub-machine guns, old carbines, machetes, knives and clubs. Optional dress, because uniforms are hard to come by. Sometimes a military blouse, but usually a resplendent shirt; sometimes a helmet, but often a

189

woman's hat; sometimes massive boots, but as a rule sneakers or bare feet. This is an indigent war, attired in cheap calico.

Every encounter with a checkpoint consists of:
(a) the explanatory section
(b) bargaining
(c) friendly conversation.

You have to drive up to the check-point slowly and stop at a decent remove. Any violent braking or squealing of tyres constitutes a bad opening; the sentries don't appreciate such stunts. Next we get out of the car and approach the barriers, gasoline drums, heaps of stones, tree trunks or wardrobe. If this is a zone near the front, our legs buckle with fear and our hearts are in our mouths because we can't tell whose check-point it is—the MPLA's, FNLA's or UNITA's. The sun is shining and it's hot. Air heated to whiteness vibrates above the road, as if a snowdrift were billowing across the pavement. But it's quiet, and an unmoving world, holding its breath, surrounds us. We too, involuntarily, hold our breath.

We stop and wait. There is no one in sight.

But the sentries are there. Concealed in the bushes or in a roadside hut, they are watching us intently. We're exposed to their gaze and, God forbid, to their fire. At such a moment you can't show either nervousness or haste, because both will cause things to end badly. So we act normal, correct, relaxed: we just wait. Nor will it help to go to the other extreme and mask fear with an artificial casualness, or joke around, show off or display an exaggerated self-confidence. The sentries might infer that we are treating them lightly and the results could be catastrophic. Nor do they like it when travellers put their hands in their pockets, look around, lie down in the shade of the nearby trees or—this is generally considered a crime—themselves set about removing the obstacles from the road.

At the conclusion of the observation period, the people from the check-point leave their hiding places and walk in our direction in a slow, lazy step, but alert and with their weapons at the ready. They stop at a safe distance.

The strangers stay where they are.

Remember that the sun is shining, and it's hot.

Now begins the most dramatic moment of the encounter: mutual examination. To understand this scene, we must bear in mind that the armies fighting each other are dressed (or undressed) alike, and that large regions of the country are no-man's land into which first one side and then the other penetrates and sets up check-points. That is why, at first, we don't know who these people are or what they will do with us.

Now we have to summon up all our courage to say one word, which will determine our life or death: '*Camarada!*'

If the sentries are from Agostinho Neto's MPLA, who salute each other with the word *camarada*, we will live. But if they turn out to be Holden Roberto's FNLA or Jonas Savimbi's UNITA, who call each other *irmão* (brother), we have reached the limit of our earthly existence. In no time they will put us to work—digging our own graves. In front of the old, established check-points there are little cemeteries of those who had the misfortune to greet the sentries with the wrong word.

But let's say that fortune has smiled on us this time. We have announced ourselves with *camarada* in a voice strangled and hoarsened by fear. The word has been enuciated in such a way that some sort of sound will reach the people at the check-point, but not an overly distinct, overly literal and irrevocable sound. Our mumbling, into which we have cautiously smuggled the fragile syllables of the word *camarada*, will thus leave us with a loophole, a chance of reversing, of retreating into the word *irmao*, so that the unhappy confusion of words can be blamed on the hellish heat that dulls and addles the mind, on the exhaustion of travel, and the nervousness understandable in anyone who finds himself at the front. This is a delicate game; it demands skill, tact and a good ear. Any taking the easy way out, any heavy-handedness, shows immediately. We can't, for instance, shout '*Camarada! Irmão!*' all at once, unless we want to be regarded—and rightly so—as the kind of opportunists who are scorned in front-line situations all over the world. We will arouse their suspicion and be held for interrogation.

So we have said '*Camarada!*' and the faces of the people from the check-point brighten. They answer '*Camarada!*' Everybody begins repeating '*Camarada! Camarada!*' sportively and loudly an unending number of times as the word circulates between us and the sentries like a flock of doves.

The euphoria that sweeps over us at the thought that we will live does not last long, however. We will live, but whether we will continue our journey is still an open question. So we proceed to the first, explanatory part of the meeting. We tell who we are, where we are headed, and where we are coming from. At exactly this moment we present our passes. Troubles arise if the sentry can't read—an epidemic problem in the case of peasant and nomad sentries. The better-organized check-points employ children to this end. Children know how to read more often than adults, because schools have begun to develop only in the last few years. The content of a general staff pass is usually warm and friendly. They state that *Camarada* Ricardo Kapuchinsky is our friend, a man of good will, reliable, and all *camaradas* at the front and in the rear are therefore asked to show him hospitality and assist him.

Despite such a positive recommendation, the people from the check-point begin as a rule by saying that they don't want us to go on, and order us to turn back. This is understandable. True, the authority of Luanda is great—but then, doesn't the check-point also constitute authority? And the essence of authority is that it must manifest its power.

But let's not give up hope or become dispirited! Let's reach into the arsenal of persuasion. A thousand arguments speak in our favour. We have our documents in order: there is the text, the stamp and the signature. We know President Agostinho Neto personally. We know the front commander. We are writing dispatches, we are making Angola and its champions of right famous around the world. The bad Europeans have decamped and whoever stayed must be on their side or he wouldn't have stuck it out. Finally: Search us—we have no weapons, we can't harm anybody.

Slowly, stubbornly, the sentries yield. They talk it over, they confer off to one side, and sometimes a quarrel breaks out among them. They can send a message to their commander, who has driven to the city or set out for a village. Then we have to wait. Wait and wait, which we spend our whole life here doing. But this has its good side, since shared waiting leads to mutual familiarity and closeness. We have already become a component of the check-point society. If there is time and interest, we can tell them something about Poland. We have a sea and mountains of our own. We have forests, but the trees are different: there isn't a single baobab in Poland. Coffee doesn't grow there, either. It is a smaller country than Angola, yet we have more people. We speak Polish. The Ovimbundi speak their own language, the Chokwe speak theirs, and we speak ours. We don't eat manioc; people in Poland don't known what manioc is. Everybody has shoes. You can go barefoot there only in the summer. In winter a barefoot person could get frost-bite and die. Die from going barefoot? Ha! Ha! Is it far to Poland? Far, but close by aeroplane. And by sea it takes a month. A month? That's not far. Do we have rifles? We have rifles, artillery, and tanks. We have cattle just like here. Cows and goats, not so many goats. And haven't you ever seen a horse? Well, one of these days you'll have to see a horse. We have a lot of horses.

The time passes in agreeable conversation, which is exactly the way the sentries like it. Because people rarely dare to travel now. The roads are empty and you can go days without seeing a new face. And yet you can't complain of boredom. Life centres around the check-points these days, as in the Middle Ages it centred around the church. The local market women set out their wares on scraps of linen: meaty bananas, hen's eggs as tiny as walnuts, red piri-piri, dried corn, black beans and tart pomegranates. Clothing-stall owners sell the cheapest garments, garish scarves, and also wooden combs, plastic stars, pocket mirrors with the likenesses of known actresses on the back, rubber elephants, and fifes with keys that move. Any children not on active duty play in locally-woven shirts in the neighbouring fields. You can encounter village women with clay jugs on their heads on their way to get water, walking from who knows where to who knows where.

The check-point, if composed of friendly people, is a hospitable stopping-place. Here we can drink water and, sometimes, purchase a couple of litres of gasoline. We can get roast meat. If it's late, they let us sleep over. At times they have information about who controls the next stretch of road.

The time to leave approaches, and the sentries go to work. They open the road—they roll away the drums, push away the stones, move the wardrobe. And afterwards, when we're about to drive off, they walk up to us with the one universally-repeated question: Do we have any cigarettes?

Then there is a momentary reversal of roles. Authority passes into our hands because we, not they, have cigarettes. We decide whether they get one, two or five cigarettes. Our sentries put down their weapons and wait obediently and patiently, with humility in their eyes. Let's be human about it and share evenly with them. They're in a war, fighting and risking their lives. Once the cigarettes are bestowed on them, they raise their hands in the victory sign, smile—and among shouts of *'Camarada! Camarada!* we set out along the road into the unknown, into the empty world, into the mad, white scorching heat, into the fear that awaits us at the next check-point.

Roving thus from check-point to check-point, in an alternating rhythm of dread and joy, I took the road from Luanda to Benguela: 600 kilometres of desert terrain, flat and nondescript.

Benguela: a sleepy, almost depopulated city slumbering in the shade of acacias, palms and kipersols. The villa neighbourhoods are empty, the houses locked up and drowned in flowers. Indescribable residential luxury, a dizzying excess of floor space and, in the streets before the gates, orphaned cars—Chevrolets and Alfa Romeos and Jaguars, probably in running order although nobody tries to drive them. And nearby, a hundred metres away, the desert—white and glimmering like a salt spill, without a blade of grass, without a single tree, beyond redemption.

I spent some time walking the border of the two quarters, and then I went downtown. I found the lane in which the general staff for the central front was quartered in a spacious two-storey villa. In front of the gate sat a guard with a face monstrously swollen by periostitis, groaning and squeezing his head, obviously terrified that his skull would burst. There was no way to communicate with such an unfortunate; nothing existed for him at that point. I opened the gate. In the garden boxes of ammunition, mortar barrels and piles of canteens lay on the flower-beds in the shade of flaming bougainvilleas. Further on, soldiers were sleeping side by side on the veranda and in the hall. I went upstairs and opened a door. There was nothing but a desk inside, and at the desk sat a large, powerfully-built white man: Comandante Monti, the commander of the front. He was typing a request to Luanda for people and weapons. The only armoured personnel carrier he had at the front had been knocked out the day before by a mercenary. If the enemy attacked now with their own armoured personnel carrier, he would have to give ground and retreat.

Monti read the letter that I had brought him from Luanda, ordered me to sit down—on the window-sill, because there were no chairs—and went on typing. A quarter of an hour later there were footsteps on the stairs and four people came in, a television crew from Lisbon. They had come here for two days and afterwards they would return to Portugal in their plane. The leader of the crew was Luis Alberto, a dynamic and restless mulatto, sharp and gusty. We immediately became friends. Monti and Alberto knew each other from way back, since they both came from Angola and perhaps even from right here in Benguela. So we didn't have to waste any time making introductions and getting to know one another.

Alberto and I wanted to drive to the front, but the rest of the crew—Carvalho, Fernandez and Barbosa—were against it. They said they had wives and children, they had begun building houses outside Lisbon (near Cascais, a truly beautiful spot), and they weren't going to die in this mad, senseless war in which nobody knew anything, the opponents couldn't tell each other apart until the last second, and you could be blown away without any fighting simply because of the crazy screw-ups, the lack of information, the laziness and callousness of blacks for whom human life had no value.

In other words, they expressed a desire to live.

A discussion began, which is what Latins love most of all. Alberto tried to sell them on the argument that they would shoot a lot of tape and make a lot of the money they all needed so badly. But it was Monti who finally assuaged them by saying that at that time of day—it was almost noon—there was no fighting on the front. And he gave the most straightforward explanation in the world: 'It's too hot.'

Outside the window the air was rippling like tin in a forge; every movement demanded effort. We started getting ready to hit the road. Monti went downstairs, woke up one of the soldiers, and sent him into town where, somewhere, there were drivers and cars. A Citroen DS and a Ford Mustang turned up. Monti wanted to make it nice for us, so he designated as our escort a soldier named Carlotta.

Carlotta came with an automatic on her shoulder. Even though she was wearing a commando uniform that was too big for her, you could tell she was attractive. We all started paying court to her immediately. In fact, it was Carlotta's presence that persuaded the crew to forget about their houses outside Lisbon and travel to the front. Only twenty years old, Carlotta was already a legend. Two months earlier, during the uprising in Huambo, she had led a small MPLA detachment that was surrounded by a thousand-strong UNITA force. She managed to break the encirclement and lead her people out. Girls generally make excellent soldiers—better than boys, who sometimes behave hysterically and irresponsibly at the front. Our girl was a mulatto with an elusive charm and, as it seemed to us then, great beauty. (Later, when I developed the pictures of her, the only pictures of Carlotta that remained, I saw that she wasn't so beautiful. Yet nobody said as much out loud, so as not to destroy our myth, our image of Carlotta from that October afternoon in Benguela. I simply looked up Alberto, Carvalho, Fernandez and Barbosa and showed them the pictures of Carlotta taken on the way to the front. They looked at them in silence and I think we all chose silence so we wouldn't have to comment on the subject of good looks. Did it mean anything in the end? Carlotta was gone by then. She had received an order to report to the front staff, so she put on her uniform, combed out her Afro, slung the automatic over her shoulder, and left. When Comandante Monti, four Portuguese and a Pole saw her in front of staff headquarters, she seemed beautiful. Why? Because that was the kind of mood we were in, because we needed it, because we wanted it that way. We always create the beauty of women, and that day we created Carlotta's beauty. I can't explain it any other way.)

The cars moved out and drove along the road to Balombo, 160 kilometres to the east. To tell the truth, we all should have died on the winding road, full of switchbacks that the drivers took like madmen; it was a miracle that we got there alive. Carlotta sat beside the driver in our car and, since she was used to that kind of driving, she kidded us a little. The force of the wind threw her head back, and Barbosa said he would hold on to Carlotta's head so the wind wouldn't tear it off. Carlotta laughed, and we envied Barbosa. At one of the stops, Fernandez proposed that Carlotta move to the back with us and sit on our knees, but she refused. We rejoiced out loud at his defeat. After all, Fernandez had clearly wanted Carlotta to sit on his own lap, which would have ruined everything since she didn't belong to anyone and we were creating her together, our Carlotta.

She had been born in Roçadas, not far from the border of Namibia. She had received her military training a year ago in the Kabinda forest. She wants to become a nurse after the war. That's all we know about this girl who is now riding in the car holding an automatic on her knees, and who, since we have run out of jokes and calmed down for a moment, has become serious and thoughtful. We know that Carlotta won't be Alberto's or Fernandez's, but we don't yet know that she will never again be anybody's.

We have to stop again because a bridge is damaged and the drivers have to figure out how to get across. We have a few minutes, so I take a picture of her. I ask her to smile. She stands leaning against the bridge railing. Around us lie fields, meadows perhaps—I don't remember.

After a while we drove on. We passed a burned-out village, an empty town, abandoned pineapple and tobacco plantations. Then a profusion of tamarisk shrubs that evolved into a forest. It got worse, because we were driving to the front on a road that had been fought over, and there were corpses of soldiers scattered on the asphalt. They aren't in the habit of burying the fallen here, and the approach to every combat zone can be recognized by the inhuman odour of decaying bodies. Some additional fermentation must take place in the putrid humidity of the tropics, because the smell is intense, terrible—so stunning that, no matter how many times I went to the front, I always felt dizzy and ready to vomit. We had jerrycans full of extra gasoline in the lead car, so we stopped and poured some on the corpses, and covered them with a few dry branches and roadside bushes; then the driver fired his automatic into the asphalt at such an angle that sparks flew and a fire started. We marked our route to Balombo with these fires.

197

Balombo is a little town in the forest that keeps changing hands. Neither side can settle in for good because of the forest, which allows the enemy to sneak to within point-blank range under cover and suddenly attack the town. This morning Balombo was taken by an MPLA detachment of a hundred people. There is still shooting in the surrounding woods because the enemy has retreated, but not very far. In Balombo, which is devastated, not a single civilian remains—only these hundred soldiers. There is water, and the girls from the detachment approach us freshly bathed, with their wet hair wound around curling papers. Carlotta admonishes them: they shouldn't behave as if preparing to go out for the evening; they ought to be ready to fight at all times. They complain that they had to attack in the first wave because the boys were not eager to advance. The boys strike their foreheads with their hands and say the girls are lying. They are all sixteen to eighteen years old, the age of our high school students or of the fighters in the Warsaw uprising. Part of the unit is joyriding up and down the main street on a captured tractor. Each group makes one circuit and hands the wheel over to the next one. Others have given up contending for the tractor and are riding around on captured bicycles. It is chilly in Balombo because it lies in the hills; there is a light breeze and the forest is rustling.

As the crew films, I walk along with them, snapping pictures. Carlotta, who is conscientious and doesn't let herself be carried away in the euphoria of victory sweeping the detachment, knows that a counter-attack could begin at any time, or that snipers lurking under cover could be taking aim at our heads. So she accompanies us all the time with her automatic at the ready. She is attentive and taciturn. We can hear the tops of her boots rubbing together as she walks. Carvalho, the cameraman, films Carlotta walking against the background of burned-out houses, and later against a background of strikingly exuberant adenias. All of this will be shown in Portugal, in a country that Carlotta will never see. In another country, Poland, her pictures will also appear. We are still walking through Balombo and talking. Barbosa asks her when she'll get married. Oh, she can't say—there's a war on. The sun sinks behind the trees; twilight is approaching and we must leave. We return to the cars, which are waiting on the main street. We're all satisfied because we have been to the front, we have film and pictures, we are alive. We get in as we did when we drove here: Carlotta in front, we in the back. The driver starts the motor and puts the car in gear. And then—we all remember that it was exactly at that moment—Carlotta gets out of the car and says she is staying. 'Carlotta,' Alberto says, 'come with us. We'll take you out to supper, and tomorrow we'll take you to Lisbon.' Carlotta laughs, waves goodbye, and signals the driver to start.

We're sad.

We drive away from Balombo on a road that grows darker and darker, and we drive into the night. We arrive late in Benguela and locate the one restaurant still open; we want something to eat. Alberto, who knows everyone here, gets us a table in the open air. It's splendid—the air is cool and there's an ocean of stars in the sky. We sit down hungry and exhausted and talk. The food doesn't come for a long time. Alberto calls, but it's noisy and nobody hears us. Then lights appear at the corner and a car comes round and brakes sharply in front of the restaurant. A tired, unwashed soldier with a dirt-smeared face jumps out of the car. He says that immediately after our depature there was an attack on Balombo and they have given up the town; in the same sentence, he says that Carlotta died in the attack.

We stood up from the table and walked into the deserted street. Each of us walked separately, alone; there was nothing to talk about. Hunched over, Alberto went first, with Carvalho behind him and Fernandez on the other side of the street, with Barbosa following and me at the end. It was better for us to reach the hotel that way and disappear from each other's sight. We had driven out of Balombo at a crazy speed and none of us had heard the shooting begin behind us. And so we hadn't been fleeing. But if we had heard the shots, would we have ordered the driver to turn back so we could be with Carlotta? Would we have risked our lives to protect her, as she had risked hers to protect us in Balombo? Maybe she had died covering us as we drove away, because the boys were chasing around on the tractor and the girls were doing their hair when the enemy appeared out of nowhere.

We are all culpable in Carlotta's death, since we agreed to let her stay behind; we could have ordered her to return. But who could have foreseen it? The most guilty are Alberto and I: we are the ones who wanted to go to the front, so Monti gave us an escort—that girl. But can we change anything now, call it off, run the day backwards?

Carlotta is gone.

Who would have thought that we were seeing her in the last hour of her life? And that it was all in our hands? Why didn't Alberto stop the driver, get out, and tell her: Come with us because otherwise we'll stay and you'll be responsible! Why didn't any of us do that? And is the guilt any easier to bear because it is spread among the five of us?

Of course it was a tragic accident. That's how, lying, we will tell the story. We can also say there was an element of predestination, of fate, to it. There was no reason for her to stay there, and further-more it had been agreed from the start that she would return with us. In the last second she was prompted by some indefinable instinct to get out of the car, and a moment later she was dead. Let's believe it was fate. In such situations we act in a way we can't explain after-wards. And we say, Your Honour, I don't know how it happened, how it came to that, because in fact it began from nothing.

But Carlotta knew this war better than we did; she knew that dusk, the customary time for attack, was approaching, and that it would be better if she stayed there and organized cover for our departure. That must have been the reason for her decision. We thought of this later, when it was too late. But now we can't ask her about anything.

We knock on the hotel door, which is already locked. The owner, a massive old black man, opens up and wants to hug us because we've made it back in one piece; he wants to ask us all about it. Then he looks at us carefully, falls silent, and walks away. Each of us takes his key, goes upstairs, and locks himself in his room.

Translated from the Polish by William R. Brand and Katarzyna Mroczkowska-Brand.

PEREGRINE HODSON

A JOURNEY INTO

AFGHANISTAN

E arly in the morning we arrived in Teremangal, a border town just inside Pakistan. It had rained the night before and the winding streets were thick with mud churned up by pack animals laden with supplies.

'Stay here, Abdul, don't talk to anyone. Wait for a man called Mahmoud.' So said my guide, who promptly disappeared into the jostling crowds of men. With a sense of unease that was almost pleasurable, I was on my own. Camel trains laden with great beams of rough-cut wood swayed past; small boys in ragged shirts threw stones at dogs that darted between the hooves of horses; chai sellers carrying trays of steaming tea stepped gingerly through the slush and horse-droppings; while beside me a couple of Pathans haggled over the price of a saddle. Everywhere there were men wrapped in dun-coloured *petous* and carrying guns.

I was squatting by the side of the road with the sun on my back and the smell of wood-smoke in the air, but my thoughts were elsewhere: between images of Kipling and memories of charades. Three days before I had been lying on my bed at Green's Hotel in Peshawar, looking at the fan going round in the ceiling. At the time it had seemed faintly amusing that life could counterfeit cliché so realistically. Now I sensed, fleetingly, how a schoolboy dream could become a nightmare. I took refuge in the everyday: don't bother trying to understand what's going on, I told myself. Think of breakfast. Patience.

Two men were walking purposefully towards me. I turned away from them and stared at the hills on the other side of the valley. There was nothing to worry about, absolutely nothing to worry about. The two men were coming closer. Where on earth was Mahmoud? The men stopped in front of me. Damn.

'Abdul?' The taller of the men was smiling. 'My name is Mahmoud.'

I stood up and we shook hands.

Mahmoud was a broad-shouldered Tajik with a black beard and a bandolier of bullets hanging from his shoulder. He smiled too often and too easily for my liking. His companion was an Uzbeki with deep-set eyes and a sparse, wispy grey beard who seemed to be

---

Peregrine Hodson's companions found his name difficult to pronounce; he was therefore given the name 'Abdul'.

203

embarrassed to be in the company of the big, laughing Tajik. His name was Anwar. His clothes were of sun-bleached, grey cotton and there was a pistol in his belt.

'Come, Abdul,' said Mahmoud. 'We must meet the others now, and then you can have something to eat. Chai, kebabs, nan—we have plenty of food here.'

I pulled my knapsack onto my back and followed them through the streets, watching the faces of the passers-by to see whether they noticed I was foreign. The few who glanced at me showed no surprise. It was reassuring. Mahmoud had a taste for the melodramatic and warned me repeatedly with stage whispers and extravagantly secretive gestures to be on my guard—'Whatever you do, don't look suspicious'—until I had begun to feel like someone wearing a false nose and beard.

Eventually, at the end of a little lane, we came into a straw-littered courtyard. Some men were sitting on ammunition boxes, drinking glasses of green tea and laughing; nearby a boy in a gold-embroidered cap plucked a chicken.

Mahmoud called one of the men over and spoke to him in a dialect that I couldn't understand. I watched the man's face carefully. It was middle-aged but heavily lined and difficult to interpret. At first his eyes were guarded and several times he looked at me as if to check what Mahmoud was saying. Gradually his face relaxed and at intervals he nodded in agreement. Then he shook my hand and smiled while his companions, who had been silently gazing in our direction, turned to each other and began talking in lowered voices.

'He says you are *mehman*, his guest, and you are welcome for as long as you like.'

Mahmoud pointed through a cloud of flies into the shadow of a doorway. 'Here you will eat and sleep until it is time to go,' he said. 'Anwar and I have many things to do before the journey starts. We must buy horses and provisions and check the weapons; and everything costs money, doesn't it? Wait for us: we will see you later when you meet the others. Don't go anywhere else, otherwise the Pakistan police may see you and then . . .' He clenched his pudgy fists, one on top of the other, as if they were handcuffed. 'Who knows? Pakistan prison isn't a good place, Abdul. Be careful.'

I kicked off my muddied shoes and stepped into the room which was to be my home for the next few days. I laid my pack in a corner and sat down beside it. Shortly a boy's figure appeared in the brightly-lit doorway. I unpacked my Persian grammar and studiously ignored him. Nevertheless, I could sense him scrutinizing my appearance: the comparative newness of my clothes; the slight differences of style—the collar and sleeves—between Afghan and Pakistan shirts; my thick woollen socks and the strange disjointed letters of the book I was reading.

His parents had been killed in a raid, he told me, and, after burying them and saying goodbye to his remaining brothers and sisters, he had made the journey to Pakistan with his uncle. That was three years ago, and since then they had lost touch with each other. Yes, one day he would cross the border and find his elder brother, *Insha'allah*. Until then he had to stay here, cooking for the groups of mujahedin. It was hard work, but the master of the *chaikhane* was a good man; he had enough to eat and, little by little, he was saving some money. Later he would join the mujahedin, but guns were expensive and almost impossible to buy for someone who was not a member of a group. He told me all this in a matter-of-fact voice without a trace of bitterness.

'My parents are *shahid*. One day I will return. Now I must prepare the midday meal. The men will be coming soon and they will be hungry—they have been working since before sunrise.'

They came later that evening in twos and threes. The younger ones had Lee-Enfields slung over their shoulders, and the way they carefully undid them, placing them reverently by their sides, showed that they had only just received them. The others had Kalashnikovs, and they too seemed only half-familiar with their weapons. The oldest couldn't have been more than twenty-five and when they looked at me they nervously avoided meeting my eyes. Finally, one of them came up to me and offered a boiled sweet.

'Are you French?'

'No, I'm English.'

'Are you a doctor?'

I explained that I wanted to write about the people of Afghanistan. He paused as if my answer was somehow meaningless. Then his features lit with a sudden idea.

'And are you coming with us to Nahrin?'

'*Insha'allah*—if God wills.'

'Then you are a *mujahed*.'

The next day I met Sa'id, one of the leaders of the group. He had a fine face with a prominent nose; his flowing black beard and deep-set eyes reminded me of an early Byzantine icon. He had spent some time in England and so, for the first time in several days, it was possible to talk in English.

'When I was in London I stayed with Mr and Mrs Robinson in Battersea. Do you know them? They were very kind to me; every morning they gave me jams at breakfast. I liked the strawberry jam very much indeed. Sometimes in the evening Mr Robinson tried to persuade me to drink wine, but I refused because it is *haram*—forbidden by my religion.

'London is a big city. When I first arrived I couldn't believe the size of the buildings. And so many ladies. I think English ladies are very beautiful because you can see their faces, but the clothes they wear are very strange. Sometimes it was difficult for me not to look too closely.' His eyes searched mine to see whether I had registered the full significance of what he said.

There was a dull rumble. At first I thought it was thunder, but the sound grew in intensity. There was a sporadic rattle of small arms fire and then, as the jets swept over us, the sharp rhythmic sound of DSHKR guns echoed from the hills around the town. Sa'id leaped to his feet and ran outside on to the wooden veranda where he stared into the sky, shielding his eyes against the afternoon sun.

'*Shuravi*—Russians.'

He was obviously frightened and had difficulty translating his thoughts into English.

'*Kojah*? Where are they, Abdul, can you see them?'

By the time I joined him the planes had disappeared. Then, from the other side of the mountains, came the muffled sound of explosions.

'We are very close to the border, Abdul. The *Shuravi* know we are here, so they bomb the villages on the other side to make it difficult for us to travel. All the people leave and then there is nothing for us or our animals to eat.'

It was several minutes before Sa'id left the veranda. After we sat down, I noticed that he was still trembling.

'When the jets come, Abdul, everyone is frightened—and the sound of the bombs is terrible. I have lost the hearing in my right ear. Immediately the people hear the *Shuravi* approaching they hide among the rocks and under the trees, but the women have nowhere to go because, by our custom, they should not leave the walls around the house. Some of the houses have cellars but, because our families are large and the cellars are small, not everyone can fit inside. Then it is a difficult choice.

'The mujahedin have their training camps some distance from the town. We can see the jets dropping bombs on the town and each one of us thinks of our families. Since the spring the *Shuravi* have bombed us often. They come two or three times a week and each time ten or fifteen people are killed, sometimes more. The day before we left a bomb hit a building where many people had sheltered; twenty-three people were *shahid*—martyred. All this is difficult to believe, but you will see it with your own eyes, *Insha'allah.*' For several minutes Sa'id was silent. Then, finishing the remains of his tea, he smiled and left me.

For the rest of the day I was alone and passed the time by writing my diary. Now and again there was the sound of gunfire, but the jets did not return and I assumed it was merely the mujahedin in high spirits, practising with their newly-acquired weapons. At some point, I fell asleep.

When I awoke the room was in darkness, and a hurricane lamp was being set down beside me. As the flame grew and cast its light across the room, I saw a small group of men sitting in a semi-circle facing the lamp. I recognized Mahmoud and Sa'id, but there were others whose faces were new to me. One man had clothes which seemed of a better quality than the others. He was wearing a brown tweed waistcoat over a white cotton shirt and trousers. On his head was a white, embroidered skull-cap.

Mahmoud noticed I was awake and called me over to be introduced. First of all he turned to the man in the white skull-cap. He seemed slightly older than the other mujahedin, and unlike them he was clean-shaven except for a neatly-trimmed moustache. His eyes were watchful and intelligent, and when he heard himself being described as a very learned man and a university professor, the corners of his eyes wrinkled humorously. He was called Wakil.

'He speaks English too. Go on, Professor, say something in English.'

The Professor hesitated. I sensed he was reluctant to reveal his ignorance in front of the others, but then he stretched out his hand in greeting. I had momentarily forgotten that my name was Abdul, and introduced myself as 'Peregrine'.

'Hallo, Mr Pelican, and how is your health?'

As we solemnly shook hands I knew we would be friends.

Before I could say anything in reply, Mahmoud was introducing me to the next man. 'And this, Abdul, is a very important man. He is the nephew of Abdul Haq and the leader of the group. His name is Nazim Khan.'

Mahmoud's face adopted an expression of false gravity and, as he gestured to the man sitting opposite, I thought I detected the flicker of a smile pass between them.

Nazim Khan had a weak face. The eyes were evasive and almost feminine, with unnaturally long eyelashes, the mouth was small with a sensual lower lip and his moustache was the sort that sixteen-year-olds grow to prove their manhood. I had an instant sense of foreboding which increased when he smiled and his upper lip drew back slightly like an animal at bay.

Once the plates and dishes had been cleared away after our evening meal, we talked more about the coming journey to Nahrin. It was going to be difficult. Some of it would be through territory patrolled by the Soviets, and there would be long marches by night of sixteen hours or more. The Professor hoped that I would be able to keep up and advised me to buy supplies of sweets for energy and pain-killers in case my legs suffered from cramp.

'Even if you are very tired you must go on. In some parts the country is very dangerous and no one will be able to wait for you. The food will be very simple—rice, bread and tea—not like the good food you eat here. While you are here you must eat as much as you can because you will need the strength later.'

The next afternoon, we met in a dusty field where last-minute preparations for the journey were being made. Boxes of ammunition, guns, sacks of oats and harnesses were strewn everywhere. The horses and mules were hanging their heads in the heat while, nearby, Nazim Khan and the older members of the group sat and talked in the stifling shade of a tent.

I joined them but it was difficult to follow their conversation. However, it was obvious that Nazim and Mahmoud were being criticized by the others. The Professor beckoned me over and whispered, 'These words are not good. Guns and money. Very difficult.'

I nodded as sagely as I could and propped myself against a saddle to piece together what was going on, but they were talking too fast and my concentration began to wander. At last the argument resolved itself and Nazim Khan asked me to take a photograph of the men standing beside the piles of ammunition. A dozen men grabbed the nearest gun or anti-tank rocket they could find and posed with suitably grim expressions. Nazim Khan was in the middle, blithely unaware of the barrel of a Kalashnikov cradled comfortably in his neighbour's arms, pointing directly at his temple. After I had taken a couple of photographs, it was time to make our farewells. Mahmoud embraced me fondly. I should contact him without fail when I returned to Peshawar, when he would be able to offer me a good price for my tape recorder. Only when the quiet Uzbeki shook my hand did I realize that Anwar was remaining in Pakistan. Sa'id embraced me, then looked into my face and said: 'Do not be afraid, Allah is with us. *Khoda hafiz*, may God protect you.'

We had been travelling for a week, and had reached the territory of the Hesb Nasr: a rival group of mujahedin who were notorious for ambushing travellers, stealing their weapons and skinning their victims. As a precaution Nazim Khan decided to make a long detour across a monotonous plain broken at intervals by gullies, some several hundred feet deep. One moment there was a cavalcade of men and horses in front, the next moment they had disappeared. It was easy to understand the origin of travellers' tales of powerful wizards and enchanted caravans vanishing without trace.

At noon we rested briefly by a stagnant pool under a grove of poplars where a roguish old Uzbeki with a chai stall did brisk business, selling warm bread and chai at exorbitant prices. From there the landscape changed, becoming less harsh. We entered a range of gently undulating hills and valleys. Whenever possible I walked alone: the blisters from the previous seven days had made me irritable and the strain of being continuously in the company of the mujahedin was beginning to tell. But solitude was hard to come by. One mujahed in particular, a man with a long, stupid face and a hat with drooping canvas ears, made my life a misery. Whenever I thought I had finally escaped him, he would pad noiselessly up behind and abruptly hiss my name. If I slowed down he dawdled, if I accelerated so did he. I stopped and let him overtake me only to find him lurking in wait round the next bend. It began to be surreal, reaching a grotesque climax as he intoned garbled fragments of English: 'I am a clock. You are my book. This is Friday.'

My head began to spin. He started reciting an obscure version of the alphabet: 'A-B-D-F-N-G-R-P-S . . .' and my patience snapped. I spun round and shouted a string of choice Anglo-Saxon expletives. He gave a fishy smile, and was silent for a few minutes; then the litany of rubbish began again. Barely able to control myself, I told him he had the brains of a sheep and that I preferred my own company. As an afterthought, I added that I was practising *zikhr* meditation, and found his presence intrusive.

For several hours I journeyed by myself, following the bootmarks in the dust, now and then glimpsing the horses and mules which were taking a different route on the other side of the valley. In the late afternoon I reached the brow of a hill overlooking a dusty plain. Several men from the group, including the idiot hanger-on, were sprawled on either side of the path examining each other's weapons. I perched myself on a rock, and was enjoying the view when I heard a burst of sniggering. Turning round I found the barrel of an anti-tank rocket launcher aimed in my direction by the idiot. One of the men was explaining the firing mechanism. As tactfully as possible I told them that in England pointing an anti-tank rocket at a person's head was *bi'adab* and would be seen as a serious breach of etiquette.

They talked about the merits of their weapons, but I had seen and heard enough about their guns, the topic bored me and I took no part in the conversation. Disgruntled, I began to write my diary and later, when they set off, I ungraciously refused their invitation to keep pace with them.

I was the last to arrive at the camp that night and the group was already gathered around Nazim Khan listening to his description of the following day's itinerary. He beckoned me to sit beside him. The next moment there was an almighty bang and a slap of hot air hit me in the face. Six feet away, an anti-tank rocket had exploded. The launcher was propped on the ground, still pointing in my direction—the rocket had missed me by inches. By the time anyone realized what had happened, the rocket had detonated harmlessly in the hillside a quarter of a mile away.

There was a stunned silence. Then everyone began shouting at a man with a smoke-blackened face—Sediq. The thought that I had almost had my head blown off was curiously finite. I felt nothing and went off to look for some corn plasters. As I was loosening the cords of my pack a mujahed with a disarmingly simian face wandered up to me.

'*Allah fazl*,' he murmured. 'God is excellent.'

Our accommodation for the night was a long, low building. Before the war it had been a roadhouse; now it was a staging post for groups of mujahedin passing through. Inside, there were posters of Ayatollah Khomeini, flanked by the charred flags of the United States and the Soviet Union. Supper was dull but plentiful, provided by some taciturn men who seemed quite inoffensive, although the professor described them in a whisper as friends of the unsavoury Hesb Nasr.

I stretched out for the night beside two brothers who had been working in Iran for a year. They were full of praise for Ayatollah Khomeini and the government of Iran. Both brothers had saved a lot of money and were on their way to their wives and families in the north. They were simple, likeable fellows. Their main topic of conversation was the colour of tea. One preferred black tea, Iranian style, *chai siah*; the other liked green tea, *chai sabz*. Throughout the journey, at almost every *chaikhane*, they would wink at me, raising their different glasses of tea, and shout the respective colours with enthusiasm.

At daybreak we marched out under a silver-blue sky. The road wound up into another range of mountains following the meandering course of a river. Throughout the morning a bearded youth kept pace with me.

He was a tailor's son from Nahrin and had just spent a year in Peshawar; an experience which had greatly inflated his sense of self-importance. He had a huge pouch of *naswar* and supplied me with generous pinches of the stuff as we walked along.

'This is better than cigarettes. Too much smoke in your chest and you can't climb the mountains. But with this'—he shovelled another batch of *naswar* under his tongue—'your heart beats strongly and the mountains are easy.'

It was true. The miles seemed to roll by effortlessly and at

211

midday we came to a squat windowless inn at the foot of a pass. In the distance, between wisps of cloud, were mountain peaks capped with snow.

Through a low doorway, I could just make out Nazim Khan and several mujahedin plunging their hands into a large metal bowl. They called out to me to join them. I was about to step into the meaty-smelling gloom when a battered vehicle rattled to a halt behind me. A vast head poked over the side of the truck: it was Rahim, one of the men in our group.

'Come on, Abdul, climb aboard. It'll save you a few miles walking.'

In an instant I had joined him on the roof and we were jolting along between hilly meadows; red-veiled women crouched in small groups, sickles in their hands, harvesting the corn, and little boys splashed in the shallows of a river. The truck drove into a stream running across the road, the engine shuddered spasmodically, and stopped.

Water was sluiced over the bonnet and there was a sinister hiss. Then the engine was switched on again; nothing happened, only a metallic cough and a brief poltergeist knocking. In front of us the road climbed towards the clouds at the top of the pass. The sky darkened and a few spots of rain fell. Anxiously, we hung over the sides of the truck and watched the driver extract unlikely-looking bits of rubber and metal from the engine's interior. It looked as if we would be there for some time. Rahim produced some naswar and together, under a sheet of tarpaulin, we lapsed into a companionable reverie of boredom.

An hour later we were moving again, gears grinding at every turn of the road, and after a lurching, swaying climb we reached the top of the pass and another range of mountains stretched out before us in the distance, paling into the horizon like shadowy veins of alabaster. Then the road rattled down into another sunlit valley, through carefully-terraced fields of corn and barley, and at last we arrived at another hostelry which had been built into the overhang of a large cliff. The afternoon sun fell across the sloping ground in front of the crumbling adobe building and there were the rusting remains of a jeep and a truck in the corner of the inn yard. It was the end of the road; further on there was only a narrow track along the banks of a swiftly-flowing torrent.

Inside the inn, we found several men sprawled out asleep beside the remains of a meal. On the walls were more posters of Khomeini, Rabbani and a large news sheet displaying the photographs of the fifty or so local commanders of Jamiat Islami, together with their names and brief details of their lives. Many of them were in their early thirties. There was a range of physical types: Pathans, Uzbeks, Tajiks and others I could not identify. Some looked as if they had stepped from the pages of Thomas Hardy's Wessex, while others looked Mongolian. In one corner of the room there was a lurid picture of a mujahed bayonetting a Russian invader off the top of a mountain.

Just as dusk was falling the others arrived, footsore and weary. On the way they had heard the sounds of gunfire in the surrounding hills, presumably a skirmish between Hesb and Harakat factions who were in dispute over the valley's administration. Rahim and I had been asleep for several hours and heard nothing. Looking at the exhaustion on the group's faces I was glad I had taken the lift on the truck.

The evening meal included some pieces of meat and vegetables, and the men's spirits revived. After eating, several people sang and I was called upon to give another rendering of 'The British Grenadiers'. Next to me a man called Maulawi, who had joined us two days before, was in fine form, smiling and clapping his hands in time with the tune.

Later in the evening he introduced me to a friend of his called Yusuf.

'And what do you think of Ayatollah Khomeini?'

I described the superficial view of him held by most people in the West and disassociated myself from it.

'I admire and respect his desire to establish an Islamic society, but as an outsider I find it difficult to understand . . .' My voice trailed away; I was on uncertain ground.

'His methods?'

'Perhaps.'

'How could you? How could any Westerner, any non-Muslim understand'—Yusuf was lost for words—'the true meaning of Ayatollah Khomeini's message to the world? In Europe and America you think of the hostages, the war with Iraq, the political prisoners and executions. You forget your own history. How many people died as a result of the revolution in the Christian religion four hundred

213

years ago?'

I thought hard for several seconds before I realized he was talking about the Reformation. I hadn't expected this sort of conversation; it was unnerving.

'Ayatollah Khomeini is a new force in the Third World. He is neither capitalist nor communist. He uses the language of religion to speak to the hearts of men. That is why he is so important. He is raising the consciousness of the Third World, not by political ideology or machines or money, but by the word of God.'

We talked about the war and his hopes for the future. The war was a test of Islam. Many people would die but, in the end, victory was certain. The struggle in Afghanistan was a battle between a dying political system and a living religion. The Russians were mad to think they could conquer a people who were under the protection of God; it was like a fly attacking an elephant.

As we talked I felt as if I had stepped through an invisible barrier into another dimension governed by fundamentally different laws, where the ordinary world that I had previously known and accepted had only marginal significance. Here, a man's body was a shadow, death was a process of life and the only truth was the mystery of God's purpose.

I said farewell to Yusuf and went out into the inn yard. The stars stretched across the shadows of the mountains and a horse whinnied softly in the darkness. A bright crescent of light shone in the night sky: the moon of Islam, a recurring symbol of the faith, utterly beyond the power of man to dislodge it from its place in heaven.

We left the inn before dawn, following the course of the river down through narrow gorges, hidden from the sun, with the chill of the night still clinging to the rocks. In places the torrent plunged into deep caverns, smoking with spray, to re-emerge in an explosion of white water. The thunderous drumming of the river reached an intensity that made conversation impossible as the noise snatched our words away, dashing them into the seething volume of water rushing past below us.

At one point, the path crossed a fast-flowing stream. A bridge of saplings with flat stones placed on top of them spanned the current and I watched a mule, laden with ammunition boxes, being led across it. The animal was nervous, and just as its front legs reached the other

214

side, its hind legs missed their footing. It toppled into the swirling waters, almost pulling the driver in as well. Two men leapt to his assistance and grabbed the halter to take the strain, while another, cursing, jumped into the foam and started beating the mule like a madman. For a minute or so, it looked as if the ropes tying the mule's load would have to be cut, and the ammunition lost, but somehow the creature was whipped and hauled on to the further bank with its burden intact. I crossed over and the driver showed me his hand: across the back of it and between his thumb and forefinger, a runnel of flesh had been torn away.

Further on we came to the steaming surface of a hot spring where several of us stripped to our underclothes and immersed ourselves in warm, rusty-coloured water to wash away the grime of the past few days. By now the sun was almost overhead and its rays began to penetrate the cliff walls on either side of us. Thereafter the path left the river, and with the sound of the waterfall still thrumming in our heads we descended into a valley of yellow corn enclosed by fantastically-coloured rock formations of deep purple and green. After the cool of the past few hours, it was like entering a furnace, and one of the drivers wove a garland of leaves around his head to protect it from the sun. At midday we arrived at a glade of poplars from where a truck would take us on to the next stage of the journey.

We clambered on and set off. The road followed a river which, as we descended, changed from a powdery blue torrent to a lazy brown meander. We stopped at several villages along the way. On each occasion Maulawi was welcomed with obvious affection by people who embraced him and kissed his hand. In the late afternoon we pulled into the ruins of a small town. It was a tableau of desolation. A month before it had been attacked by helicopter gunships and nearly all the drab, nineteenth-century stone buildings had been damaged or destroyed. A strong wind was sweeping through the street, raising a grey cloud of dust that covered people's faces and turned them into expressionless masks with darting eyes. One of the townspeople invited me to have tea with him, and I listened to his description of the day when the helicopters came while we shelled pistachio nuts and his brother stroked the head of a tiny bird cupped in his fingers.

It was Maulawi's last evening with us, for the next day he was returning to his own village. During the time we had travelled together I had come to like his cheerful good humour and the prospect of bidding him farewell saddened me. After an unappetizing bowl of rice garnished with a gnawed sheep's vertebra, we talked about Persian poetry. Hafiz was a charming sensualist, Sa'adi was a man of wisdom, but as for Jalaluddin Balkhi Rumi! There was a true poet! One could read his poetry for a thousand years and still not reach the hidden depths of meaning.

Just as we were going to bed a party of Hesb Islami entered the town. Their arrival worried Nazim Khan who gave me strict instructions not to leave the room where I was staying, and ordered two mujahedin to sleep one on either side of me, each armed with a pistol.

The following morning we loaded a truck with the guns and ammunition and climbed aboard. It was a sad contraption, falling apart with rust, and when the engine started it threatened to push its way through the disintegrating bonnet. The men were in good spirits for the worst of the journey was over. As we rumbled across the plain and into a series of winding gorges a mujahed beside me told me about his family in Nahrin.

Suddenly, a figure stepped into the middle of the road. The driver sounded the horn but, instead of moving aside, the man merely waved his hand motioning us to halt. Beside me Rahim fumbled with his rifle, but it was too late: as he did so a volley of gunshots exploded from the cliffs around us. We had driven into an ambush. I looked round. No one had been hit. Either our attackers were useless marksmen, or they were aiming away from us. After several seconds the firing subsided and the driver switched off the engine. For a moment there was utter silence.

The figure in the middle of the road unhitched a megaphone from his shoulder.

'Nazim Khan! You are surrounded. If anyone touches a gun my men will fire, only next time they will kill. Do you understand?'

To emphasize the point another scatter of shots rang out.

'Enough! I wish to speak with Nazim Khan.'

No one on the truck moved. Nazim Khan was sitting in the driver's cab with Maulawi and the Professor. Cautiously we scanned our surroundings. In front and behind, guns pointed down at us from rocks and crevices in the cliffs. Thirty yards to our right, among a collection of boulders, slight movements were visible. On our left there was a wide sweep of open ground sloping down to a river. A high-pitched whine came from the megaphone.

'Nazim Khan! I know you are there. Come out!'

The door of the cab remained firmly closed.

'You refuse to come out, so we will come and get you.'

The figure with the megaphone beckoned two men from behind some rocks who walked slowly towards the truck. Behind me someone hissed: 'Don't shoot them. Wait and see what happens.'

One of the men banged on the door of the truck.

'Nazim Khan! Which one is Nazim Khan?'

The door opened slowly and as Nazim Khan emerged the man pulled at his hair, flinging him to the ground.

'Coward!'

The word hung in the air and we all avoided each other's eyes. Nazim Khan scrambled to his feet and I glimpsed his face; it was as white as paper. The other man kicked him in the small of the back and he stumbled forwards. Half-turning Nazim Khan shouted back over his shoulder to us: 'Don't shoot, for the love of Allah, don't shoot. Don't—' A rifle butt slammed into the back of his head.

One of the men unfastened Nazim Khan's pistol. Then, gripping his arms, they dragged him away and disappeared behind an outcrop of rocks at the bend in the road.

'Get out of the lorry,' said the megaphone.

We clambered down, some of the men with their guns still strapped to their shoulders.

'Go to the side of the road and don't move.'

A few of us edged away from the track, discreetly choosing the meagre protection of a low bank that would give us cover against any shooting from our right. The sun grew hotter.

I lit a cigarette. Another shot rang out above us. Our ambushers were nervous. I wondered whether I was looking at the scene before a massacre.

'Put your guns in the truck.'

Reluctantly the men unshouldered their weapons and placed them in the back of the truck. There was a buzz of flies. Minutes passed and the sweat began to pour down our faces. Some men moved slowly to one side and squatted down to urinate. I did the same, taking the opportunity to check the lie of the land in case the shooting started. Run underneath the cliff, over the road and then

217

across fifty yards of open ground to some rushes by the river's edge; dive in and hold my breath—it was pretty hopeless. Having my head blown off on a dusty road in Afghanistan seemed a prosaic way to die.

There was no sign of Nazim Khan so the Professor and Maulawi set off towards the bend in the road holding a white length of turban above their heads. There were no warning shots and the men encircling us eased their positions, letting their heads show above the rocks.

Half an hour later Maulawi and the Professor reappeared with Nazim Khan and we smiled with relief. Something had been agreed; at least we would know what was happening.

A large bruise covered one side of Nazim Khan's face, almost obscuring the eye; his lips were bloody. He spoke with difficulty. We had no choice but to surrender our arms. The leader of the ambush was called Kheir Mahomet, who was mad and wouldn't listen to reason. The men were to stay behind while he, the Professor and Maulawi were taken with the guns and ammunition to Kheir Mahomet's village. Nazim Khan turned in my direction: 'You will come with us, Abdul!'

Several of our ambushers emerged and took charge of the lorry. Nazim Khan and Maulawi got into the driver's cab while the Professor and I hoisted ourselves into the back. Then a strange thing happened: the five men who had been travelling with Maulawi nodded to our ambushers and they all climbed aboard together and began laughing and joking with our captors, turning over the Kalashnikovs, the rocket-launchers and DSHKR guns like children with a collection of new toys. The truck lurched off leaving the rest of the group in a cloud of dust surrounded by men with guns. As we rattled along, I asked the man beside me what was going to be done with us; he said nothing—merely drew his hand across his throat and smiled.

Half an hour later the truck drew up, the arms were swiftly unloaded and our captors spirited them away into some trees at the side of the road. Nazim Khan disappeared in the company of Maulawi and his men and our captors drove off, leaving the Professor and me by the side of the road. My sense of unreality intensified when some old men appeared, greeted us courteously and invited us to accompany them for a glass of tea. We followed them through a field of ripening corn to a courtyard in the shade of a huge mulberry tree. A pot of steaming green tea and two warm nan loaves were placed before us while the elders of the village appeared in twos and threes. A little later Nazim Khan and Maulawi emerged from a nearby building followed by the village chief who had organized the ambush. He seated himself at one end of a large carpet in the shade. Nazim Khan took his place at the other, sunlit end of the carpet while the rest of us arranged ourselves on either side, facing one another. Kheir Mahomet then spoke, saying how fortunate the village was; now they had guns they were safe and could defend themselves against the *Shuravi*. The arms were necessary and God had been generous in providing them. Sweat was pouring from his forehead and several times he seemed to lose the thread of what he was saying. I looked around at the faces of the old men. Only a few nodded their heads in agreement; most were grave and solemn. There were murmurings of the bad reputation that would befall the village.

Then Nazim Khan replied. The guns were for the *jihad*, for the people of Nahrin to defend themselves. He appealed to the elders: surely it was wrong for a Muslim to steal from his brother Muslim? The arms had been bought in Peshawar, then carried for ten days with great difficulty over rivers and mountains. Now all the efforts of the men were lost. For the love of Allah, where was the justice?

At this, the old men looked even graver, and several took Nazim Khan's part to remonstrate with Kheir Mahomet. He smiled sardonically. The old men could think and say what they liked; the arms were staying with him. He rambled on with a malarial glitter in his eye: a spy had told him that some of the arms were destined for the lord of the neighbouring territory. He had already killed several of his men and if he received any more arms he would pose an even greater danger. Taking the arms was an act of self-defence. Further discussion was pointless; the arms remained with him. Brushing aside any other comments from the assembly, Kheir Mahomet walked away.

Our attention turned to the ambush. How had Kheir Mahomet known about the truck and the load of arms? Was it really just coincidence that Maulawi lived in the neighbouring village? And why had Maulawi's men been allowed to keep their weapons? They protested their innocence, but the perfunctory way they expressed their regrets implied that they were not unduly troubled by the morning's events. Had the smiling Maulawi secretly contacted Kheir

219

Mahomet the previous evening? Had he, indeed, planned it all along, all the way from Peshawar? Nobody knew.

That evening Maulawi invited us to have supper at his mosque and then stay the night there. Before the meal he led the prayers for our group and afterwards he was brave or brazen enough to sleep among us. The backbreaking efforts of the past ten days wasted, the men in the group accepted the rice impassively. Their attitude reminded me of a passage in the Odyssey in which, after a swathe of men had been devoured by the Cyclops, the survivors sat down and ate a meal on the seashore. Then, when they had finished eating, they lay down and fell asleep. But the stoicism of their actions could not conceal the lines of exhaustion and disappointment in their faces. I was tired too, as if I'd been swimming against an invisible current all day, and I was glad to find oblivion in the cramped darkness with the rest of them.

It took us several more days to reach Nahrin, and I remember arriving only as a series of disconnected images.

A man with a hideously scarred face and a stump where his right arm should have been greeted us and embraced the Professor tenderly. I noticed what I thought were slices of water-melon placed on the shoulders of a horse, presumably to cool the skin where the ropes had chafed it, but when I looked closer I saw that it was an expanse of raw flesh. What had seemed like the black water-melon seeds were flies, feasting on yellow pus which frothed at the edges of the wound like a sherbet dip.

We came to a field of melons. The Uzbeki who was travelling with us suddenly ran to a brushwood shelter and emerged with a plump, middle-aged woman at his side, who was his mother. He shouted to the members of the group to wait while he gathered armfuls of the round, heavy fruit which he then tumbled at our feet. His mother stood at one side smiling with happiness that her son had returned safely, in such a state of excitement that her *chadogh* slipped repeatedly from her face.

In the late afternoon we entered one of the outlying villages of Nahrin and after wending our way through leafy, walled streets we arrived in the courtyard of a little mosque. One by one I said farewell to the members of the group. The two brothers who had worked in Iran shouted for the last time *'Chai siah!' 'Chai sabz!'* Sediq gave me a

220

fumbling handshake and looked away; Latif, who had taught me to pronounce the words '*la illaha illa lahn*', embraced me and commended me to God. The Professor promised to contact me soon and Rahim vowed that he would buy me as many shish kebabs as I could eat when we met each other again. Amin'allah was staying with friends nearby and said that we would easily find each other.

The time I had spent in the men's company and the distances we had travelled together had led to several deep but unspoken friendships. Now we were saying goodbye to one another. It seemed extraordinary that our lives should part so easily and suddenly. When they had gone I sat down by the side of a still, green pool and watched some children filling vessels of water. I was a stranger, an observer, an unnecessary mouth to feed. The others were returning to the welcome of their family and friends. I was alone.

An old man then emerged from the doorway of the mosque with a glass of chai and some dusty sweets which he placed on the ground beside me. He looked into my eyes, then gazed up at the sky and looked once again into my eyes. After a moment he nodded and smiled. The gentleness of his presence eased the heaviness from my heart, and I became more at peace.

Towards evening a man led me to the home of Abdul Haq, commander-in-chief of Nahrin and the surrounding area. Abdul Haq was away in the mountains and would not be back till the following day, but his second-in-command and a dozen fellow mujahedin were staying at the house. Lamps were lit and we seated ourselves under the portico, where plates of rice and lamb were brought for us. When the meal was over, pillows and cotton quilts were laid out and I lay back to sleep with the sound of cicadas sussurating in the moonlit garden.

I am inside one of the stalls in the bazaar. On the shelves are fist-sized crystals of salt, cubes of evil-looking soap the colour of congealed mutton fat, and boxes of state-manufactured matches and jars of naswar. I am drinking a glass of chai with the owner of the shop, Said Mansour.

'It is getting harder to earn a living. Many things are two or three times the price they were before the war—that is, when I can get them—and then the people have no money to buy them. A few years ago the town was famous for its pistachio nuts; they were one of the

221

main sources of the town's income. Now production is less than half, the men are away fighting, and the nuts fall from the trees unharvested. We can do nothing. We cannot buy or sell in the larger towns because the state controls them. Without buying and selling in the towns it is impossible for places like Nahrin to carry on indefinitely. Money has to flow from the towns into the country like water into the fields. The *Shuravi* are trying to stop the flow so that the country will wither. Men say this is a war of religion, a war of politics, a war of freedom. Maybe so. But I say this is also a war of money. Everyone needs money: to buy flour or rice, medicine or kerosene. The *Shuravi* know that without money we cannot survive. They bomb us, but that is only to make their real objective happen sooner. What is their real objective? I will tell you: they want to turn us into beggars. Then, when we have nothing to eat, they will offer us a handful of grain and tell the world how kind they are. They will mend the irrigation channels which they destroyed and say how they improved the primitive agriculture of backward peasants. They think they can treat us like dogs, starving us and beating us until we obey them. What fools they are. Our Muslim brothers all over the world know what is being done to us. They will not forget this war.

'Help from other countries? There was a time when I thought that Europe and America would help us. Several foreigners have visited the town since the war began. They stay for a week or so, take photographs of planes and smoke, and then they leave. I know that you can earn a lot of money from the pictures you have taken. But what will we receive? Nothing. Each time we ask such people for doctors and medicine, we wait and no doctors come. Only, perhaps, another journalist. Your people come and look at our suffering and sell it for money in their own countries.'

He asks how often there is news of Afghanistan in newspapers and on the television, and when I tell him he is crushed with disbelief. I try to explain how Afghanistan is a distant country and the war is just another item occupying far less than one percent of world news coverage.

Dust Muhammad, the watchmaker, has two shirts. One is khaki-coloured, ex-army issue, given to him by a deserter from the State army; the other is of fine blue cotton embroidered with white silk. Today he is wearing the blue one. It reminds me of ones that used to flutter in multi-coloured rows in Portobello Road, or hung from the shoulders of summer holiday holy men with shoulder bags full of mysticism at fifty dollars an ounce.

We are having breakfast together in one of the chaikhane by the bazaar or, to be more accurate, I am eating while Dust Muhammad watches me. He is poor and unwilling to accept hospitality which he cannot repay. There is a wireless playing in the background, the music is oddly familiar and suddenly I recognize the melody—'Yesterday' by the Beatles. For a moment, the emaciated young man with a wispy beard sitting in front of me could be the ghost of a traveller on the hippy trail to Kathmandu.

We have talked several times before, but this is the first time Dust Muhammad has mentioned that he was in prison. I ask him whether I may tape the conversation and he invites me back to his room, over the stables of the caravanserai.

It is completely bare except for a cotton quilt and blanket in a corner and a table and chair beside the door. The table is scattered with cogs, hairsprings, screws, bits of wire and shells of transistor radios that are beyond repair. He spreads the blanket on the earth floor and I switch on the tape recorder. To begin with, his voice is taut with nerves and he stumbles over the words.

'At three o'clock in the morning, in the month of Mizan, I was on my way to the *kargat* of my brother mujahedin when the Soviet occupational forces surrounded the party of men I was with, and captured us. We were kept in Khanageh for two nights and tortured. Then eleven Russian armoured cars and a Russian jeep took us in chains to the airport at Khunduz. We spent another three months there under Russian torture. Then we were taken to the town of Khunduz where I was for another twenty-one months. I was hung by the ankles and tortured with electricity and put in a cell which was so small that I could barely stand up.'

'For eight months we were taken out of our cells three times a week and beaten and tortured. They questioned us about our weapons, and asked whether we had received them from America, but we answered "We fight you with our faith." Our interrogators were Khad agents with two or three Russian supervisors. They even pulled the hairs from our beards.'

'In another part of the prison there were Muslim women: we could hear their voices. We had no books, no pens, no paper. I wanted very much to obtain a copy of the Qur'an. One day I noticed one of the guards: he looked a good man and I said to him, "You are a brother Muslim. Help me. Please bring me a copy of the Qur'an." He said nothing but later brought me the book, which I kept hidden from the authorities. I learned it by heart.

'After twenty-one months I was put to work on a building project inside the gaol. One afternoon, when there was no one looking, some of us tied our turbans together, lowered ourselves over the walls and escaped. From there I made my way to Nahrin and have been living here for a year.'

Dust Muhammad pauses for a moment.

'Listen, helicopters.'

Sure enough, there is a faint clatter in the distance.

'Do you want to continue?'

Dust Muhammad's voice is neutral but, even so, the question seems like a challenge and I have to restrain myself from responding like a schoolboy to a dare.

'I don't know, what do you want to do?'

'I have almost finished. I would like to give a message to the people of your country.'

We agree to complete the tape. While he speaks, I feel a growing tension in my chest like waiting in line to buy a ticket at a station when the train is already on the platform. I look round the walls of the room, the low ceiling, the sunlight shafting down through the narrow window and know, with absolute certainty, that if there is a raid I have to be outside, under an open sky.

'*Tamam shod*—it is finished.'

I thank him and, as I pack the tape recorder away, the sound of a jet becomes audible. I try not to appear nervous but my hands and fingers fumble disobediently with the straps of my satchel. People are already running towards the hillside at the north of the town. Dust Muhammad is calm.

'You must go, but I will remain here.'

I try to persuade him to come with me but he is unmoved.

'Some places are safer than others, but nowhere is completely safe. I don't mind. I'm used to it.'

I say goodbye and hurry downstairs into the street below, but my relief to be out of the cramped room vanishes with the realization that I have no idea where to go. I make for the garden with the mulberry tree.

The attack begins. The roller-coaster swing between fear and relief leads rapidly to a blankness of mind. An old man sitting next to me gazes expressionlessly at the ground. Each time there is an explosion he hunches his shoulders and, as the planes scream into the distance, he raises his head and his shoulders relax once more. One plane comes in. The old man and I wait: we are both afraid of dying. There is a thunderous bang and the old man dips his head down further. But the sound of the explosion means we are both alive. Our neighbour's death is not our own.

The sound of the jets grows fainter and I get up to take some photographs; a chorus of voices tells me to wait. I ignore them and set off up the hill to get a view of the town which is partially obscured by thick smudges of rust-coloured smoke. From nowhere there is a sudden, terrifying roar and I run for cover, almost falling on top of someone huddled in a foxhole. I tumble in beside a young man and a few seconds later the bombs start falling again. From where I am I can watch the planes coming in over the ridge on their bombing runs, very low, no more than a couple of hundred feet. The explosions seem to be getting closer, and irrationally I imagine they are working methodically across the town towards where we are. A jet sweeps over the crest of the hill, less than a hundred yards away, and I watch two bombs falling diagonally from it. Then the stunning unreality of what is happening disintegrates in a massive double drumbeat which shakes the ground around us and another cloud of smoke rises above the trees.

The boy pulls at my shirt and shouts something: he is shuddering and gasping with fear and his words are unintelligible. I hear the word 'Allah' several times. Asking him something is like talking to a man pulled from a frozen lake. He jabs at the sky with his hand and buries his face in the earth again. Then, on the hillside above us, there is a burst of heavy gunfire; I curse at the invisible fool whose pointless heroics are almost certain to draw more bombing or rocket attacks in our direction. The gunfire goes on in bursts for several minutes, then finishes as abruptly as it began. From the edge of the foxhole I see a helicopter wheeling away. There is no sign of anyone else on the hillside and it takes several seconds for me to grasp that I have been cursing a helicopter gunship attack.

People begin to stir. The first to move are shouted back by those who are still under cover, but others follow them and emerge into the streets. A young man runs up to me.

'Come, come, there are *shahid*.'

I follow him without enthusiasm. We hurry through a maze of mud-walled streets and come to a mound of rubble across our path. Coming in the opposite direction a group of men is carrying a bed on which there is the inert form of a twelve-year-old boy. The blast has caught him below the waist; he is covered with dust and one of his feet is missing. My camera is ready. I check the light meter, adjust the focus and press the button. I am surprised by the methodical way I react, as if the mechanics of recording the reality are more important than the subject-matter. Perhaps by taking a photograph I diminish the horror, hiding my eyes behind the camera. But only a moment is captured. The boy's suffering is not confined to the photograph. I have only one roll of film, and as the boy rocks and sways on the shoulders of the men and is borne out of sight, I take two photographs.

'Come this way,' says my guide and, forcing myself not to think, I plod after him, my mind still juddering from the compression of time into seconds. What do the Soviet pilots think as they 'press the fire control button'? Is there the same absence of emotion which I seek as I press the button of the camera? Do we both, for an instant, lose our humanity in machines?

There is a sound of crying, of a woman in high-pitched grief. The next moment a boy of five, wearing a turquoise-blue shirt that comes down to his bare knees, races out of a doorway in tears. He might just have been bullied by a friend, or smacked by his father. Two old men are standing in the middle of the street and one of them calls out to the tearful boy: 'Child, is your mother lost?'

The little boy stops running in mid-stride and stands there with his mouth open in a wordless cry. The nearest old man turns to his companion. 'His mother is lost.'

The words have no visible effect on the man's lined face: he gazes into space. The little boy has disappeared.

'Follow me over here,' calls my guide and we step across a carpet of leaves and torn-off branches into the garden of a house. A small crowd has gathered round four bodies stretched out in the blasted remains of a melon patch, the heads and torsos covered with blankets. The feet are splayed slightly, like those of someone napping on the lawn under a newspaper on a hot Sunday afternoon. The legs are dusty and streaked with blood.

Some men are carefully placing the bodies on charpoys. I take two photographs: one of the men covering the bodies with blankets, another of someone's grieving face. I always wondered what sort of people took such photographs. My guide is waiting for me and we set off again. Just then there is the sound of helicopters and people begin running for open spaces, away from the houses. Someone shouts, 'Don't all go to the same place. Spread out,' and the young man and I lie down in a dry irrigation channel. But the helicopters only circle for a few minutes and then swerve away into the distance. Perhaps they are also taking photographs of the damage.

We walk across a field of baked earth and my guide tells me that he is the sole survivor of a family of seven, all killed in previous raids. He is not yet twenty.

In the sparse shade of a bush, there is a man lying on a charpoy. Half his leg has been blown off. Under a film of yellow dust and sweat his face is very pale. An old woman sits beside him and makes ineffectual efforts to cover her face with her chadogh as we approach. The man greets me courteously.

'*Jan e jour, khoub hasti, kheir amadi*. How are you, are you well, welcome.'

I ask him whether I may take his photograph. His face is open and smiling.

'Of course, I don't mind. Please, take as many as you wish.'

Once again I am surprised by my attention to focus, foreshortening and shutter-speed. I take two photographs. I thank him and he says something in reply, but he is unnaturally talkative and I cannot understand. I guess that at the moment he is in shock and not in too much pain. I manage to find a few crumbling Norvegin tablets at the bottom of my satchel which I tell him to take when the pain begins. Norvegin is about the same strength as aspirin. I reach out to say goodbye and the blood on his hand and arm has dried in

227

patches on his skin like an obscure map. '*Khoda hafiz*', we say to one another, '*Khoda hafiz*'. As I walk away the old woman bends forward and helps him to drink from a glass of green tea in her hand.

L ater I met Abdul Haq at last, and a handful of mujahedin. They asked me how many people had been killed in the bombing. I told them of the dead and wounded that I had seen. They asked me to describe the location of the damaged house, and even as I answered I realized the gulf that lay between us: the corpses I had seen were mere forms, covered in dust and blood, but they had been friends and neighbours of the men in front of me.

We waited in the shade of a tree for the sun to set behind the mountains. A mujahed with a sandy beard and humorous grey-green eyes, who introduced himself as a geography teacher, told me of his attitude towards death.

'For me it is not important. It is *qismet*—my portion of destiny—or *taqdir*. I do not fear death, for it is already decided. I do not know the place or time, but God knows. That is why I am not afraid, because it is God's will.'

I told him that the people of Europe and America admired the bravery of the mujahedin.

'Wouldn't they fight like us if the *Shuravi* invaded?'

'Perhaps it would be a different kind of war.'

While we were talking Abdul Haq's eyes were continually scanning the hills on the other side of the river. But he missed nothing of the conversation and explained that when people were killed their relatives were strengthened by the belief that the souls of the *shahid* would, without a shadow of doubt, enter Paradise.

As the sun disappeared into the mountains, Abdul Haq judged it safe to re-enter the town.

Later we sat together by the light of a kerosene lamp. Three golden lights came swaying towards us along the road and some shepherds, two men and a boy, appeared like refugees from another time to ask for payment for supplying meat to the mujahedin. A meteorite grazed the darkness like a stone cast across the frozen surface of a deep lake. It was time to say my final farewells, for the next morning it had been arranged for me to start the return journey through the Panjshir and Nuristan to Pakistan.

LEONARD FRANK

THE

DEVELOPMENT

GAME

Development, as in Third World Development, is a debauched word, a whore of a word. Its users can't look you in the eye. Among biologists, the word means progress, the realization of an innate potential. The word is good, incontestable, a cause for celebration. In the mouths of politicians, economists and development experts like myself, it claims the same approval, but means nothing. There are no genes governing the shape of human society. No one can say of a society, as a gardener can of a flower, that it has become what it should be. It is an empty word which can be filled by any user to conceal any hidden intention, a Trojan horse of a word. It implies that what is done to people by those more powerful than themselves is their fate, their potential, their fault. A useful word, a bland word, a wicked word, a whore of a word. Development in the mouths of Americans has a lot in common with psychotherapy in the mouths of Russians.

No. This is nonsense. There is nothing sinister about 'development'. It is simply a useful word to describe the achievement of desirable goals: higher incomes, better nutrition and so on. There are no serious disagreements about what is desirable, and by repeated use the word has achieved a validity of shared understanding. That is all.

I'm happy. I'm alone. I am sitting on a balcony with my feet up, perfectly relaxed. My left arm grills in the sun; my right, in the shade, is still cold from the night. Up here, there is not enough air to filter the light from the sun nor enough to store its heat. I am crossed by a sharp diagonal shadow, happily divided. On a low table by my elbow is a pot of green tea, brought to me by a slavish servant. Next to it are papers and an unopened report. Beyond this rest-house are mountains: mountainsides, mountain valleys, mountain peaks, snow, high passes, the Himalayas, the roof of the world.

There are few perfect moments for a man like me, and now I shiver at the perfect moment. I am here, but not here. I am suspended between these mountain tops. I have arrived, but no one knows I have arrived. The officials have not been informed; the other mission members have not yet caught up. For a moment I am free.

Photo: Philippot/Sygma

'You don't want Botswana. You want Pakistan!' The Korean man calling from Geneva had an explosive way of talking. 'Pakistan. North-west Frontier. Beautiful place. Mountains. It's a good place for a person like you. Famous place for you Westerners. The Great Game and all that. Never mind Botswana: you want Pakistan. Next week. Before the snows come. Very beautiful.'

It sounded like a good idea. There are so many development-aid people in Botswana you can't find anything to finance any more. I asked about the Afghan war.

'No, no. No war. Forget about the war. These people are very poor. Nobody has done anything for them. No development. They need development. You have to go before the snows.'

I don't want to know about the war next door. They don't want me to know. Or about the opium traffic. These are two things I don't want to know too much about. And politics. I don't want to know about politics either.

We are six on the mission to the North-west Frontier: an old Japanese, a Korean, an American, a Bangladeshi, a Dutch girl, me. I'm Canadian with a French mother. None of us have been here before. None of us have previously met. The Korean who brought us together does not know us either. He got my name from an Indian I once worked with in Manila and he phoned me at my Paris number.

How did the world get this way? It's all quite rational but it's too complicated to think about. OK: the Japanese, because Japanese money is becoming important; a Bangladeshi, because they are cheap and brown; a Korean, because the mission organiser is Korean; an American to punch statistics; a Dutch girl sociologist for the soft and warm. A mix of people because this time it's an international agency. I'm in charge; I make the big decisions. We've got four weeks to come up with a project for, say, thirty million dollars. Routine.

This job is a question of damage limitation. Damage to yourself. You spend your time in places you don't want to know with people you would not choose. I would not choose them; they would not choose me. You get canny: you don't notice anything you don't need to notice; you schedule work so you can stay at international hotels. You keep the conversation bland. The American is a racist but I'm ignoring it. The younger Korean is upset because his marriage is failing, but I don't want to know. People were not meant to go to a different country every month and live intimately with a group of strangers. When people and places change too much your mind can't cope. You become confused and your memory goes. Once I proposed marriage to a woman in France, but by the time I had visited Venezuela, New Guinea and Zanzibar, I had forgotten.

There is something disturbing about the people in this valley: they look just like me. They are poor peasants, but they look just like me. They have fair complexions, rosy cheeks and straight noses. Some of them are blonde with blue eyes. I am used to my target group being browner. I saw two little blonde girls playing, and they could have been from California, except for their dirty faces. Perhaps the children have dirty faces because it rarely rains and the water from the melted snow is too cold for washing. There is no one I would ask about this.

Their dogs are just like ours. Cocker spaniels seem most popular. The people like to sit in garden chairs on the grass under the trees, and fondle their dogs. They grow apricots and apples. Apples! People in my projects grow mangoes, paw-paws, bananas, passion-fruit. They don't grow apples. I suspect an elaborate joke is being played.

Tomorrow we go to another valley, the next day another. We are looking for valleys to develop.

The old Japanese is related to the emperor of Japan. My father managed a supermarket. Last night we shared a room. He snores. I found myself trying to trace the invisible hand which took him from his childhood and me from mine and brought us together on the North-west Frontier. I stopped myself. At breakfast we talked about golf courses in Japan, women in Manila and the relative merits of Intercontinental and Holiday Inn hotels.

233

These people are poor. Very poor. They may look like me but the truth is that they are very poor people. They scratch a living without enough land or water. They can't feed themselves. Every year the government distributes subsidized wheat at great expense, but many of them are too remote to be reached. The men have to leave their homes to look for work elsewhere. The ecology is collapsing. There are no longer enough trees to provide firewood for the long winters. Because the trees have been destroyed there are deadly mud-slides which bury villages, and floods which destroy the crops.

Three-and-a-half million Afghan refugees make the situation worse—but they are not our concern. The refugees are under separate administration and for us they hardly exist. We pass their camps and caravans, and the officials direct our attention elsewhere. The bases of mujahedin fighters do not exist for us at all. We are skilled at not seeing.

The peasants here sell nothing and buy little. There are no markets; they hardly deserve the name peasant. For half the year they are cut off by snow; for the other half transport is too expensive to be worthwhile. These people are wretched. Only the lightest and most valuable crops are worthy of investment. Opium poppies are ideal, but we have decided that, for us, opium poppies do not exist.

In summary, these people have a resource constraint, a market constraint, an infrastructure constraint and a technical possibility constraint. They are a suitable target group. Their appearance is deceptive.

'OK, but if we define it as an opium-producing region the project will have to come under the US-assisted OEDD programme to co-ordinate it with other international funding for opium poppy substitution. If we do that, the terms of the US money mean we'll be stuck with a law enforcement component. And that means we'll have to channel funds through the NPSEB of the Federal Government. Bad news. Better to define the region as free of opium poppies and make the project part of the SDD without enforcement so we can by-pass the OEDD and locate it directly in the DCD of the PG. It will facilitate disbursement no end. Of course the Americans and

UNCAD will be pissed-off at not getting a piece of the action, but there's no shortage of co-financing agencies. Everyone wants a part of the North-west frontier these days.'

'Right.'

How did the world get this way? It's simple enough. Let me remember the story. Towards the end of the Second World War the rich countries, seeing a need for reconstruction in Europe and safeguards against economic instability, brought into being the International Monetary Fund and the International Bank for Reconstruction and Development—the World Bank. With the introduction of America's Marshall Plan for Europe, the World Bank was free to turn its attention to the poorest countries of the world. By providing scarce capital on favourable terms it permitted investment beyond the existing resources of these countries. Moreover the World Bank was able to provide the missing expertise. The success of these pioneering efforts led to a network of international development banks working under the World Bank's fatherly eye. Nowadays Third World nations can call upon a wide range of international and bilateral agencies to support them in their development efforts, and multinational missions of experienced 'development professionals' can be readily assembled in response to particular needs. There! Now I can sleep.

Except you could say—I've heard it said—that the World Bank is, in reality, an American organization, and its origins were not idealistic but opportunistic. It has loaned money to make the poorer countries import manufactured goods and export their raw materials. It has sought to tie the world to it with the intimate bond of debtor to creditor. It has insisted on projects designed by its own people to enforce its politics at the expense of local needs. It has made the great post-war political discovery: development finance is cheaper than colonialism but just as effective—the difference between a wonder-drug and gross surgery. We are the missionaries representing America's moment of vision, now far removed from us. Restless capital is seeking out the remotest Himalayan valleys, made interesting by heroin on New York streets, by the Russians across the border and by the need of a friendly dictatorship to survive an election. We are all foreigners, but we are all Americans. None of us knows Pakistan but we all know what is good for it.

Now I can't sleep.

The truth is that money is simply the way of our world. We are the honest brokers who stand between the ignorant poor and the powerful rich. We control capital with careful planning; we guarantee that governments will not use aid for selfish or despotic ends. We stand in the path of an irresistible force and try to keep it decent.

Now please let me sleep.

'It's absolutely amazing. They are the most fantastic people. Do you know that their culture is tied up with the Persians and the Chinese? They don't really belong with the rest of Pakistan at all. You should talk to the people in the villages. They know exactly what they want. They are very well organized, very articulate. Sociologically it's amazing. The whole community is devoted to building these incredible irrigation works. Have you been up in the mountains to look at them? They build these stone channels high on the mountainsides—sometimes water has to travel five miles along sheer rock faces before it reaches a patch of soil. They could give Western engineers some lessons. And the social structure is completely intact and self-sufficient. All the labour is organized by the community and they make sure everyone shares the benefits. These people are geniuses! All the trees and livestock are managed on a community basis too. And have you seen how dignified they are? They smile because they don't feel belittled by the outside world yet. We have to be very careful here; they have something very valuable. We should go gently. Otherwise I can't agree with development here.'

I expect the Dutch girl's right. But where does it get us? The government wants to spend lots of money fast; the agency wants to lend it. She's naive. She burdens me. She does not understand the simplest fact of a bank's life: a return next year is worth having but a return in ten years' time isn't worth the trouble of calculation. Capital and care don't mix, and she had better decide who is paying her, the agency or the peasants.

I find the beauty sickening. I sit on the veranda with five companions not of my choosing. Some of them read reports, pretending to work. All of us have run out of safe things to say. In front of the veranda are mountain flowers, then the big river, then the mountains. If I look up, it's all snow-capped peaks, like meringue-topping. I don't want it. It's like a deceit, a sneer. The people are poor, the mountains a logistical nightmare. Everything is vertical instead of horizontal. Road building will cost twice the average. The sky here is an absurd blue, totally clear. It draws you up into it. Thank God we are returning to the Intercontinental in Peshawar tomorrow.

At least two people in the mission are mad. They have made the mistake of confusing what they say they are doing with what they are doing. The American carries his own computer around with him and is entering all the official statistics he can find. He wants to calculate the impact of all our possible investments in the region. The madness takes the form of obsessive scrupulousness about the data and analytical techniques. If two figures contradict each other—as they always do—he sweats over reconciling the difference and weighting the averages. He is trying to create a single economic model which will go from the daily milk consumption of migrant pastoralists in winter to the indirect macro-economic benefits of oil import substitution. His eyes are glued to his computer; it is impossible to get him to attend meetings any more. He only leaves his chair to go jogging, returning as dead-eyed and haggard as when he left. I tell him to relax. I tell him—exaggerating slightly—that half the statistics come from village clerks who made them up and the other half are manipulated by the government for policy purposes. And anyway, the figures don't matter very much. There will be a project: they want to borrow; we want to lend. His economic calculations will just be the window-dressing. It's politics, not economics, I tell him. At this he flies into a fury, standing up and knocking over his chair. He insists that he is a professional and that I should respect his expertise and integrity. I drop the subject. He's an experienced expert; I know that in the end he will convince himself that the convenient figures are the right ones.

Leonard Frank

The Korean is also mad. He is forty, has had half his stomach removed, drinks a bottle of whisky every night and compresses his leisure into intense bouts with the pornography he carries around with him. At home his wife has given up on him because he is never there. He fawns on the old Japanese who treats him like a servant, requiring him to prepare food and give massages in addition to his duties as an agriculturalist. His problem is that he genuinely likes the peasant farmers and, astonishingly, speaks enough Urdu to talk to them. This sympathy conflicts with his method of work, which is to start with what he thinks the peasants should be doing in ten years' time and work backwards. Each time he follows this line of thinking he discovers that the peasants would have to be forced to change their lives in ways they would not like. His inability to reconcile the idea of the peasants becoming Korean with the idea of them being happy sends him to the whisky, the pornography and, on one occasion, to my room at four in the morning. There he drunkenly asserted that he was a simple man, a peasant educated by accident, not like the aristocratic old Japanese whom he must respect but secretly disliked.

I've learned more about the Korean than any of the others. During the long night I came close to being involved in his emotions and caring about his problems. I only saw the danger with the coming of the dawn, when I understood it would be best to a take a firm line and give him a deadline for his overdue report. After he left I felt dizzy, like a man walking on a cliff edge.

The old Japanese is not mad. His life is the game and he plays it well. The Dutch girl is not mad because she isn't in the game yet. I'm not mad; I know the rules.

'We are very interested in the mountain area. We want to do something for our people quickly. We don't want your six-year project; we want two years, three years. The people up there hardly know the government exists. They wonder what the government is doing for them. They see the refugees receiving all sorts of international aid and they wonder why they are not getting anything. It is a restless place. You should not think so small. We want to make an impact. You should join these people to the rest of Pakistan. You should be building tunnels through the mountains and making truckable roads right

238

up to the border areas. There are huge barren areas you could irrigate with large-scale irrigation schemes. Take our word for it. If you give us money we can do it. We can move people from the crowded areas to these new schemes. We can open up the region to new crops and industries. You are too timid. Agricultural research and improved farming are not enough. We want results. It's a priority area. The government is ready to move. We know what we have to do; you do not need to work it out in detail. Just release the money and we will do the rest.'

My head aches. We are back from the Himalayas. Do not disturb me in my Intercontinental room. I close the curtains. The hotel rooms in Pakistan have videos because there is nowhere to go. No bars, no night-clubs, no women. Not officially. The film is *On Golden Pond*, about a cranky old American played by Henry Fonda and a crusty old woman played by an actress whose name I used to know. Every month I learn the names of a hundred new people and a hundred new places and then forget them. Like a prostitute, I am a master of forgetting, but it's an inexact science. In the film I notice that, one, the couple have plenty of money; and, two, they've got a lot of time on their hands. I turn it off in favour of going through the pile of reports from which I will make my report.

In Peshawar they have blown up the PIA office, the railway station, the Khyber Mail Express, a bazaar, the Afghanistan office and the third best hotel—twice. At our hotel someone shot a white woman by the swimming pool, but I am told that the killing was religious not political. I ask my government guide whether the Intercontinental is likely to be blown up, us in it. For some reason he imagines me an ally and launches into a reckless analysis of the situation. The official line is that the Russian-backed Afghan government is responsible, even though on one occasion they seem to have bombed themselves. The imputed motive is that the bombings will stir up resentment among the Pakistan populace against the Afghan refugees, who are already disliked for taking over the most profitable businesses. If the refugees become unwelcome, Pakistan will no longer be able to support effectively the mujahedin fighters who mingle with them. My confidant is not convinced by this version. He tells me that he is a supporter of Benazir Bhutto and a rapid return to democratic government. He believes that his own government is bombing itself to create a security crisis which will give it an excuse to continue martial law.

There are more complexities. He is very indiscreet. I've no idea whether he is right or wrong. Finally he notices my indifference and stops talking, embarrassed. I ask him again whether he thinks our hotel will be blown up. I tell him it is a management consideration. He replies that I need not worry, the bombers seem interested in killing only local people.

I don't like change but there is one new fact I must accept. Japan. The Japanese asks me quietly about vacant posts in international organizations. Can I help him place his men? He is sad about Japan's apologetic posture in the development world. The war is long over, but, although Japanese money is important, his country has not been given the influence to match its contribution. It is a humiliation. He wants to change things softly, softly. I encourage him and the inevitable. He has invited me to Japan, and I am ready to stop being American and to become Japanese. I'm tired of new places but I suppose I will go.

This Dutch girl is a nuisance. What are they doing sending a young woman to a Moslem country anyway? The officials do not listen to her, and her inexperience is a problem for the rest of us. For her it is an important discovery that the official world does not match the real one. She visits villages and reports back to us at dinner that the irrigation schemes are not working the way the government says they are, or that the veterinary employees are selling drugs they should give away. She tells us that money for building primary schools has gone into the pockets of contractors and local politicians. The official figures on truck transport are wrong because they neglect the Afghanis who own most of the trucks. And so on. She's like a detective excited at uncovering a vast conspiracy. We make non-committal replies and try to change the subject. The older Japanese says nothing and finds an excuse to leave the table.

You have to make a choice about the world you live in—the real world or the official world. Nowadays I live in the official world. The real world is infinitely complex, and even the people who are part of it don't understand it. And we are here for only four weeks, most of that in office meetings. When you discover that the official world does not correspond to the real world, you can either accept the official version or make your own judgement. It's always best to take the government figures. That way you save yourself work and don't tread on the toes of anyone who matters. We are here, after all, as guests.

'Look, we want to lend you the money you are talking about, but one valley is not enough. One valley doesn't have the absorption capacity. We need a minimum of two, and preferably three, valleys. We want at least a million people. Otherwise Geneva won't like it. Frankly, they will say it was not worth the expense of sending out a mission. We want to give you a project but you'll have to take away some valleys from someone else and give them to us.'

I spend my life in other people's offices. Here the officials are polite and intelligent, and invariably insist on tea and biscuits. In this case it's an administrator in the British mould—a cultured, literate generalist. I employ my usual technique of letting the man speak while I doodle in my notebook, pretending to note his views. We are getting along well when three French people are shown in to pick up their tourist authorizations. The occasional bombing of the border area by Russian MiGs had not inhibited the promotion of tourism by a government department not responsible for defence matters.

The two Frenchmen and one woman seem unduly taken aback by my presence and offer me a confusion of greetings. They look unlikely mountain trekkers: two of them, a middle-aged couple, are overweight, while the third is a fit young man. For French people on an expensive holiday, they are oddly un-chic. The woman's hair is poorly cut and her make-up is clumsy. All of them are cheaply dressed. They look away from me in order to avoid conversation; I'm convinced they are not French. While the official signs the papers and talks about snow leopards and the rare hawks to be found in the mountains, I examine their shoes. They look like Adidas and Nikes but in fact they are cheap imitations. Now I am convinced they are Russians posing as tourists; no wealthy Frenchman would wear imitation brands.

241

After they leave, the official returns to our conversation apologetically, explaining that he has been told to encourage tourism. I shrug and tell him I understand.

'We have decided we can give you two more valleys. We will give you an American valley and one which was going to the Germans. We want to reduce bilateral funding in favour of international donors. But we have to have assurances that you will release the money fast.'

'No problem. I'll tell Geneva.'

Someone always gets sick on these trips. Foreign food, foreign bugs, unhealthy hotel life. Usually it's the stress that does it. People were not meant to live this way. First it was the old Japanese with his aches and pains, now it's the Bangladeshi. It will not be the American, who is too dry for any disease to take, and the Dutch girl has vitality on her side. I am saving myself and I doubt it will be me. The Bangladeshi has some sort of burning in his stomach and is vomiting all the time. Last week he told me he was homesick and missed his children. What could I say? Illness is an embarrassment to everyone and, in a way, unprofessional. We all have to work harder. If it gets serious it becomes a management problem. We'll have to decide whether to evacuate him to the American hospital or send him home. Either way he doesn't get paid and will probably not be hired again.

I'm tired of this mission. I don't like Moslem countries: they make your life difficult. All over the world men are much the same: you can unwind with them in bars, talk about money and politics and women. Here they don't drink in public and don't admit to lust. The will of Allah suddenly comes into the middle of a business discussion. A meeting stops because it's time for the Chief Secretary to pray. The whole place seems slightly out of focus. The same government which uses sophisticated economic analysis is also keen on cutting the hands off criminals and public floggings. You hardly see a woman on the streets and, when you do, she is covered from the top of her head to her toes. I caught myself trying to catch a glimpse of an ankle just to check whether the woman was young or old, fat or slim. Next month it's the Gambia where the hotels are full of English women holidaymakers going topless.

'OK, what we'll do is this. We'll keep the six-year concept but make a four-year first phase to satisfy the government. We'll go for a small-farmer development package, with increased government staff and transport in the region, but we'll include pre-feasibility studies for the large construction projects so they can't say we ignored them. Logistically and socially the large-scale projects are bad news. We'll include them in the total package but auction them off separately to co-financing agencies. There are plenty of development agencies who would be happy to pick them up. Pakistan is a success story, don't forget: it can pay its debts. And this is the hottest region right now. We'll put in a good-size road component, but we can't touch the ecological problems—too long-term. We'll put in something for research to cover our critics. And I want something on the soft and warm—an appendix on social factors. OK? We're getting there. We're in business.'

We've done the Himalayas, we've done the provincial government and we've cleared the federal government in Islamabad. After twenty-seven nights together, the mission has dispersed. The old Japanese and the American have taken the report to Geneva. The Korean has gone to Korea, the Dutch girl is staying on to do some research of her own. Research for research's sake. The Bangladeshi was sent home four days early. I've shed them; I'm alone in the Karachi Sheraton. So tired. My job is over and I have five nights to kill before I need to be in Washington for a briefing on the Gambia mission. I try—not very hard—to remember the names of officials in Peshawar and I am pleased to find that already I cannot.

I take a long hot bath and wrap myself in an extravagance of towels. Then I take a walk around the hotel's restaurants and cafés, looking at the foreign women without focusing my attention on any particular one. Probably I am smiling. I don't need company; I've had enough of company. Back upstairs, I phone room service to order beer and something simple and Western to eat. They are showing *Close Encounters of the Third Kind* on the video and I settle back on the bed to watch. I have lots of pillows and the dinner tray on the bed next to me. I run a calculation through my mind to see how much I've earned, then I get lost in the film. Then I fall asleep.

GRANTA

NOTES FROM ABROAD

China
Orville Schell

everal years ago, I attended a banquet hosted by the Mayor
of San Francisco for a delegation of actors and directors
from China's film industry. After the dinner and the speeches
extolling cultural exchange and friendship, it fell time for
the ritual exchange of gifts. The leader of the Chinese delega-
produced a square flat box with characters on the front saying
'handicraft work'. The Mayor received it respectfully, and, with the
synthetic enthusiasm politicians have in inexhaustible reserve,
thanked her Chinese counterpart profusely. Then, she held up the gift
for the American guests to see, to an audible gasp of disbelief. It was a
ceramic plate, topped with a protective bubble of plastic that
enveloped a small, fuzzy white kitten made out of spun polyester. It
looked like a miniature taxidermist's trophy; it was not only void of
political meaning and thoroughly un-Chinese, but also utterly bereft
of artistic inspiration.

As the banquet guests headed for the door, I walked over to
examine the kitten more closely, hardly able to believe that an official
delegation from the People's Republic of China had chosen it as a gift
to the mayor of a prominent American city. On the cat's white fluffy
face, there was a red felt nose and two pink plastic eyes. The insides of
its furry ears were tinged in light blue. And around its neck was a
crimson bow which might have come from a package of pre-tied
stick-on Christmas ribbons. The plate looked like a mock-up for a
Hallmark card, rather than a present from a Communist
country—much less a country with the oldest continuous living
civilization on earth.

I turned the plate over, and was surprised to see that it had been
made in Jingde, a town in Jiangxi Province renowned for its fine
porcelain since the Ming Dynasty. It seemed almost unimaginable

that the country which had produced Tang poetry, Sung landscape-painting, Ming porcelain and Qing fiction could have produced such kitsch as this.

Back in China a short while later, I discovered that cat plates had become ubiquitous. Whole sets were being sold throughout the country in gift shops, along with statues of Jesus made out of shells, decorative plastic shrimps, lamps in the shape of naked women, with frilly shades which looked as if they had been made out of lingerie, T-shirts saying ZUOLUO (transliteration for 'Zorro') and MODERN DANCE (with a blond couple fox-trotting), thermos bottles emblazoned with Bambi-like fawns, ersatz jade carvings, garish coloured glass vases filled with gaudy artificial flowers, bunches of blindingly green plastic grapes with which people had begun to festoon stores and restaurants as if they were Italian trattorias. Kitsch is abundant in every country, but here there was nothing of any artistic merit—virtually nothing in any of these shops, or even in the large Friendship Stores (set up in the sizeable cities specially to make China's very best goods available to foreign visitors) which would have made an appealing gift.

*O*ver the past ten years, I have always returned to China with a sense of anticipation. But recently I have found myself becoming more and more dispirited by the aesthetic poverty of the country. After being in China a few days, I begin to feel I have contracted a low grade infection. My symptoms have included wanting to withdraw into books which have absolutely nothing to do with China, dwelling over meals long after they are finished, taking extended showers, and lingering in hard-to-find quiet places as if some part of me were trying to make a surreptitious escape from my new surroundings. The sad truth is that urban China has become so defoliated aesthetically that living there is a form of extreme sensory deprivation.

The irony is that while Mao was still alive, I hardly noticed this. The militant denial of the aesthetic sense in the name of politics and revolution was what was absorbing and distracting. As Mao proclaimed: 'There is in fact no such thing as art for art's sake...'

Going to China to see art was as absurd as going to Iceland to see palm trees.

But in the wake of the Third Plenum of the Eleventh Party Congress in December 1978, when Deng Xiaoping consolidated his power and redefined China's policies, the country began to change. With the revolution called off, and the resurgence of the notion of 'art for art's sake', China's aesthetic defoliation was all too apparent. Chinese students were beginning to flood abroad to study and live. They began singing western operas, dancing classical ballet, writing psychological novels and poetry, and painting abstract expressionist works of art. It was a dramatic and exciting change. But the artistic shortcomings a visitor might previously have seen as necessary and inevitable sacrifices for the revolution could not now be so easily forgiven. The basis for this cultural disorientation precedes Mao. Over the last century, China has repeatedly repudiated itself in a series of quests for new forms of cultural and political salvation. Most western countries, at least in modern times, have constructed national identities around notions of pluralism, but China has almost always tried to centre its cultural and political life around a unifying orthodoxy. Whenever it has cashiered one such orthodoxy, its leaders have immediately tried to rally the masses around a new one.

One can see traces of all of China's past identities as one walks through cities such as Canton, Shanghai, Tianjing and Beijing, and looks around at the buildings. It is as if each street were a cross-section of the country's architectural past.

First, there are the few remaining traditional buildings, which, with their sloping tile roofs and post-and-beam constructions, have escaped the ravages of China's modern revolution. And, while they are often either run down beyond repair or so ardently restored that they look unreal, they are nevertheless a reminder of China's old culture, when its people had a specific understanding of what it meant to be Chinese.

The next layer, transplanted from London, Paris or New York, consists of those western-style structures built by foreigners at the turn of this century, in such cities as Shanghai, Quingdao, Dairen, Canton and Beijing. Once evocative of an alien foreign elegance, these dilapidated embassies, consulates, banks and corporate headquarters recall an era when China was once before undecided as to how western ideas about science, art, freedom and democracy might fit together with what was left of its battered traditions to produce something other than cultural schizophrenia.

The third layer of buildings was inspired by 1950s Stalinist architecture, and went up after 'liberation'; their sheer dead mass is an attribute Soviet architects have long confused with grandeur. Such bulky paeans to socialism as the Beijing and Shanghai Exhibition Halls are embellished with non-functional colonnades, strange steeples topped with communist stars and pretentious entrance-ways. These outlandish period pieces look as bizarre in China as the Temple of Heaven would in Leningrad.

A fourth layer of building began in the late fifties when the Russians stopped playing the role of 'socialist big brother' and abandoned the Chinese to their own devices. Local architects built various large projects like the Beijing railway station and the Great Hall of the People, which look like stage sets for an epic Hollywood adventure set in some long-lost civilization of the Mid-east. They also instituted a genre of sombre, square brick and concrete edifices more like warehouses than places of human habitation. Even in the fifties, they looked twenty years old.

With the rise to power of Deng Xiaoping in the late seventies, China began its fifth and most prolific building period. Thousands of high-rise apartment buildings, office buildings and hotels shot up in China's cities in an effort to fill a critical need for living and working space. The construction boom has left China littered with cold, bare, cell-block-like structures with little but dust or mud between them. Even those few new skyscraper office towers, such as the Union Building in Shanghai and the China International Trade and Investment Building in Peking, as close as China has come to effecting a 'modern' semblance, still have a strange and awkward ungainliness.

Should an archaeologist in the distant future dig up a Chinese high-rise complex from this period, he might be surprised by the unrelieved squareness of the buildings, the poverty of decoration inside and the dull clothing of their denizens. He might well wonder to what cataclysmic event these artistically impoverished people were reacting; what evolutionary imperative had caused such a complete suppression of colour and design during this inter-regnum of Chinese history. For these Chinese buildings are not simply examples of practical minds trying to economize in order to accomodate a people desperate for space; they are a form of extreme anti-design which harkens back to that revolutionary period when any expression of style, architectural or otherwise, was considered dangerously bourgeois. When visiting friends in their cheerless dormitory-style homes, I was often struck by the irony that even the animals in Chinese zoos had more attention paid to the design of their living environment than the average Chinese.

Clothing is perhaps the second physical feature noticed by a visitor to a foreign country. During the 'ten lost years' (1966-76), one could look down any lông street in China and see nothing but the officially approved colours: blue, khaki and grey for the masses, and dark blue or black for ranking Party officials. Almost everyone wore 'Mao suits', an egalitarian style of dress first introduced by Sun Yatsen after the fall of the last dynasty in 1911. The garb provided not only a practical unisex style of clothing, but also a shroud to hide all individual distinguishing features. Any change from the standard uniform—a ribbon in the hair, a piece of jewellery, a coloured handkerchief—was considered a dangerous deviation: a clear expression of the kind of individualism the Party feared and wished most to suppress.

During the mid-seventies I often studied carefully the dress of Chinese women for signs of warmth and self-expression. I discovered only one minuscule window in which women felt free to adorn themselves. This was the small triangular space directly under their chins between the lapels of their Mao suits. Here one would sometimes see a pretty button or a brightly coloured piece of blouse peeking out. Otherwise only small children and minorities like the

Tibetans and Mongolians were allowed to dress with colour or flamboyance. It was not surprising that stage and film directors, looking for some romance and brightness for their productions, included roles for minorities to exploit the theatrical value of their costumes.

In the explosion of interest in fashion which has marked China these past few years, introducing cosmetic surgery, modelling schools, fashion magazines and fashion shows all across the country, one sees China struggling back towards a notion of sartorial beauty. But more often than not, this notion is imitative of the West. Western wedding gowns are now the style for marriages. Dresses and skirts, trouser-suits, high heels and stockings, and even hot pants, have taken over women's fashion. Tight pants and T-shirts with inscriptions in English are *de rigeur* for young men. In fact so popular have blue jeans (called 'cowboy pants') become in China that they featured in a recent Beijing rock and roll song.

> Wa wa cowboy pants!
> Wa wa cowboy pants!
>
> When my guy wears cowboy pants
> He looks so slick and agile
>
> When my girl wears cowboy pants
> She is so sleek and lively.
>
> Oh why, oh why, oh why,
> Do cowboy pants cast such a spell over me?

Once forbidden as 'spiritual pollution', pop music now blares away everywhere in China. People listen to non-stop medleys of sugary love ballads by Taiwanese song stylists, bastardized versions of 'Red River Valley', 'Frosty the Snowman' and Jimmy Rogers's 'Hobo's Lullaby' ('Will there be any freight trains in heaven, any box cars in which we can ride?'), Hong Kong rock and roll in Cantonese, western classical selections such as Schiller's 'Ode to Joy' from Beethoven's Ninth, Hawaiian hula music, Madonna and synthesizer Bach all played one after the other.

These miscegenated musical offerings spew forth endlessly inside stores, restaurants, airports, taxis, trains, discos, and even over government controlled radio and television stations, not to mention from the millions of ghetto-blasters now the rage in China. Not long ago the Chinese were listening to heroic proletarian songs like 'The Screws of the Revolution Will Never Rust', 'We Will Follow Chairman Mao to Eternity' and 'All Commune Members Are Sunflowers'.

When one hears such songs now, it is hard to recall how different China was when there were only eight officially approved dramas, and the Party controlled all newspapers, publishing houses, museums, schools, radio and television stations, arts academies and universities; when artists and intellectuals were hounded, reviled and finally left with a choice between ceasing all activity and silently trying to inure themselves to the propaganda around them, or surrendering their intellectual and aesthetic independence by becoming Party hacks. Art, literature, music, theatre, film: wherever the individual human imagination might fall out of step with the 'correct line', the Party aimed its awesome defoliating power. The gracelessness of China's new architecture, the poverty of decoration, the didacticism of its arts and music and the baggy drabness of officially acceptable clothing were only the most obvious emblems of the way in which the cultural flora of the country had been scorched to its roots.

This scorching left the Chinese living in an aesthetic vacuum, starved of anything bright or remotely stylish, so that when the door was again thrown open to the outside world, it began indiscriminately sucking up new things. Most of what people reached for was crude and lacked any but the most imitative inspiration. Having been repressed for so long, China's aesthetic sensibility would not easily or quickly rebound even if the Party had stopped suppressing all aesthetic self-expression. Too many Chinese had forgotten what beauty is. Perhaps the greatest irony of Mao's revolution is that by so ruthlessly suppressing the independent growth of China's own arts, it made China more vulnerable than ever to exactly those invasive outside forces the Party feared most.

Deng Xiaoping's new policies created a curious paradox. After years of trying to seal itself off from the outside world, China now seems hell-bent on opening up. Where formerly China prided itself on its anti-imperialist purity, now everywhere one looks one sees signs of cultural invasion from the West. Calendars featuring blonde models abound. Young Chinese eagerly take Christian names. Western Christmas tree decorations festoon everything from restaurant and hotel lobbies to stores and offices. It is indeed a culturally deranging experience to walk into a Peking restaurant in the middle of August and find it hung with shiny red and silver mylar stars and chains of blinking Christmas-tree lights. People are buying 'mo-deng' (modern) stuffed couches and armchairs which, while they may suggest western modernity to their purchasers, are actually as hideously designed and graceless as any I have ever seen. One is assailed by paintings of romantic alpine scenes at sunset, kewpie dolls with heads that wobble on springs, plastic bottles in baroque shapes containing air freshener and vases of plastic flowers in day-glo colours.

The Party still endlessly exhorts 'the broad masses' to take only 'the best' from the West and combine it with 'the best' from the East. But such a neat formula of integration has proved infinitely difficult to execute. Even the most scrupulously careful cultural borrower has difficulty determining an objective basis for selection. Moreover, the seductive power of a firmly-rooted western culture is magnified by China's own cultural uncertainty, all too easily overwhelming and devaluing the indigenous culture. This is an old problem for China, whose historical sense of inadequacy in the face of the more powerful West, coupled with the disintegration of its own sense of cultural or national essence (*guocui*), has always put China in double jeopardy when borrowing from abroad.

Attemps to introduce an element of Chinese-ness into all this borrowing too often end up being gratuitous and irrelevant. For example, western fashion has by now virtually dominated the Chinese market. How does one Sinify western dresses and suits? The fabric of a dress designed in an obviously imitative western way can be stamped with prints of the Great Wall or embroidered with a few Chinese characters, silk neck-ties may be imprinted with traditional landscape paintings. But such efforts only contrive nondescript hotch-potches. The results are something like several jigsaw puzzles which have been mixed up and then forced together to form no coherent image.

Is it surprising, then, that China ends up producing cat plates as official gifts?

But if kitsch cat plates are a far cry from real art, they are also a far cry from socialist-realist propaganda. They may negate the very notion of 'art', and be examples of the worst kind of borrowed western-ness, but a few years ago their existence would have been unthinkable. They represent an artistic nadir, but paradoxically also a new groping towards the world of colour and design, which owes no allegiance to politics or Party. This in itself is a step forward of enormous significance.

A year and a half ago, having travelled across northern China by train, I was in Beijing waiting to return home. I had become so depressed by the endless string of grey provincial cities filled with grim soul-less buildings, colour-less streets, monotonous clothing and horrendous pollution that I could hardly wait to leave. Then, during my last night in the Capital, an acquaintance invited me to a screening at the British Embassy of a film called *Yellow Earth*, which had recently been completed by a young Chinese director, Chen Kaige from the Beijing Film Academy. Having seen numerous Chinese films, all of which were still confined and stunted by the unseen ideological boundaries within which artists had to work in China, I expected little.

But the film surprised me: it was spellbinding. The story—acted, filmed and directed with a beautiful but unpretentious simplicity—took place in the *loess* (yellow earth) hills of Shanxi in the 1930s, and recounted the tale of a peasant girl who was married against her will in a traditional ceremony, and finally drowned while trying to run away. The haunting barrenness of Shanxi and the hardness of peasant life were captured with a truthfulness that left me almost in tears.

But what struck me most about this film was its indelible Chinese-ness: it drew its inspiration not from the Party line or the West, but from the nativist sensibilities of those Chinese who made it. There was about it, moreover, an aura of freedom, which made me feel the film was its own master, doing its own bidding, as a true work of art must. One work does not make an artistic renaissance, but after the suffocation of so many years of socialist realism and kitsch, I could not but be uplifted by this single wonderful film. For what it seemed to suggest was that if the Party was at last willing to release its grip, China would once again find a new and genuinely Chinese aesthetic sensibility, with which it might slowly refoliate its denuded artistic landscape.

Notes on Contributors

Redmond O'Hanlon was in the Amazonas in the summer of 1985. Parts of his previous travel book, *Into the Heart of Borneo*, originally appeared in *Granta*. 'Amazon Adventure' is from a longer work-in-progress that will be published by Hamish Hamilton. **Salman Rushdie** went to Nicaragua in July 1986 for the seventh anniversary of the Sandinista revolution. 'Eating the Eggs of Love' will be included in *The Jaguar Smile: A Nicaraguan Journey*, to be published by Picador on 30 January at £2.95. He is currently at work on a new novel. **Timothy Garton Ash** is a Fellow of the Woodrow Wilson International Center for Scholars, and the author of *The Polish Revolution: Solidarity*. **Ryszard Kapuściński** is the author of *The Emperor* and *Shah of Shahs*. 'A Tour of Angola' will be included in *Another Day of Life,* which Picador publish on 8 February. **Norman Lewis**'s new novel, *The March of the Long Shadows*, will be published in April. He is now writing a book about the indians of South America. **Hanif Kureishi** is the author of *My Beautiful Laundrette*, and is currently working on a new film about the Brixton riots. **Colin Thubron**'s most recent travel book is *Among the Russians*. 'A Family in Nanjing' is part of a longer work-in-progress which will be published by Heinemann in Autumn 1987. **Peregrine Hodson**'s *Under a Sickle Moon*, from which 'A Journey into Afghanistan' is taken, will be published by Century Hutchinson on 8 January. He works in banking in London, and is now writing a book about Japan. **Martha Gellhorn** settled in Cuba at the end of the Spanish Civil War. A new edition of her collected war journalism, *The Face of War*, was recently published by Virago. **Amitav Ghosh** is the author of one novel, *The Circle of Reason*. He lives in Delhi. **Leonard Frank** has spent fifteen years in development work. None of the people and events described in 'The Development Game' bears any relation to real people or events. Leonard Frank lives in Paris. **Orville Schell** is the author of *To Get Rich is Glorious: China in the Eighties*, and a book about meat. He lives in Bolinas, California.